MULTIPLE-CHOICE & FREE-RESPONSE QUESTIONS IN PREPARATION FOR THE AP PSYCHOLOGY EXAMINATION

(SECOND EDITION)

Michael Sullivan

Hopkinton High School
Hopkinton, Massachusetts

D&S MARKETING SYSTEMS, INC.
1205 38th Street • Brooklyn, NY 11218

w w w . d s m a r k e t i n g . c o m

ISBN # 0-9787199-2-1

Printed in the U.S.A.

◆ TABLE OF CONTENTS ◆

AP Psychology

Introduction

It would be pretty easy to make the case that every high school student should take psychology before they graduate. In the first place, it's no accident that psychology is perennially one of the most popular majors on college campuses – it is a terrifically interesting field, so almost all high school students will find it accessible and intriguing. But the major selling point for such a proposal is the relevance of psychology. Whether or not a student plans to go to school after grade twelve, a fundamental understanding of human behavior, emotion and mental processes will serve them well in life. As many of my students say, "psychology is everywhere!" The more one knows about principles of human perception, the more aware and insightful about even the most mundane events one becomes. The more one knows about learning and motivation, the easier it is to understand and even influence the behavior of others in the workplace and in the world at large. The more one knows about human judgment, decision making and attitudes the better able one is to think for themselves and to wisely evaluate the thinking of others. The more one knows about psychological disorders or the roots of personality, the more sensitive and tolerant one becomes. In fact, it's hard to imagine teaching and learning about psychology without making connections to one's own life. After all, psychology is *about* one's own life – one's perceptions, thoughts, feelings, motivations, quirks and quest for happiness, fulfillment and meaning.

The Advanced Placement Psychology curriculum is designed to give you a "university level" look at this very broad field while you are still in high school. This book can serve most of the functions of a full-length, hardcover college psychology textbook in your preparation for the advanced placement examination. It provides all the content and practice you need in order to excel on the AP exam. You may wish to secure another text to serve as a resource; this is especially true if you are preparing entirely on your own. If you do, make certain it is a college level introductory text. There are literally dozens of such texts available, and most of them would serve you very well. A simple way to find one is to scout a local university bookstore and thumb through the selections there, but it may be even easier to peruse the websites of various publishing companies on the internet. Some teachers of advanced placement psychology believe that the textbook choice is the single most important decision one makes in preparing for the exam. If, however, you are taking a legitimate psychology course taught by a capable and diligent instructor, you are obviously at an advantage no matter what text you use.

The practice items you will see in this book *will* prepare you for the kinds of questions you will see on the test itself. Those items are useful both for practice and for "diagnosis" of strengths and weaknesses. **Each chapter includes a set of multiple choice items** that mirrors the range of difficulty and breadth of content you will encounter on the AP Examination. If you follow the directions for **time management** and self discipline that this book provides, each section will give you a true sense of where you stand in that particular unit. Later, when you try one of the **three full length practice examinations**, you will discover that it's pretty easy to identify your weaker and stronger content areas. This will make your studying more effective and less time consuming.

   In each chapter there is an "Essay Themes" section, which highlights the "big picture" of each unit. Of course, there's no guarantee that those themes will show up on a particular essay, but reflecting on them will certainly help you to bring the unit into focus and help you tie what otherwise might appear to be a bunch of disparate "facts" into a coherent whole. The essay portion of the exam (the authors of the test prefer to call it the "free response" section) will almost always ask you to think thematically, so we'll practice that kind of thinking all along the way in this book.

   Psychology is such a multi-faceted field that it is difficult to study it *without* thinking thematically! And there is a great deal of overlap between the many subfields within the discipline, even though there are many who actually contend that 'psychology' isn't really one discipline at all anymore. Such thinkers might argue that study of say, "personality theory" is very different in content and approach from the study of " the biological bases of behavior", but the AP curriculum still emphasizes study of each of those and much more under the one umbrella of 'psychology'.

   The Advanced Placement Psychology Examination is made up of **100 multiple choice items** (worth 2/3 of your entire exam score) and **two free response or essay questions** (collectively worth 1/3 of your overall score). There is no choice on the free response section as there is, for example, on the AP US History test. Every student is asked to "present a cogent argument" in response to the same two items. The multiple choice section lasts **70 minutes**; the free response section, distributed only after the multiple choice portion has been collected by the test proctors, is **50 minutes long**. There's no hard and fast rule on this, but in very general terms students tend to feel more "rushed" on the essays than on the multiple choice. Again, disciplined time management is especially important on that part of the examination. You should try to adhere to the pacing guidelines suggested at various points in this book; **the importance of time management on the AP Psychology Examination cannot be overstated**.

   Advanced Placement Exams are scored on a **one to five scale**. Most colleges and universities award advanced placement credit for scores of three or above; some accept only four's and five's, and a very few highly selective schools will only grant credit for a five. The College Board and the Educational Testing Service have conducted at least two "comparability studies" to validate the test. They found that high school advanced placement psychology students perform at least as well as college students on advanced placement exams, which indicates that those students are indeed receiving a genuine "college intro psych" experience.

   Generally speaking, of over 50,000 test takers, 67 – 70% each year earn a score of three or above in AP Psychology. Despite what you may hear from teachers and other students, there is no strict threshold for any particular score. Your score is more of **a ranking** of how you performed in comparison to all the other test takers than it is anything else. There is no cut-off established beforehand for "four-ness" or "five-ness". For instance, if there was a year in which students did poorly nationwide on one essay, the overall raw scores would be lower, but students who were the best of the best, however good or not so good "best" was that year, would still receive "fives".

There are fourteen content areas in the AP Psychology curriculum, although this book breaks one of those, "Cognition", into its two major parts, "Memory" and "Thought and Language" and incorporates "History of Psychology" into the rest of the program rather than treating it separately. **Most units will make up 7 to 9 percent of the multiple choice items** on the big exam. You'll see some exceptions to this, although that won't impact your preparation very much. The percentages do *not* apply to the free response section of the text. Anything is fair game in those. The authors of those questions try hard to reference concepts from several different content units in each free response item. Their basic goal in developing free response prompts is to come up with fair but challenging questions that will differentiate between student levels of mastery, not to cover any particular content area. So it's a losing battle to try to use previous tests to predict what might be on this year's exam. In the past there has been a very loose tendency to place one "harder science" item (on "statistics and methodology" or "biopsychology" for example) with a "softer science" question (from "personality theory" or "social psychology" for instance), but items are not written or chosen based on thinking like "we need a 'memory' question – we haven't had one of those in years" or "we have to come up with more difficult questions because the students are doing too well!". It isn't done that way.

COURSE OUTLINE

I. Research Methodology and Approaches (6-8%)

The meat of this unit focuses on experimentation in the social sciences. You will learn how to design and critically evaluate experiments. You'll also study other kinds of research: naturalistic observations, longitudinal and cross-sectional studies, correlational research, the case study approach and survey methodology. There's a bit about statistics in this unit – don't worry, you don't need to be a "math person" to understand these basic concepts!

II. The Biological Bases of Behavior (8-10%)

This unit does frighten people, but mastery of it is essential for understanding of later topics. You can't really claim to understand 'psychology' if you don't know about the biological underpinnings of what we do, think and feel. By the time you're finished here, you'll have a nice grasp of how specific brain regions seems to operate, how the body sends its messages through neurons in the brain and through the glands of the endocrine system and how a "genetic predisposition" can give us a push in one behavioral direction or another.

III. Sensation and Perception (7-9%)

Many college psych textbooks break this into two separate chapters, but the AP curriculum quite reasonably joins them together. That makes for a large unit, but fortunately many of the concepts can be demonstrated to you, which makes them easy to assimilate and retain. Basically, the 'sensation' part of this unit covers the physiological information gathering systems in humans, while the 'perception' segment involves study of the psychological interpretation of that sensory input.

IV. States of Consciousness (2-4%)

Like many students, you'll probably find this a very high interest topic, although it has relatively small weight on the AP Exam. The main focus here is on sleep and dreams: why do we sleep? what are the characteristics of a "typical" night's sleep? do dreams have significance, or do we simply attempt to attach significance to what is essentially random brain activity? what is the nature of hypnosis – is it an "altered state of consciousness" or is a hypnotized subject simply very relaxed and thus more suggestible than he would be otherwise? You'll also learn a bit about the action of psychoactive drugs in this mini-unit.

V. Learning Theory (7-9%)

Here you will learn about classical conditioning, operant conditioning, social or observational learning and some different types of cognitive learning. Some of the best known studies in the history of psychology are in learning theory; you'll find it pretty easy to remember Ivan Pavlov's classical conditioning of salivation in dogs, John B. Watson's classical conditioning of fear in a little boy, and Albert Bandura's famed "Bobo" study in which young children imitate the aggressive behavior of adult models. This unit is very important because it foreshadows your later study of the "behavioral" school of psychological thought in units on motivation, personality theory, abnormal psych and treatment.

VI. Cognition (including Memory and Thought and Language) (8-10%)

Here is another topic that is often split into two chapters in textbooks. Concepts in memory are often easy to actively demonstrate, and it's easy to think of real life examples of such phenomena, so they should be relatively easy to remember! The second half of the unit focuses on human judgment, planning and decision making and on language acquisition. The latter topic serves as a nice lead-in to the unit on developmental psychology, so this book is organized with that in mind.

VII. Motivation and Emotion (7-9%)

In this book, this unit is placed *after* Developmental Psychology, although the AP Psychology curriculum places it here. Either sequence is easily defensible. Stop someone on the street and ask them "what is psychology?", and they may well say "it's the study of why people do what they do" – and that is the thrust of the first part of this chapter, which is yet another example of a topic which is sometimes split in two in college psych textbooks. In the second half of the unit, we will examine how human emotions unfold, whether or not they are universally experienced and perceived, and the nature of specific emotions like love and aggression.

VIII. Developmental Psychology (7-9%)

Again, this book is laid out a bit differently than the AP unit chronology, in that this unit is placed immediately after the unit on Cognition, and is then followed by study of Motivation and Emotion. You'll understand more on the reasoning behind that placement later. Developmental Psych is the study of how humans progress through life in terms of physical and social growth, thinking and moral reasoning.

IX. Personality Theory (6-8%)

This will supply you with a nice overview of the big "schools of thought" in psychology, which is essential for success on the AP Psych Exam. Several free response questions on past AP Psychology Exams have revolved around those major perspectives, and you'll see a whole lot of overlap between this unit and several others in the course, so give it careful attention.

X. Testing and Individual Differences (5-7%)

This used to be referred to as "intelligence and assessment", and that pretty much tells you what it is about. You'll learn about several theories which attempt to define 'smart', and various ways to try to assess that elusive quality. You'll also explore the concepts of reliability (the consistency of the scoring of a test) and validity ("does this test really test what it says it tests?") in assessment, and there'll be powerful connections here to your own educational experiences.

XI. Abnormal Psychology (7-9%)

Many people think this is 'psychology'; the study of the characteristics and origins of mental disorders. It *is* a very important and quite fascinating topic, but it is only one of many under the big tent of 'psychology'. It's also almost always placed rather late in psychology textbooks and curriculum progressions. In Abnormal Psych you'll learn about several different categories of psychological disorder (ranging from mood disorders to anxiety disorders to various kinds of schizophrenia) and you'll explore the issue of where to draw the lines which define clinically 'abnormal' behavior. You'll undoubtedly leave this unit more sensitive about the complexities of human behavior and dysfunction.

XII. Treatment of Psychological Disorders (5-7%)

Your study of this unit will go well if you got a good grip on the major theoretical perspectives in psychology during the chapter on Personality Theory. There is significant overlap between the two topics, but in this chapter you'll focus more on specific therapeutic techniques used by clinicians from different psychological orientations – psychoanalytic strategies to uncover unconscious conflict, cognitive techniques to restructure self destructive thinking, behavioral approaches designed to model or condition healthier behaviors, drug interventions from the biomedical perspective, and more.

XIII. Social Psychology (7-9%)

Because this is almost always placed at the end of textbooks and course outlines, it sometimes gets less attention than it deserves. Don't overlook it! For one thing, it carries substantial weight on the AP Exam, but more importantly, it contains engaging material which is readily linked to your own lives. Social Psych is the study of individual behavior in group and societal context. The specific topics in this unit include obedience to authority, conformity to group pressure, helping behavior, group dynamics, attitudes, prejudice and attraction. That's a pretty broad menu, and it makes for stimulating discussions!

XIV. History of Psychology (2-4%)

You'll pick up what you need to know in this area in the course of your study of the units mentioned above.

Top Ten Things to Remember in Taking the Multiple Choice Section of the AP Psychology Exam
(an introduction to tips that will be referred to later in this book)

10. If you are well prepared, you probably won't feel rushed on the multiple choice, so you **can probably afford to slow down**!

9. **Practice time management**, using the review items at the end of each chapter and the three full length practice examinations in this book. Knowing about pacing strategies is not the same thing as being able to actually execute those strategies – the only way to gauge your ability to do that is to try them! You might also ask your teacher to design his or her unit tests to mirror the pacing of the actual AP Exam, to give you year long practice in time management.

8. As you proceed through the exam, **make a mark next to items you want to revisit** later. You may not have time to review all 100 items, so it'll be useful to have highlighted those that most require a second look

7. If you do have "review time" after running through all 100 questions, look only at those you marked earlier. While recent research conducted by Justin Kruger and others suggests that one shouldn't be afraid to review and actually change answers on multiple choice questions, on a strictly timed exam like this one **it's simply not feasible to re-evaluate every decision you've made** during the course of the test.

6. The items in the multiple choice section are arranged in **order of difficulty**, based on pretesting data and the judgment of the committee that constructs the test, so it is an especially useful strategy not to "out think yourself" on items placed early in the test. Sometimes well prepared students feel an answer is "too easy" and talk themselves out of it, but it's important to remember that items early in the test *are* likely pretty easy for a well prepared student!

5. **Consider covering the answer choices as you read the stem** of each question, and try to answer before looking. This can make some of the distractor items less distracting! It takes practice to get yourself to actually do this consistently, so try it out early in the year when answering review items at the end of each chapter.

4. There is a small section in this book, immediately preceding the three practice exams, entitled "Preparation to Take the Examination". Try some of the exercises in that section. Learning "test taking strategies" isn't enough for you to succeed on a challenging standardized test – there's no substitute for knowing the content! But **practice with process of elimination and other techniques can certainly help on specific items**. Again: *knowing about* such approaches is not enough – you have to try them out.

3. The multiple choice section of the AP Psychology Exam is **worth 2/3 of your total test score**. That's a lot of weight. Lots of students (and their teachers!) "worry" more about the free response section of the test, but do not underestimate the importance of these 100 questions.

2. This book will help you **space your practice** over the course of the school year, but you should also **do the same for your studying**. Generally speaking, "distributed practice" is more effective than "massed practice", although last minute cramming can be valuable if you're essentially "relearning" material you had already "mastered". If, however, you're trying to assimilate new material in large amounts at the last minute, you are going to struggle.

1. Use the "test preparation" **graphic organizers** provided for you at the end of each chapter, or, better yet, make your own. Simply engaging in the process of creating a visual representation of the material you know or wish to know is an invaluable learning tool – it's very hard to create a graphic organizer unless you have a pretty good grasp of the stuff you're representing. And a 'graphic organizer' can have any kind of visual layout that works best for you. There are all kinds of suggested formats available, but individually tailoring the look of it so it makes sense to *you* is the best approach.

Top Ten Things to Remember in Answering the Free Response Questions on the AP Psychology Exam

10. From the start of the school year, **practice pacing**. Time yourself on essays your teacher gives you on unit tests. That will help you gradually develop an internal "clock" which will serve you well on the AP Exam in May.

9. **Budget your time**. Actually write down your projected "start" and "finish" time when you begin writing. This step can help discipline you to give fair treatment to both of the essays. You might consider giving yourself 22 or 23 minutes on your first essay, and the same amount on your second, which will still leave you a few minutes at the end to go back and add a flourish or clean up a loose end. Also remember that the two free response questions have equal weight; even though one might look bigger than another, don't let that fool you!

8. **Do the item you know best first.** This is to insure that you get full credit for what you really know. It's pretty frustrating to spend a lot of time on an item you're struggling with only to get to a question you know very well with too little time to do it justice.

7. **Highlight key elements of each question** and respond directly to them. If the question asks you to "compare *and* contrast", it'll hurt you if you don't actually do both, and the best way to avoid such an oversight is to highlight everything you need to do.

6. Take a breath and **reflect for a moment**. You may only have moments to do this, but that little snippet of time can help you focus on what you know, how to organize it and how to express it to a reader.

5. **This is a specific kind of writing and time is very much a factor**, so you don't need an introductory paragraph, especially if it is only going to restate the question, nor do you necessarily need to follow a strict "five paragraph essay" format. The free response prompts are often laid out in a kind of outline format. You can use that layout as an organizing principle in your essay, perhaps by simply beginning a new paragraph for every new concept you're asked to consider. Look at the free response questions in the practice exams at the end of this book and you'll get a sense of how this would work.

4. **A fellow human *will* be reading this**, and he or she deserves your consideration. Those readers are very capable people, and they're usually pretty nice too, so they want to give you the credit you deserve, but it's your job to make that easy for them. So you do want the occasional paragraph break (!), you do want to remember **this is an essay**, not a series of short answers, and you do want to write as legibly as you can.

3. Think of your audience as a very intelligent but uninformed child. He or she can understand things quite well, but doesn't know anything about the field, and it's your job to **"teach" them what *you* know about it**.

2. **Say it clearly, and move on**. You don't have the time to do much else, and the readers appreciate it when students are direct and concise. Continually reminding yourself of what your audience needs and wants can help guide you in the writing process.

1. **Use terminology from the field of psychology**. Your goal is to impress upon the reader that you thrived in a rigorous college level psychology course, and that you're not merely relying on episodes of "Law and Order" or "CSI" or "Oprah" for your knowledge.

Chapter I

Statistics and Research Methodology

Introduction

At the end of this and every section of the book there is a set of practice multiple choice items. Use them! It will be easy for you to tell yourself that you've done enough having read the content summary, but doing the practice items diligently, and timing yourself while you do so, will be very important in your preparation.

This opening unit on research methods basically introduces you to how psychologists do their work. Partly because "popular psychology" is often seen as lightweight and largely intuitive, real psychologists and the teachers who construct the advanced placement exam are committed to presenting psychology as a social *science*. This unit introduces students to the scientific methodology that is used to gather all the data that is then reported in the textbook that you are reading and the classes you are taking. For as long as the advanced placement psychology program has existed, this unit has been a significant area of focus on the AP Examination. Simply stated, you are in trouble on the test if you do not give this unit your full attention.

Experimentation In Psychology

The meat of this chapter revolves around **experimentation** in psychology. Most people refer to research in general as 'experimentation', but an experiment is a specific type of research, just as **correlational research, case study approaches, survey approaches, naturalistic observations, cross sectional studies** and **longitudinal studies** are. You must have a basic understanding of how each of those is conducted, with a sense of their strengths and limitations as well.

The basic goal in an experiment is to determine if some variable you manipulate (the **independent variable** or **IV**) has a cause and effect relationship on some outcome that you measure (**the dependent variable** or **DV**). Essentially, you are testing the effect of the independent variable on the dependent variable. Students have lots of trouble discriminating between these two types of variables, so be sure to know them. You might want to think of the independent variable as like an intravenous treatment in a hospital; the doctor "puts something into you" with the IV and then measures what effect it has on you.

A researcher states a **hypothesis**, which is a prediction of the effect of the independent variable on the dependent variable, and then attempts to control for possible **confounding variables** (variables that might account for a difference between groups in the experiment). This concept also gives students difficulty, so here's an example: if you were testing the effect of two different teaching styles (the IV) on AP Psychology examination performance (the DV), you would want to make certain that any difference between the two groups on the AP Exam was in fact the result of being taught differently. You would not want one group to do better than the other because one took the exam when bright and fresh at 9 a.m while the second group took the test at 4:30 p.m. after a full day of classes. You would not want one group to take the exam in an air-conditioned room while the second group slogged through the thing in unpleasantly hot conditions. The differences in time of day and testing environment might account for the differences in performance between the two groups, so you need to control for those possible confounding variables.

While you are not likely to see this on the AP Exam, more than trying to "prove" their hypothesis, social scientists actually try in their research to *disprove* **the null hypothesis**, which is the statement that the independent variable will have *no effect* on the dependent variable. No matter what data was gathered in the experiment described above, it would be difficult to say that one had *proven* that one teaching style was superior to all others. But the data could at least suggest that using a particular approach had *some effect* on performance.

Experimenters must also endeavor to gain a **representative sample of the population** they are studying, and assign volunteers to **control** and **experimental groups** such that each group is representative of the whole population as well. That way, one can **generalize** from the outcomes of the experiment to the entire population. Random selection of subjects and random assignment of them to experimental or control groups is generally all that is needed to insure that you have a representative sample overall and in each of your groups. To choose **"at random"** simply means that all members of the population have an equal chance of being chosen. Another way to insure representativeness in each group is to use **group matching**; in that procedure, one systematically assign individuals to each group to guarantee balance. If you used group matching to choose fair teams for an informal basketball game, you might place the two best players on opposite teams, the two worst players on opposite teams, and so on.

Often, it is necessary for experimenters to establish **operational definitions** (a definition of a concept or phenomenon which provides for specific ways to measure whether that thing exists or occurs) of the concepts they are studying. This helps especially in the measurement of the dependent variable. It is difficult to measure something that is poorly defined. And having clear and precise operational definitions allows for **replication**, in which other researchers repeat an experiment to confirm its conclusions. Replication is an essential component of the scientific method.

You must also know about **double blind** procedures designed to eliminate possible experimenter bias, and the use of **placebos**. In a double blind, neither the participants in the study nor the experimenters or the experimental assistants who gather the data know which participants belong to the control group and which belong to experimental groups. A group receiving a placebo actually gets no treatment (or independent variable) at all, to account for a possible "placebo effect" in which a participant's *belief* that they are receiving a treatment may produce an outcome rather than the treatment or IV itself.

It is unlikely that you will see this on the AP examination, but just in case: sometimes **counterbalancing** is utilized in conducting an experiment. This is done when the order of presentation might influence the outcome of the research. A simple example: if you were asking volunteers to identify four different tastes, it would be wise to give some volunteers the samples in order from #1 to #4, while others received sample #2 first, followed by #3, #4 and #1. If all possible orders were presented to at least some of the participants, you could guarantee that the order in which volunteers tasted samples didn't influence their judgment.

There is a strict set of **ethical guidelines** that researchers must adhere to, and you ought to familiarize yourself with considerations such as **informed consent, confidentiality, use of volunteers only, the right of those volunteers to discontinue participation in the experiment at any time, conducting studies which have an absolute minimum of deception or stress, and the obligation to debrief fully** after the experiment is completed.

Later, in the unit on learning theory, you'll learn about a well known study in the classical conditioning of fear, in which behaviorist John B. Watson conditioned a very young orphan (known as Little Albert) to fear a white rat that the boy originally liked. Even without the details you will examine in that later chapter, you can see some obvious ethical issues (an awful lot of distress imposed on the child and lack of informed consent, just to mention two) in this work from 1920. In the last unit of this course, on social psychology, you'll learn about Stanley Milgram's work in the early 1960's on obedience to authority; this too sparked much ethical debate and contributed to the standards that now exist in the field of psychological research. Milgram asked male volunteers to "teach" word pairs to other volunteers, using painful electric shocks as punishment for incorrect responses. In fact, the "learner" was part of the experiment, and did not actually receive shocks, although the teacher did not know that as he heard the learner pretend to yell in protest and pain in a nearby room. Milgram's real intent was not to study the effect of punishment on learning, but to examine whether an individual would obey an authority figure (the researcher conducting the study) even when doing so would cause harm to another. Did Milgram place his volunteers under too much stress? Was there too much deception inherent in his research design? Did he inform volunteers that they had the right to discontinue participation at any time? (in fact, he did not – that present day guideline evolved pretty much as a direct response to Milgram's study) Was his post-study debriefing sufficient to relieve any distress his work may have caused? You may be able to consider these questions more deeply as your studies progress, especially after you examine Milgram's research further at the end of the course.

Other Research Methods

There are several other ways to conduct studies in psychology. One of those is through **correlational research**. The aim here is to examine the link (the co-relationship) between variables; do two variables tend to occur together, and, if so, in what direction? For example: does the weight in pounds of professional baseball players correlate with the number of home runs players hit? If so, is it that heavier players tend to hit more home runs (a positive correlation), or that home run totals go *down* as weight *increases* (a negative correlation), or is there no apparent statistical connection between the two variables? The strength of such correlations is measured in **correlation coefficients**. A "perfect" positive correlation is represented as $r = +1.0$, a "perfect" negative correlation as $r = -1.0$. In real world research, you would never get a perfect correlation, in which the two variables you are studying always move in exact proportion to each other. But, as one example, you might find a rather strong positive correlation, perhaps $r = +.70$, for height and weight in American males. Taller individuals do tend to be heavier than shorter individuals. A key point to remember is that, no matter how strongly correlated two variables are, one can not assume that one variable causes the other to occur. As you can read in almost any college psychology textbook, one can "never infer causation from mere correlation".

Some psychological research is done through the use of **surveys**. Two things you must consider in administering a survey are **demand characteristic** and **social desirability bias**. At times those who are taking a survey sense what the researcher seems to want of them; they then supply the responses they feel they're expected to give. This is demand characteristic, and it is one argument for keeping the person who is administering the survey "blind" as to the hypothesis or the agenda of the lead researcher. That way, the administrator cannot unwittingly cue the respondents. In social desirability bias, the survey respondent offers responses they deem to be socially acceptable. For example: if asked to report the number of times they drink alcohol per week, college students may well give responses that are in line with accepted standards of the culture, especially if they feel their actual behaviors are excessive in either direction.

In **naturalistic observations**, a researcher unobtrusively observes subjects while the subjects do whatever they do in a "natural" setting. This is an attempt to see what people and other animals really do in typical environments and scenarios, as compared to what they *report* they do on surveys or self-report inventories.

Case study approaches serve a similar purpose in that they take a single case which has already occurred and study its elements and implications. Often, such real life cases offer the opportunity for insights that one could never or would never attempt to gain through artificially designing an experiment. One of the more famous case studies in psychology comes from 1964. A 28 year old woman named Kitty Genovese was assaulted near her apartment in Queens, New York. Over the course of thirty minutes, she was stabbed repeatedly; she eventually died of her wounds. When the police investigated, they found over three dozen individuals who'd heard the commotion and the victim's cries for help, but had done nothing. Only one person called the police, and then only after Genovese had passed away. While controlled studies into what has come to be called *the bystander effect* have since been conducted, they largely only confirmed what psychologists had already learned from this tragic case study.

In a **longitudinal study**, researchers follow the same subjects over an extended period of time. Film maker Michael Apted made a movie in the mid-1960's he called "7 Up". In it, he interviewed a number of seven year olds in England. Since then, he's tracked those individuals down every seven years to make other documentaries (entitled "14 Up", "21 Up" and so on). The result is a compelling series examining the lives of the same people over the course of a lifespan. Such an approach obviously takes many years and intensive commitment, and there is a potential problem with losing subjects along the way (sometimes called *subject mortality*), so **cross sectional studies** are often conducted instead. In these, one examines a representative sample of different ages here and now.

Statistics In Psychology

There are some statistical concepts an AP Psychology student must know as well. Most college textbooks provide a summary of major concepts in statistics in an appendix at the back of the book. If you are using such a textbook in conjunction with this one, do not overlook that section.

Descriptive statistics do what they say they do – they summarize quantitative information about some group. **Inferential statistics** involves the analysis of data to determine whether they are the result of mere chance or are actually the result of a manipulation made by the researchers.

The concept of **statistical significance** is important. A finding is generally deemed to be statistically significant if there is a 95% or greater chance that the differences between groups in an experiment are not merely due to chance occurrence. An AP Psychology student does not have to know how to calculate a value for statistical significance, but should certainly understand it conceptually. Likewise, a well prepared student will have a basic grasp of **normal and skewed distributions**, **percentiles** and **the three measures of central tendency (mean, median and mode)**. If data about a variable are graphed and fall on a symmetrical, "bell shaped" curve, the distribution is referred to as a "normal distribution" or a "normal curve". In a skewed distribution, scores tend to cluster in one direction or another. The "skewedness" of such a curve is determined by the rare scores, the outliers. Thus, if a distribution is pushed to the right, with the hump of the curve at the high end of scores, this is called **a negative skew**, as the less typical scores are on the low end of the distribution. In **a positively skewed distribution**, high scores are the outliers. This is counterintuitive for many AP students, so be careful with it. In our later study of intelligence and assessment, you will encounter examples of normal distributions for intelligence quotient (IQ) and S.A.T. scores. There are visual representations of those distributions in chapter eleven of this book.

A **percentile** score tells you where you scored in comparison to others. If, for example, you scored at the 84th percentile on an exam, it means you performed as well as or better than 84% of those who took the same text. Finally, **the mean** is the arithmetic average of a set of values, **the median** is the middle value in a set, such that half the values fall above it and half below it (remember to put the values in order first! the median value of the set of scores 3,8,5 is five, not eight...it is just such a seemingly simple item on the multiple choice section of the AP Exam that messes some people up, if they are moving too quickly), and **the mode** is the value that occurs most frequently in a set of scores.

There are a few more statistical concepts that you are less likely to encounter on the AP exam but which we will quickly summarize anyhow:

- **the gambler's fallacy:** in figuring probabilities, many people commit this error – essentially, they wrongly assume some occurrence is "due" to happen even when that occurrence is purely a matter of chance; if you are playing a card game and "need" an acc, you cannot assume that you are due for an ace because you haven't had one for a long time – if the cards are being shuffled appropriately, every time a card is dealt you have a 1 in 13 chance (since there are four aces among the 52 cards in the deck) of receiving an ace.

- **polygons:** a flashy name for a line graph; you might see reference to the term, but it shouldn't trouble you on the exam.

- **histograms:** a flashy name for a bar graph; again, just recognizing that you might see the term is all you need to worry about.

- **scatterplots:** a graph with lots of dots on it, signifying data points; this is what you'll be looking at when analyzing correlational research, which we explained earlier.

- **pie charts:** they look like a pie, cut into pieces...that's all.

- **scales of measurement:** numbers can be used in different ways, and you may need to know that so you don't try to do calculations with some set of numbers that aren't really useful. For example:

  - you would not do some quick arithmetic and announce that "the average number on our girls' basketball team is 13.6". The numbers in that case are simply *names*; this is **nominal** data.
  - if numbers assign an order to some set of things, those numbers are **ordinal data**. A "top 25" list of college football teams, which gives no other information but who is #1, who is #23, and so on, is ordinal data.
  - if a set of numbers also tells you the difference between individual data points, you have **interval data** (it tells you *the interval* between the tenth number and the eleventh number); an example of interval data are S.A.T. scores; if the tenth highest score on the S.A.T verbal section was a 610, and the eleventh highest score was a 590, we of course know the order of finish but also the gap between the two, twenty points.

- **ratio data** has an "absolute zero" or absolute starting point, while interval data does not; this allows you to do computations with ratio data that you cannot do meaningfully with interval data; for instance, if one book weighs 3 pounds and another book weighs 1 pound, we know the interval between them (two pounds, of course), but we can also say that the first book is three times heavier than the second book, since there *is* such a thing as no weight.

This is not a particularly large unit, but it is necessary that you have a good grip on it in order to understand much of the data you encounter throughout your year of study and also to succeed on an exam which places a premium on mastery of this material.

Name Hall Of Fame

(If you don't know these names, you don't know psychology... in fact, these may be the few names you would actually have to directly recall on an AP Psych exam)

In this unit, there really are no clear cut, "first ballot" inductees into the Name Hall of Fame. However, in your study of experimental methodology, you've heard about **John B. Watson** and his (in)famous work in classical conditioning with a young orphan named **"Little Albert"**. You also explored **Stanley Milgram's** study on obedience to authority, often referred to in high school classes as "the electric shock study". Both of these offer much material for a debate on ethics in research methodology, and the Milgram study in particular provides a marvelous opportunity to discuss multiple variations one can build onto the basic design of a study (the Milgram study is not really an 'experiment' per se, as it did not have two or more experimental groups or an experimental group and a control group, but many would scc that as nit-picking). Many teachers and textbooks refer to the example of **"Clever Hans"** to introduce the idea of using the experimental method and implementation of a double blind procedure. Hans was a horse who won acclaim in Europe for his alleged ability to count and do other tricks not typically within the skill set of a horse. It turns out that his owner was not a charlatan, but *was* unconsciously guilty of signaling Hans when he approached a correct answer to the owner's queries. This was revealed only once a set of questions was given to Hans by a questioner who did not himself know the answers; thus, he was unable to cue the animal. Hans, who was certainly a bright horse but not a magically gifted one, now had no unconscious signal to read, and his performance dipped to chance percentages.

Finally, there are names which are usually associated with the history of psychology which might come up on the AP Exam. Two that are notable are **Wilhelm Wundt**, who established the first formal psychology laboratory in Leipzig, Germany in 1879, and **William James**, the great American psychologist whose textbook, Principles of Psychology was published in 1890 but is still respected for its insights. Other names from the history of the field, like **Hermann Ebbinghaus, Edward Thorndike, Alfred Binet, Sigmund Freud, John B. Watson** and **Ivan Pavlov**, to name but a few, will be covered in other content areas: Thorndike, Watson and Pavlov in Learning Theory, Ebbinghaus in Memory, Freud in Developmental Psychology and Personality Theory, and Binet in Testing and Individual Differences.

Essay Themes

One of the most common themes in past advanced placement psychology exam essays has been the **designing and critiquing of experiments**. In the first decade of the program, almost one third of the free response items revolved around this theme. This does not mean that the authors of the test are "due" for another such question anytime soon, but it does say something about the importance of knowing all you can about how to conduct research in psychology.

It's also a good general rule for every unit in this course to reflect upon areas of controversy and debate which require genuine critical thinking, as these offer rich topics for intelligent essay test construction. For example:

- are the conclusions any particular researchers reach valid? that is, did the research they conducted truly test what it claimed to test, can the results be reliably replicated, and is the procedure sound?
- is there a trade-off between adherence to ethical research standards and the "need to know"? is what we learned from Stanley Milgram's research into obedience to authority "worth" its ethical compromises? is it ethical to require placebo groups in a study designed to evaluate the effectiveness of a new drug when volunteers randomly assigned to that group might thus miss out on the benefits of the new medication if it *does* turn out to be effective?

Test Preparation: Statistics and Research Methodology

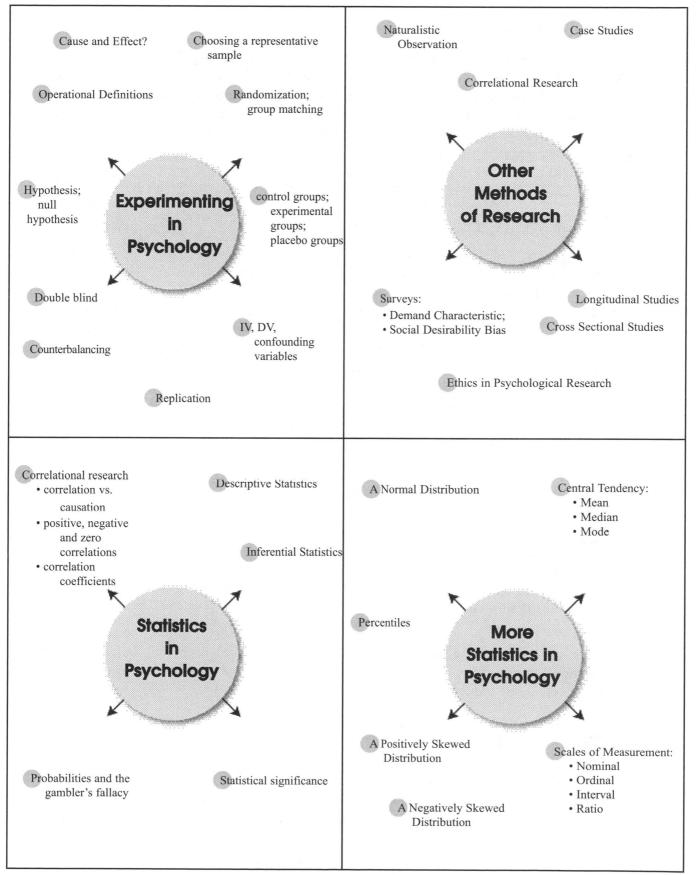

Cause and Effect?

Choosing a representative sample

Operational Definitions

Randomization; group matching

Hypothesis; null hypothesis

Experimenting in Psychology

control groups; experimental groups; placebo groups

Double blind

Counterbalancing

IV, DV, confounding variables

Replication

Naturalistic Observation

Case Studies

Correlational Research

Other Methods of Research

Surveys:
• Demand Characteristic;
• Social Desirability Bias

Longitudinal Studies

Cross Sectional Studies

Ethics in Psychological Research

Correlational research
• correlation vs. causation
• positive, negative and zero correlations
• correlation coefficients

Descriptive Statistics

Inferential Statistics

Statistics in Psychology

Probabilities and the gambler's fallacy

Statistical significance

A Normal Distribution

Central Tendency:
• Mean
• Median
• Mode

Percentiles

More Statistics in Psychology

A Positively Skewed Distribution

Scales of Measurement:
• Nominal
• Ordinal
• Interval
• Ratio

A Negatively Skewed Distribution

Practice Items

- **time yourself** on this section, and record how long it takes you; this information will be useful to you later on
- if you work at the pace you will need on the actual AP Exam, this section should take you no more than 10 minutes and 30 seconds
- if it takes you only three minutes and you get them all correct, more power to you! if you are done in less than seven minutes and you make 3 or more errors, then you ought to consider slowing down a bit
- THESE SECTION ITEMS ARE **NOT** IN ORDER OF DIFFICULTY!

1. "This new drug will have no effect on levels of depression". This is a statement of

   (A) generalizability
   (B) demand characteristic
   (C) the null hypothesis
   (D) a positive skew
   (E) a negative skew

2. Two psychologists are debating the merits of different approaches for studying the consistency of extroversion over a lifespan. Psychologist #1 argues for a longitudinal study, psychologist #2 for a cross sectional study. The best argument psychologist #2 might offer in opposition to his colleague's position is

   (A) psychologist #1's approach would not allow for generalizability
   (B) psychologist #1's approach would not allow for selection of a representative sample
   (C) psychologist #1's approach is potentially limited by subject mortality
   (D) psychologist #2's approach offers more opportunity for consistency within the subject pool
   (E) psychologist #2's approach is the only valid method for examining development over the lifespan

3. Which of the following pairs most accurately describes problems in Stanley Milgram's research design that would render his 1963 study on obedience to authority unacceptable by today's standards for ethical research?

   (A) failure to obtain informed consent; failure to debrief subjects
   (B) failure to allow volunteers to discontinue participation at any time; failure to utilize an absolute minimum of deception
   (C) failure to maintain confidentiality; failure to secure informed consent
   (D) failure to maintain confidentiality; failure to debrief volunteers
   (E) failure to utilize an absolute minimum of deception; failure to use volunteers only

4. In administering a survey, use of a double blind procedure can help protect against

    (A) negatively skewed data
    (B) positively skewed data
    (C) reactance
    (D) randomization of responses
    (E) demand characteristic

5. For homework, an elementary school student is asked to find data about something he is personally interested in and to calculate the mean of that data. The next day, he reports to his classmates "the mean uniform number on my favorite professional football team is 51.3". His calculation indicates he does not yet understand the limitations of

    (A) ratio data
    (B) interval data
    (C) confounded data
    (D) ordinal data
    (E) nominal data

   * the next two items each refer to the following scenario:

Researchers design an experiment to test the effect of reading aloud on retention of the material read. One group of randomly assigned volunteers will read a story quietly to themselves, and a second group of randomly assigned volunteers will read the same story aloud. Both groups will then be assessed for retention of what they've read using a multiple choice test.

6. What is the independent variable (IV) in this experiment?

    (A) retention of facts in the story
    (B) the story itself
    (C) the reading of the story aloud
    (D) the items on the multiple choice test
    (E) reading

7. Which of the following would be a confounding variable in this experiment as it is presently set up?

   (A) one group reads the story aloud but the other reads it quietly
   (B) the "reading aloud" group reads the story in the classroom, and the "reading silently" group reads the story in the school library
   (C) the brightest students are randomly distributed between the "reading aloud" group and the "reading silently" group
   (D) the story is familiar to all the students
   (E) the story is unfamiliar to all the students

8. The major problem threatening the validity of a naturalistic observation is that

   (A) the subjects may react to or be influenced by the observation itself if they know they are being watched
   (B) such studies are almost impossible to measure empirically
   (C) the researcher cannot predict or control for the behaviors of the subjects
   (D) there is no counterbalancing
   (E) they only allow for the gathering of descriptive statistics

9. In an experiment in which one group receives a new drug treatment and a second group is given something they are told is a new medication but which is in fact only a sugar pill, the second group has received

   (A) a neuromodulator
   (B) the dependent variable
   (C) a confounded variable
   (D) a placebo
   (E) a counterbalanced treatment

10. If there is a 95% or greater chance that an experimental outcome is not due to chance we say the result has

   (A) criterion validity
   (B) interrater reliability
   (C) verifiability
   (D) correlational relevance
   (E) statistical significance

11. One advantage of a case study approach over a survey approach in psychological research is that

   (A) there is often a significant difference between what individuals report they would do in a certain circumstance and what they actually do in such a circumstance
   (B) over 90% of subjects have been proven to knowingly lie in responding to surveys
   (C) it is difficult to ever get a truly representative sample of respondents when administering surveys
   (D) the case study method allows for relatively easy control of confounding variables
   (E) the case study method allows for the gathering of more specific empirical data

12. What is the median of the following four IQ scores? 100, 110, 115, 135

   (A) 115
   (B) 100
   (C) 135
   (D) 112.5
   (E) 35 points

13. A teacher assigns a team of five students to observe their classmates for evidence of "helping behavior" in the school cafeteria. She asks each of them to come up with a score sheet and to simply record the number of "helping behaviors" each observes over the course of one week. Which of the following is a significant limitation of this study?

   (A) there is no way to replicate the study
   (B) there is no operational definition of 'helping behavior'
   (C) no null hypothesis is stated
   (D) there is no counterbalancing
   (E) there is no double blind procedure

14. Which of the following is the most likely value for "r" in a study examining the correlation in adult males between age in years and amount of hair on the head?

   (A) r= +1.0
   (B) r= -1.0
   (C) r= -.44
   (D) r= +.79
   (E) r= -1.17

15. A survey indicates the children who have been exposed to training in playing a musical instrument academically outperform children with no such background. School administrators in the area conclude that playing musical instruments early in childhood makes children more intelligent. This conclusion is flawed because

   (A) the administrators did not accurately identify the independent variable
   (B) survey methodology is notoriously inaccurate
   (C) there was no control for confounding variables
   (D) the administrators wrongly inferred causation from correlation
   (E) no such conclusion can be reached with only nominal data

Chapter II

The Biological Bases of Behavior

Introduction

This unit frightens many students who see "science" as a weakness, but it's not as difficult as it might at first appear, and you will have ample opportunity to revisit major concepts in it as the course progresses, since there is so much overlap between "biopsych" and the other sub-disciplines within psychology. The multiple choice section of the AP Exam will feature at least seven items from here, and it's entirely possible that at least one free response item will require some mastery of all this as well, so give the chapter careful attention.

The Neural Chain

There are billions of cells in the brain, called **neurons**, which are made up of:

- **dendrites:** the branch-like projections that receive messages from other neurons

- **the soma:** the cell body, made up of a nucleus which is surrounded by cytoplasm, all of which is held together by a membrane

- **the axon:** the "tail" of the neuron along which electrical signals are conducted; this signal results from a brief change in the electrical charge of the cell, called the **action potential**, which radiates down the axon,

- **terminals or terminal buttons:** knobs at the end of each axon from which chemical messengers called **neurotransmitters** are released into **the synapse**, the gap between the terminal buttons of one neuron and the dendrites of receiving neurons. This web of interconnections between cells is often referred to as **the neural chain**. The neurotransmitters carry information which is the foundation of behaviors and mental processes. Neurotransmitters may be **excitatory**, stimulating the firing of messages, or **inhibitory**, slowing the transmission of neural messages. For example, the caffeine in the coffee you drink increases the release of **glutamate**, the major excitatory neurotransmitter that therefore serves as a stimulant to the **central nervous system** (made up of the brain and spinal cord – everything else, that is whatever is not encased in bone, is part of the **peripheral nervous system**). Simultaneously, caffeine blocks some inhibitory activity; in essence, it is stepping on the accelerator of the car, while draining some brake fluid at the same time. If there is more excitatory than inhibitory input, then messages are sent along their way. If there is a majority of inhibitory input, messages are slowed or stopped. To complicate things a bit, some neurotransmitters can be excitatory *or* inhibitory, depending on **the receptors** to which their molecules bind. **Acetylcholine** is one example of such a chemical.

15

Some students find it useful to think of these inhibitory mechanisms as the safety catch on a gun, and the **"gun analogy"** also holds up in terms of other operations in the firing of a neuron. When there is sufficient input, the cell is **depolarized** (briefly, more positively charged inside the cell), and the neuron reaches its **firing threshold**. Once it does so, it fires in an **"all or none"** fashion. In pulling the trigger of a gun, there is a point at which the gun will fire, no matter how slowly or gently you have pulled the trigger. Pulling the trigger slowly will not make the bullet fly more slowly. After the neuron fires its electrical signal, there is a very brief **refractory period** in which the cell cannot fire again. This is analagous to the time after firing a pistol that one has to re-cock the gun in order to shoot again. It's easy to confuse the concepts of refractory period and resting state. When a neuron is in its **resting state**, it is more negatively charged inside the cell, and it *could* fire, it just isn't firing at the moment! During the absolute refractory period, the cell temporarily cannot fire at all, and during the relative refractory period that follows, it is much more difficult for the cell to fire than when in its resting state. It's not likely that you'll run into this distinction on the AP Exam, but if it comes up you'll be ahead of the competition.

When the electrical signal reaches the end of the axon it causes the release of the neurotransmitter housed in **the vesicles** of the terminal buttons. The chemical enters the synapse, where it locks into the receptor sites of the receiving neuron (**the post-synaptic neuron**; the neuron that sends the message is considered **pre-synaptic**). Any excess neurotransmitter left in the synapse is re-collected by the transmitting neuron. This is called **re-uptake**. Some neurotransmitters are "cleaned up" from the synapse not by re-uptake but by enzymes which break the chemical down.

Many textbooks use the **"lock and key"** analogy to help students understand how cells communicate, and also how drugs can act to block or stimulate neurotransmitter activity. For example, some drugs designed to control schizophrenia work like a piece of tape covering a keyhole. The presence of schizophrenia is correlated with higher than normal levels of **dopamine** activity, and several medications used to treat the disease basically do not allow that neurotransmitter (the key) to bind to the receptor site (the keyhole or lock) of the post synaptic neuron. Such a drug, one that blocks the action of a neurotransmitter, is called an **antagonist**; drugs that simulate the action of a certain neurotransmitter are called **agonists**. In a sense cocaine is a kind of agonist, although it does not so much mimic the action of dopamine as it stimulates a higher than normal level of dopamine activity by blocking the re-uptake of that chemical. Dopamine molecules are thus left out in the synapse and continue to bind to receptors, elevating the level of dopamine activity.

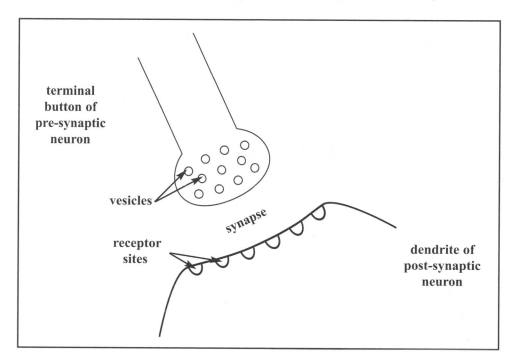

In later units on Sensation and Perception, Memory, Motivation and Emotion, Abnormal Psychology and others you will learn more about the action of specific neurotransmitters. For example, low levels of **acetylcholine** are correlated with the presence of Alzheimer's Disease. But it also clearly sends messages regarding muscular contraction as well. Some snake venoms block acetylcholine receptors, leading to paralysis and suffocation. Arousal of the **fight of flight mechanism** when an organism is under stress stimulates the release of **norepinephrine** and the natural pain killers called **endorphins**. The aptly named **Substance P** is the neurotransmitter responsible for the sending of pain messages. **Serotonin** seems connected to mood regulation and eating drives, among other things. The aforementioned **dopamine** is often linked to pleasure; several recreational drugs seem to operate on dopamine neurons. Some estimate that as many of one third of all neurons are **G.A.B.A. (gamma-aminobutyric acid)** neurons. G.A.B.A. is the leading inhibitory neurotransmitter in the brain. Many seizure disorders are correlated with lower than normal levels of G.A.B.A. activity, resulting in lower than normal levels of inhibition – simplistically stated, it's as if the brakes are failing in the car.

Finally, you might see reference on the AP Exam to the basic process by which **afferent, or sensory neurons,** carry messages to **interneurons** in the brain and spinal cord (the central nervous system) which then transmit the message out to the muscles and glands (the effectors) via **efferent, or motor neurons**. In a reflex arc, sensory input of a foreign object flying toward your eye is carried by afferent neurons directly to the spinal cord and then back out to your eye and head muscles even before your brain is engaged, and you reflexively flinch. A common trick to keep these two types of cell straight is to link "A" for 'afferent', "A" for 'approach', and "E" for 'efferent', "E" for 'exit'. And **glial cells** are pretty easy to remember because their name sounds something like 'glue', and they function as support cells which essentially hold together the message sending neurons and support their functioning.

The Nervous System

Keeping up with breaking research in the field of neuroscience requires a flexible mind which is willing to seek out, examine and accept new information that might very well challenge one's notion of what was previously considered "fact". But questions on the AP Psych Exam tend to focus on areas in BioPsychology that are not much in dispute, at least at present, and, while the people at E.T.S. constantly remind teachers and students that they are responsible for keeping abreast of the newest research, they do not expect advanced placement students to be on the absolute cutting edge in this ever evolving field.

Any such ongoing learning is facilitated by a human brain which is remarkably "plastic", in that it seems able even as we age to wire and rewire its synaptic connections in response to new situations, information and environmental stimuli. This concept of **brain plasticity** is supported by many striking examples of humans whose brains have somehow refitted themselves to compensate for the loss of function resulting from injury or illness. Among others, Matt Ridley argues that the world in which we live and function helps to "build a brain", and that our "nature" manifests itself only via interaction with the environment.

There are some old standby areas in the study of the nervous system that are essential in your preparation. You must have a general understanding of the difference between the central nervous system (the CNS) and the peripheral nervous system (the PNS), both of which were mentioned earlier. Many students struggle with the distinction between the **somatic system** and the **autonomic system**, the two subdivisions of the PNS. In psychology, 'soma' means 'body', which might help you to remember that the somatic system controls the voluntary actions of the body, while the autonomic system is largely involuntary. Many teachers teach the autonomic system by referring to it as "automatic", but students are usually familiar with the term 'autonomous' from history classes, and it is more accurate to refer to this as a system that pretty much acts on its own, as an autonomous country would. The autonomic system is further broken into **sympathetic** and **parasympathetic** systems; the former is analagous to an emergency response system (ratcheting up heart rate, dilating the pupils, inhibiting digestion and salivation to ready the body for immediate action), the latter to its opposing process, working to return you to balance. Thus, these are often referred to as **antagonistic systems**.

The central nervous system consists of the brain and spinal cord. The wrinkled, convoluted shell of the brain is called **the cortex**. It is divided into four lobes: frontal, parietal, occipital, temporal. Generally speaking (all of these summaries of the functions in each of the four lobes are open to debate and to change), **the frontal lobes** act as the executive of the brain, carrying out planning, decision making and judgment. **The motor cortex**, responsible for voluntary muscle movement, is located in the rear of the frontal lobe, near the border of **the parietal lobe**, which houses the **somatosensory area** of the cortex. This section governs the sense of touch, temperature and pain. The **visual cortex** is located in the **occipital lobe**, in the rear of the cortex. Many students find this odd and thus easy to remember – they are surprised to learn that the area of the brain given over to the processing of visual information is actually at the back of the head. Meanwhile, **the auditory cortex**, which processes information from both ears, is located in the **temporal lobes**, to the side of the head, just above the ears. Last but hardly least is the **association cortex**, which makes up a huge portion (perhaps as much as 3/4) of the entire cortex. It is difficult to localize, but it seems to be responsible for linking relevance and meaning to sensory input and, in the frontal lobe, for much of the highest level thinking that humans do.

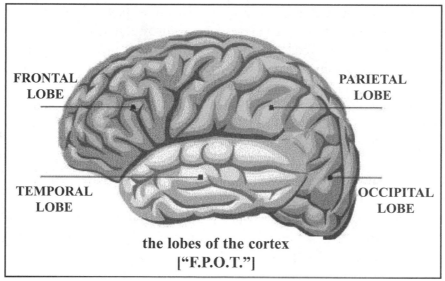

the lobes of the cortex
["F.P.O.T."]

From Psychology: A ConnecText 4/e by Terry F. Pettijohn. Copyright © 1999 by The McGraw-Hill Companies, Inc. All rights reserved. Reprinted by permission of McGraw-Hill Contemporary Learning Series.

The reticular activating system, also known as the **reticular formation**, is also difficult to place exactly in the brain. Different textbooks will tell you it is in the midbrain, others in the hindbrain or brain stem. You will not be asked on an AP Psychology Examination to place it accurately, but you should know that it is generally considered to be the area which controls the arousal to attend to incoming stimuli. In a sense, it serves as the bell which rings over the entrance to a store, signaling the proprietor that there is a customer who requires attention. **The thalamus**, located in the midbrain, is often referred to as the switchboard of the brain. It relays sensory information (for all senses but smell, which is routed through the emotional limbic system) to appropriate destinations.

In the **"hind brain"** are the **medulla**, which helps to control breathing, swallowing and blood circulation, and the **cerebellum**, which is a center for balance and coordination. A third structure in this oldest and most primitive part of the brain is **the pons**, which functions much like a bridge between brain regions, and is also believed to play a role in sleep and basic arousal.

More On The Brain

Most every college psychology textbook has a nice visual description of Roger Sperry's work with **"split brain" patients**, from which we have learned so much about the function of the left and right hemispheres of the human brain. You should be conversant with his methodology. A simple visual representation of this follows. Sperry conducted experiments on the perceptions of patients who had had their corpus callosum severed in a surgical procedure designed to control severe seizures. The corpus callosum connects the two halves, or hemispheres, of the brain. The surgery thus isolates each hemisphere from the other, which has no overt impact on functioning; however, Sperry (and his collaborator, Michael Gazzaniga) discovered that it *did* have some effect. When, for instance, he asked such a patient to look at a dot in the middle of a divided screen and instantaneously flashed separate images to the two sides of the screen, he found that the participants could not verbally report what they had "seen" on the left half of the screen. He knew they had indeed seen the image, because they could identify it by touch and through illustration using the left hand, but they couldn't *name* it. Sperry knew that the left side of the body is governed by the right side of the brain, and vice versa. From this, he surmised that the right side of the brain, the side that would've first received the image (which, remember, had been seen only by the left eye), must have limited language capability. The left side of the brain must house the major centers for language. Images flashed to the right eye, and thus the left hemisphere of the brain, were readily identified verbally by the split brain patients. In you and me, the corpus callosum instantaneously allows the two halves of the brain to communicate with each other, but the surgical procedure these patients had undergone cut that connection. Split brain patients adapt to the change over time, but Sperry's work told us much about language function in the brain. For the purposes of the AP exam, you should also know about **Broca's Area and Wernicke's Area**, structures in the left hemisphere of the brain which appear responsible for the expression and understanding of language.

Sperry's Split Brain Research

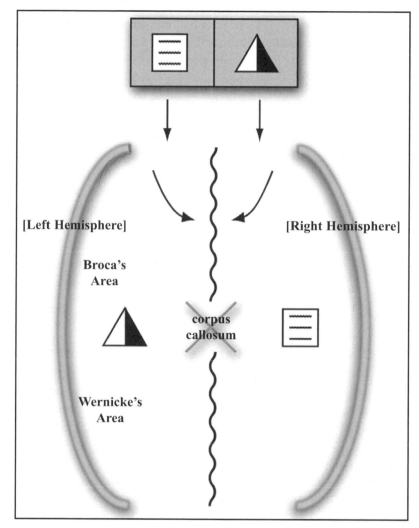

The hippocampus, the amygdala and the hypothalamus are all part of **the limbic system**, often thought of as the seat of emotion and primitive motivations. **The hippocampus** is only peripherally involved in such processes however. It seems mostly responsible for the formation of new memories. The **amygdala** is associated with anger, fear and to some extent sex drive – it may also be viewed as the spot in the brain most responsible for evaluating the "emotional relevance" of <u>any</u> incoming information. **The septum** also plays a role in fear response. Finally, **the hypothalamus** works in concert with **the pituitary gland**, located at the base of the brain, to help regulate eating, drinking and sex drive. It also joins the pituitary in directing the other glands of **the endocrine system**. Thus, the pituitary is sometimes called "the master gland".

The Endocrine System

The glands of the endocrine system secrete **hormones**, another type of chemical messenger. Unlike the aforementioned neurotransmitters however, hormones are carried in the bloodstream. Some liken the relationship between hormones and neurotransmitters to post office mail as compared to today's speedier electronic mail. **The thyroid and parathyroid glands**, in the neck, specialize in growth and metabolism. The **adrenal glands**, at the midsection of the body, near the kidneys, govern "fight or flight" responses, through secretion of adrenaline and noradrenaline (also called epinephrine and norepinephrine) and cortisol. **The pancreas**, just below the adrenals, secretes insulin which works in the metabolism of blood sugar, and, the **ovaries** and **testes** are responsible for the development at puberty of **primary sex characteristics**, which are involved directly in reproduction, and **secondary sex characteristics** such as breast development in females and growth of facial and body hair in males.

Genetics

You understand most of what you need to know about genetics in an advanced placement psychology course if you grasp the concept of **genetic predispositions.** This is the idea that humans are born with a tendency toward certain behaviors or characteristics, but only a tendency. Many students misinterpret this to mean that we "are born with" certain traits, but the concept of genetic or biological predisposition only suggests a push in one direction or another, a nudge that relies on environmental influences as well. For example, there does seem to be a genetic predisposition (but not genetic "determinism") for body weight and body fat percentage, for schizophrenia, for major depression, and so on. You will encounter more such examples in later units, especially when you examine twin studies in units on Developmental Psychology and Personality Theory.

A concept that is so often misunderstood that it is unlikely to appear on an AP Exam is that of **heritability**. This refers to the amount of *difference between individuals* that seems to be accounted for by heredity. If we were to say that body fat percentage was 40% heritability it would NOT mean that 40% of your body weight comes from genetics, but that 40% of the difference between you and some other individual seems due to genetics.

You probably already know something about **dominant and recessive genes** from biology class, and that **males have XY chromosomes and females have XX**. In that course you likely also learned that **genotype** refers to one's genetic make-up while **phenotype** refers to one's physical appearance. You probably won't even need to know all that in order to succeed on the AP exam; likewise, you will probably not be assessed on your knowledge of genetic disorders, although **Down Syndrome** is one genetic abnormality that is particularly relevant in psychology. It is caused by an extra chromosome on the 21st chromosome pair, and results in various levels of mental retardation, some limitations in physical development, and characteristic features of appearance.

Finally, there has been discussion in the past amongst members of the test development committee as to how much students should know about methods used to look at the structures and activity in the brain. Again, most college textbooks have brief descriptions of how each of the following brain imaging techniques is used: magnetic resonance imaging **(MRI)**, computerized axial tomography **(CAT)**, electroencephalograph **(EEG)** and positron emission tomography **(PET)**. For the purposes of this book and the AP Exam, suffice it to say that the first two largely look at brain *structure*, the latter two at brain *function* or activity, although there are now **"functional MRI's (fMRI)"** that do a bit of both. Currently, it is also fair to say that you would not be asked a question about any of these without reference to both the name and the acronym.

Name Hall Of Fame

There are no shoo-ins for the Hall of Fame in this unit. You may have to recognize **Roger Sperry's** name in reference to his split brain research, and you might see **Wilder Penfield's** name in regard to his work in the middle of the 20th century in mapping the motor and sensory areas of the cortex. Almost every teacher and text refers to the 1848 case of **Phineas Gage**, who was injured in a horrifying accident while doing railroad work. Gage was 25 years old, 150 pounds, and a very reliable worker, but his personality was significantly altered after a 4 foot, 13 pound metal rod was driven through his skull in an explosion. Although he somehow recovered physically from this trauma, the damage to his frontal lobes and an apparent severing of the connection between that section of the brain and his limbic system left him an impulsive, highly emotional man, unable to perform much in the way of goal directed activity. From this frightening case study, scientists learned much about the functions of all healthy human brains.

Essay Themes

While it is unlikely that you would see a free response item that was completely based on understanding of the biological bases of behavior, you still ought to have a general grip on the concept of **how neurotransmitters and hormones work to effect behavior**. You will also benefit from knowing the **basic functions of the structures of the brain** summarized in this unit outline. When in doubt in searching for a biological justification for some behavior or characteristic, you always have the concept of **genetic predispositions** to fall back on, especially as more and more such genetic tendencies are uncovered. That is also a possible topic for a critical thinking essay which might require you to organize and evaluate evidence on the predominance of biological vs. environmental influences on human behavior and mental processes.

Technological advances have provided more and more data illustrating **the plasticity of the human brain**. It has become a major area of focus in neuroscience, and thus could be important on an AP Exam.

Test Preparation: Biological Bases of Behavior

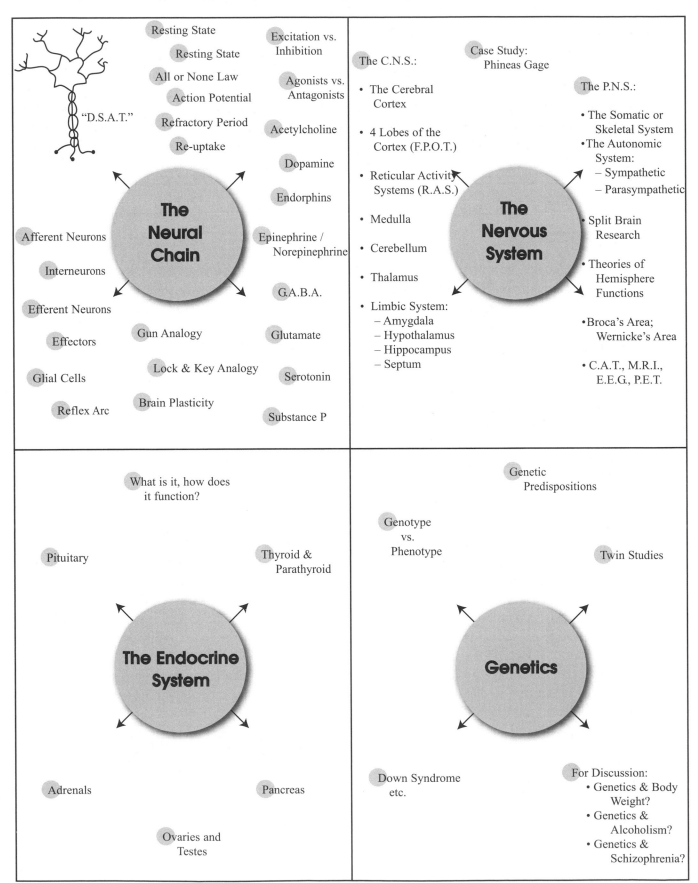

The Neural Chain

- "D.S.A.T."
- Resting State
- Resting State
- All or None Law
- Action Potential
- Refractory Period
- Re-uptake
- Excitation vs. Inhibition
- Agonists vs. Antagonists
- Acetylcholine
- Dopamine
- Endorphins
- Epinephrine / Norepinephrine
- G.A.B.A.
- Glutamate
- Serotonin
- Substance P
- Afferent Neurons
- Interneurons
- Efferent Neurons
- Effectors
- Glial Cells
- Reflex Arc
- Gun Analogy
- Lock & Key Analogy
- Brain Plasticity

The Nervous System

- The C.N.S.:
  - The Cerebral Cortex
  - 4 Lobes of the Cortex (F.P.O.T.)
  - Reticular Activity Systems (R.A.S.)
  - Medulla
  - Cerebellum
  - Thalamus
  - Limbic System:
    – Amygdala
    – Hypothalamus
    – Hippocampus
    – Septum
- Case Study: Phineas Gage
- The P.N.S.:
  - The Somatic or Skeletal System
  - The Autonomic System:
    – Sympathetic
    – Parasympathetic
  - Split Brain Research
  - Theories of Hemisphere Functions
  - Broca's Area; Wernicke's Area
  - C.A.T., M.R.I., E.E.G., P.E.T.

The Endocrine System

- What is it, how does it function?
- Pituitary
- Thyroid & Parathyroid
- Adrenals
- Pancreas
- Ovaries and Testes

Genetics

- Genetic Predispositions
- Genotype vs. Phenotype
- Twin Studies
- Down Syndrome etc.
- For Discussion:
  - Genetics & Body Weight?
  - Genetics & Alcoholism?
  - Genetics & Schizophrenia?

24

Practice Items

- remember to TIME YOURSELF, and shoot for 10½ minutes total on these 15 questions
- remember that these section items are NOT in order of difficulty
- remember that the multiple choice section is worth 2/3 of your total score on the AP Exam; this practice is very important

1. Which of the following house the auditory cortex and the visual cortex respectively?

   (A) the limbic system and the endocrine system
   (B) the sympathetic system and the parasympathetic system
   (C) the occipital lobe and the parietal lobe
   (D) the temporal lobe and the occipital lobe
   (E) the temporal lobe and the parietal lobe

2. Afferent neurons

   (A) carry neural messages into the central nervous system
   (B) are also known as motor neurons
   (C) are also known as interneurons
   (D) support the function of glial cells
   (E) support the effectors

3. In a neuron, the dendrites

   (A) are responsible for the regulation of the firing threshold
   (B) house the molecules of the neurotransmitter
   (C) are surrounded by sheaths of a fatty substance called myelin
   (D) stimulate reuptake
   (E) receive input from other neurons

4. Lower than normal levels of acetylcholine activity in the brain are correlated with the presence of

   (A) multiple sclerosis
   (B) mental retardation
   (C) autism
   (D) Alzheimer's Disease
   (E) obsessive-compulsive disorder

5. If the human brain were an orchestra, which of the following regions would be most analagous to the conductor of that orchestra?

    (A) the left hemisphere
    (B) the right hemisphere
    (C) the somatic system
    (D) the prefrontal cortex
    (E) the hindbrain

6. The band of fibers that connect the two halves of the human brain is called the

    (A) corpus callosum
    (B) cerebral cortex
    (C) the association cortex
    (D) the pons
    (E) the reticular formation

7. Which of the following are considered part of the old or hind brain?

    (A) the hypothalamus and the hippocampus
    (B) the hippocampus and the amygdala
    (C) the medulla and the cerebellum
    (D) the reticular formation and the pons
    (E) the cerebrum and the association cortex

8. Reduced control of bladder contraction and inhibition of salivation and digestion are characteristic of

    (A) cerebral entropy
    (B) endocrine activation
    (C) the firing of neural messages
    (D) parasympathetic nervous system activation
    (E) sympathetic nervous system activation

9. A split brain patient is instantaneously flashed an image of a truck to the left visual field and a cow to the right visual field. When asked to verbally report what he saw,

   (A) he will be unable to meaningfully respond
   (B) he will report seeing both a truck and a cow, but will reverse their proper placement on the screen
   (C) he will report seeing a cow
   (D) he will report seeing a truck
   (E) he will immediately try to verbally incorporate the two images into a coherent "storyline"

10. If a drug were administered to an individual to block the action of endorphins,

    (A) it would stimulate portions of the somatosensory cortex
    (B) it would essentially block the placebo effect
    (C) it would likely alleviate symptoms of schizophrenia
    (D) it might induce symptoms of major depression
    (E) it might induce symptoms of bipolar disorder

11. The tail-like portion of a neuron upon which electrical signals are carried is called the

    (A) dendrite
    (B) terminal
    (C) soma
    (D) effector
    (E) axon

12. For a brief time after firing a single shot handgun, you cannot fire the gun again. This is analagous to what in cell firing?

    (A) reaching the firing threshold
    (B) the resting state
    (C) the refractory period
    (D) the action potential
    (E) inhibitory neurotransmitter activity

13. The pleasure humans derive from food, water and sexual activity is most correlated with activity of which of the following neurotransmitters?

    (A) G.A.B.A.
    (B) Acetylcholine
    (C) Substance P
    (D) Glycine
    (E) Dopamine

14. In the peripheral nervous system, the somatic branch

    (A) operates as an opposing process vs. the autonomic system
    (B) serves as part of the central nervous system
    (C) is made up of sensory and motor neurons which largely govern voluntary muscular responses
    (D) essentially governs involuntary processes such as breathing and heart rate
    (E) essentially governs speech

15. The thalamus and the hypothalamus in the human brain are most accurately described as performing what basic functions, respectively?

    (A) the center for emotional arousal; the center for higher level decision making
    (B) the relay station or switchboard of the brain; regulation of appetite and thirst
    (C) the center for formation of new memories; regulation of sex drive
    (D) a sensory processing center; the center for storage of newly formed memories
    (E) regulation of appetite and thirst; a sensory processing center

Chapter III

Sensation and Perception

This is a big unit in the AP Psych curriculum. Happily, a very large percentage of the concepts can be demonstrated to you, which makes them relatively easy to retain. If you're in a solid AP course, your teacher will almost surely do a lot of these active learning demos. Most college hardcover texts have numerous visuals which will illustrate otherwise difficult concepts in memorable ways. So, while there is a lot to digest here, if you actively engage in the study of this unit you will certainly leave it with a new perspective on how we take in and interpret information from the world.

Sensation

'**Sensation**' refers to the process of attending to and taking in stimuli from the environment. It involves what-is-out-there and how we see or hear or taste or touch or smell it (on top of those five familiar senses we also have a sense of whole body balance or equilibrium, **the vestibular** sense, housed in the inner ear, and a sense of body part position and movement, **the kinesthetic sense**). '**Perception**' refers to the interpretation and organization of sensory information. As you will discover in this unit, it is quite remarkable how much of our sensory experience is influenced by our individual attention, memories, past experiences, previous learning and motivations. For that reason, 'perception' is sometimes called **"top-down"processing** while 'sensation' is thought of as **"bottom-up" processing**. You and your best friend might each attend to the same red chair and "see" it largely in the same manner, but your perceptions of it could be notably different. It may, for instance, remind you of a chair you sat in when asking your favorite person to the prom although it has no such significance for your friend. On an even less emotionally laden level, each of you might "see" the chair using the same basic sensory processes but one might describe it as "big", another as "small", one might add features to their recall of the chair that are not present in the actual chair, one might miss or forget fairly obvious features of the chair that the other considered prominent, and so on.

The earliest work in the field we now call 'psychology' was led by researchers like Gustav Fechner, Wilhelm Wundt, Edward Titchener and Ernst Weber in the area of '**psychophysics**'. This involved the study of the links between physical stimuli in the world and the psychological experience of those stimuli. You can see that this is the essence of what we label today as 'sensation and perception'. Several of the concepts you must learn for the advanced placement course were first examined by those men and others in the last quarter of the 19th century.

Imagine that you are ushered into an examination room with several classmates and given a set of earphones. Each of you will close your eyes and be exposed to tones of varying volume. You are instructed to raise your hand if / when you hear a tone. One goal of such a test is to determine your **absolute threshold** for hearing. This is the minimum amount of stimulus you can detect at least fifty percent of the time it is presented. If the examiner were to identify a tone that all of the students could hear, and then presented another tone and asked the students to report whether it was louder or softer than the previous tone, he or she would be measuring the **difference threshold**, or the just noticeable difference **(the JND)**. This is the smallest difference between two stimuli which a subject can detect at least fifty percent of the time. Some experts might argue that the difference threshold and the JND are not exactly synonymous, but this is a distinction that would not be made on the Advanced Placement Examination.

If a very loud tone were presented to the students and then an only *marginally* louder tone was presented, **Weber's Law** would predict that the listeners would be unlikely to notice the difference in the tones. Weber's Law is actually a formula which supports the principle that two stimuli must differ by a constant *proportion*, not a constant *amount*, for a difference between them to be detected. Simply stated, the louder a sound is, the brighter a light is, the more pungent an aroma is, the more you would have to change it, proportionally, to notice a difference. This law does not apply very well to very high and very low levels of stimulus. Anyone who has lifted weights can see this is so: according to Weber's Law, if an individual can bench press 300 pounds, a significant weight, adding only 5 pounds to the bar, a relatively small amount, should not be noticeable. Of course, it is <u>quite</u> noticeable if the lifter is already at the ceiling of their performance.

Study of detection thresholds leads naturally into study of attention. It would be much more difficult for the students taking the hearing test to perform well if they did not attend to the stimuli in the first place, or even to the *idea* that stimuli may be presented. And background interference (known as *'noise'*, which can be interference in any sensory modality, not merely hearing) can also influence one's ability to detect a stimulus. In **signal detection theory**, if a stimulus, say a tone, was presented and an individual detected it, it is called a **"hit"**. If a tone was presented and the individual did not detect it, it is a **"miss"**. If no tone was presented and the individual reports there *was* a tone, this is a **"false alarm"** (or a *false positive*) and, if no tone was presented and the listener reports that there was no tone, we use the term **"correct rejection"**. There are all kinds of real-life examples to illustrate signal detection theory, from parents listening for the possible cries of their newborn baby to radar and sonar operators and their reliability in the detection of signals.

As you might surmise from your own experience, repeated exposure to any stimulus can make you so "used to it" that you no longer attend to it. This **adaptation** happens on a "psychological" level, but can also occur on a *physiological* level – the receptors for any particular sense actually no longer respond in the same way to repeated stimulation. Developmental psychologists ingeniously determine how much infants, who can't verbally tell us about their preferences, like someone or something by how long they attend to it. Once they essentially adapt to the input they may no longer give it attention *until it changes*. This is referred to as **habituation**.

You will also have to know about **selective and divided attention** and **dichotic listening and viewing** studies. The two types of 'attention' essentially explain themselves, especially if you have ever attended a party in which much auditory, visual and olfactory stimulation is reaching your sensory system and you *choose to attend* to some of it but not to all of it. Of course, the very fact that you can attend to some of it implies that you can *divide your attention* between multiple sensory inputs. This in turn is examined in the laboratory through the use of dichotic listening tasks, in which you might be asked to wear a set of headphones which simultaneously play two competing messages, one in the left ear and one in the right. You may be asked to selectively attend to only one or attempt to divide your attention between both, and, in either case, might then be tested for what you retained from either or both sets of input. A famous dichotic viewing test superimposes two teams of men playing catch with a ball onto a television screen and asks you to attend to one group while tuning out the other. Variations are sometimes built into this – your teacher may wish to demonstrate them to you, and your text will almost certainly cover such variations.

The remainder of the 'sensation' portion of the unit involves specific study of each sensory system. The Advanced Placement Examination often ends up with more weight placed on the visual and auditory systems, although this is not by design; it may merely result from the fact that there is more "stuff" to test on in those areas. In any case, it is important to be familiar with the basics of all seven senses.

The Visual System

- **receptors:** rods and cones, located in the back of the retina; **rods** are far more numerous and are specialized for black/white, light/dark vision, while **cones** are specialized for color vision and for visual clarity or acuity. All told, there are over 120 million rods and cones in each eye. Cones are largely clustered in **the fovea** – thus, in order for us to see an object clearly, the image must fall on the fovea, which is in the center of the retina. Further, in order for us to really discern color, an image must fall on the fovea – rods predominate in our peripheral vision. The energy of the light waves the eye receives is transformed by the rods and cones into electrical signals (this process is called **transduction**) which are then transmitted to a layer of a few million bipolar cells, which in turn communicate with about one million ganglion cells (this organization, from so many rods and cones down to far fewer ganglion cells is called *summation*). The axons of those cells form the optic nerve, upon which the neural message is carried to

- **the visual cortex:** the portion of the brain responsible for the processing of visual information; it's located in the occipital lobe, at the back of the head.

- **The blind spot:** at the point where the optic nerve exits the back of the eye, headed for the visual cortex, there are no rods and cones, and thus no receptors for vision. An image that falls directly on the blind spot would not be seen, although head and eye movements and the teamwork between the two eyes, each compensating for the other, allows us to avoid "blind spots" in our vision. The following highly simplified representation may help you in visualizing all this:

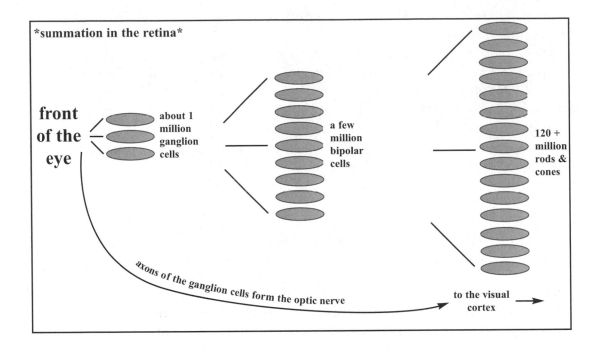

- in **trichromatic color vision theory** it is thought that there are three different types of color receptors, which are specialized for red, green and blue but which overlap as well, combining to allow for seeing other colors. This is sometimes called Young-Helmholtz Theory
- **in opponent process color vision theory** states there are two kinds of cones, one of which responds to red and green, the other to blue and yellow, while the rods, of course, process black and white input. As one color in each pair is excited, the other is inhibited. Thus, if you stare for about 30 seconds at a green dot, and then avert your gaze to a neutral background, you will likely experience a *red* **color afterimage**. The intense exposure to green inhibits red, but when that exposure stops there is an "overshoot" effect to red. Most individuals who are considered "color blind" actually do see some color, but have trouble discriminating the differences between certain hues.
- **dark adaptation:** the process of the rods and cones adjusting to changes in levels of light; rods and cones adapt, for instance, when you enter a darkened movie theater, although the rods do so for a longer period (up to 40 minutes or so!)

The Auditory System

- **receptors: hair cells,** located on the basilar membrane in the cochlea; the energy from sound waves is **transduced** into electrochemical energy, and sensory neurons then carry that information to the auditory cortex
- **auditory cortex:** the portion of the brain responsible for processing hearing; located in the temporal lobes

- **conductive deafness:** deafness resulting from blockage of the transmission of sound waves; ear wax, for example, blocks the conduction of sound waves through the auditory canal, just as damage to the bones (the ossicles) in the middle ear might impede the transfer of sound waves from the eardrum to the oval window, so the information never reaches the hair cells in the cochlea
- **perceptive deafness:** deafness caused by damage to the hair cells or the auditory nerve. The following greatly simplified visual may help you picture the basic auditory mechanism

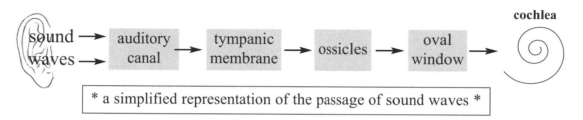

* a simplified representation of the passage of sound waves *

- **place theory:** the theory that suggests we identify the pitch of sounds according to the location of vibrations on the basilar membrane. This works something like plucking a string on a violin or guitar while pressing down on the string at different spots on the neck
- **frequency theory:** the theory of hearing that suggests we identify the pitch of sounds according to how rapidly the nerve impulses fire. At very high frequencies, nerves fire one after another **(the volley principle)**, since no one cell could fire quickly enough to accommodate such frequencies, and in the auditory cortex the number of impulses fired per second is "translated" into hertz, the unit of measure for the frequency of a sound

The Olfactory System

- **receptors: olfactory cells** located in the nasal cavity; there may be as many as 100 different kinds of olfactory receptor sites, and about 10 million total olfactory cells
- **olfactory cortex:** located in the temporal lobes; this is "wired" closely with the amygdala and the hippocampus, both of which are in the emotional limbic system, which may account for the power of emotionally charged memories triggered by smells. All other senses are "wired" through the thalamus, the relay station of the brain. By the way, the phenomenon of a sense cueing a memory is called *redintegration*
- **anosmia:** the term for the loss of the sense of smell
- **pheromones:** chemically produced odors which send signals (of sexual readiness, territory etc.) to other members of that species

The Gustatory System

- **receptors: taste cells**, clustered in groups called taste buds, located on the tongue; their sensitivity tends to decline with age, especially in the case of those specialized most for **bitter** and **sour** tastes. The other two types of taste cells respond largely to **sweet** and **salty**, although many older textbooks do not include recent research which indicates there is less specialization than was once thought. Likewise, many older texts may have "tongue diagrams" that suggest specific <u>localization</u> of each of these taste areas on the tongue although we now know that these taste locales are *not* so strictly localized
- **much of the sense of taste comes from the sense of smell**, which you can demonstrate to yourself by holding your nose while beginning to eat anything with a strong taste that is *not* sweet, sour, salty or bitter – if you then release your nose, you should get a burst of that "flavor", which is really an olfactory phenomenon

The Somasthetic System

- **receptors:** several different types located in **the skin**; the Advanced Placement Examination would <u>not</u> include questions about specific receptors like Meissner corpuscles, Ruffini endings or Merkel disks however
- **sensory cortex:** located in the **parietal lobe** at the crown of the head. The left parietal lobe receives information from the right side of the body, while the right parietal lobe gets the information from the left side of the body. The more sensitive the area of the body is, the more surface area in the cortex is given over to that body part
- **gate control theory of pain**: the theory which suggests there is a kind of "gate" in the spinal cord which opens and closes to both allow pain messages through to the brain and to stop those messages – substance P activity in the spinal cord would open the gate while the release of endorphins would essentially close the gate

The Kinesthetic System

- **receptors:** in the joints and muscles, which give us information as to **body part** position and movement

The Vestibular System

- originating in the semicircular canals in the inner ear, governing **whole body position and balance**

You might find it interesting to do a bit of research on *synesthesia*, a fascinating ability in some to vividly experience one sense in terms of another; that is, to "see" musical notes or to "hear" certain colors. You're not likely to need it for the AP Exam, but it's certainly fun, and mystifying, to read about.

Perception

As we've already seen, 'perception' involves how we interpret sensory input from the top down; that is, from our brain/mind down to the world "as it is". You may hear reference to the synonymous term **organismic variables**, which includes all the things an individual organism brings to each sensory experience and which thus can make that sensory experience into a very different 'perception'. For example, each of us has a different **frame of reference**. A 7 foot tall man might describe an alleged bank robber as rather short while a young preschooler would be more likely to describe the same bank robber as being quite tall. Each of us is also often influenced by **perceptual set** (also called **perceptual expectancy**), in which what we expect to see, hear, taste, touch or smell *actually influences* what we experience. A closely related concept is that of **schema**, which is a kind of framework we have in our heads based on previous experience. If asked to look at a photo of an office, we already expect certain things to be part of that office and might well be surprised to see things that do not fit our "office schema". A professional football player given a quick look at a panoramic image of a play in motion would be better able to "remember" details of that image because his experience has supplied him a schema for where particular players would most typically be. **Context**, the impact of the surrounding environment on our judgments, can also play a significant role in our perception of images and events. There are also **contrast effects** in perception. A gray bar on a white background can appear to be a different shade of gray than the same gray bar on a black background.

According to **gestalt psychologists**, humans have a tendency to want to organize their perceptions into meaningful units or wholes. We "finish off" incomplete images based on our prior knowledge (this is called **closure**), we group **similar** perceptions together, as we do items in close **proximity** to one another, and objects that seem to "flow" together (called **good continuation**). We also sometimes **infer** the presence of something we cannot directly perceive, again based upon previous exposure to similar situations. For example, when driving we do not need to directly see the rest of the road over the horizon to infer that there is indeed a "rest of the road".

We also infer things about the shape and size of objects even when the image we "see" of it changes. If we see a plane in the sky, we know it is a large plane even though the image of it that falls on our retina (called the **proximal stimulus**) is tiny. We know it is a **constant size (the distal stimulus**, referring to how the thing really is in the world) despite its appearance. For **shape constancy**, many textbooks use an example of a door viewed from multiple angles. If you see the door closed, or ajar, or wide open, you still perceive it as a door, despite the differing shapes projected onto your retina.

There are at least two theories as to how we recognize multifaceted items in the world. How, for instance, do we know that the letter 'K' is the letter 'K'? According to **feature analysis theory**, we first break it into its pieces and decide what those features could comprise. Support for this comes from the Nobel Prize winning work of David Hubel and Thorsten Weisel, who discovered that there are cells in the brain (conveniently labeled **feature detector cells**) which are specialized to fire only in response to particular angles or lines in the visual field. Conversely, according to **prototype matching theory**, we have stored a small number of models or paradigms of each letter and compare each new whole to those prototypes.

All good college textbooks will include reference to several cues for perceiving depth or distance, and many will have useful visuals of each. Here is a quick list of those most likely to show up on an Advanced Placement Exam:

Each of the following is a **monocular depth cue**, meaning that they require only one eye. Look around the room you're sitting in and you can find an illustration of many of these:

- **accommodation:** changes in the curvature of the lens to adjust and focus on objects at various distances; when you squint at an unclear object in the distance you're basically trying to accommodate
- **brightness:** objects nearer to you appear brighter than those further away
- **elevation:** objects further away from you appear to be higher in the visual field; if you asked a child to draw her house and then asked her to draw her grandmother's house, she would likely place it higher in the picture to signify its distance from her own home
- **interposition:** objects nearer to you appear in between you and objects which are further away
- **linear perspective:** parallel lines seem to converge as they move off into the distance; think of how a railroad track would appear to you as it recedes into the horizon, or simply look at how the tiles on the floor below you seem to narrow and come together as distance from you increases
- **motion parallax:** objects near you appear to move more quickly than objects further away from you; think of how slowly an airplane seems to move in the sky when it is far away but then how speedy it is as you view its landing from an airport window
- **texture gradient:** objects further away from you are not as precise and detailed in their appearance, while objects closer to you are more distinct; again, look at the floor or perhaps at the ceiling and you can see this distance cue at work

the following are binocular depth cues – you need both eyes for these:

- **convergence:** as an object moves closer to you, your two eyes converge on it, and you feel tension in the ciliary muscles of the eye
- **retinal disparity** (also known as **binocular disparity**): each eye actually receives a slightly different image of any object you are viewing, and the two are put together in the visual cortex. In the 1990's, it was shown that there are cells in the visual cortex that respond specifically to binocular disparity. The nearer an object is to you, the more difficult it is to combine the 2 images, which might account for why you "see double" as you view your own finger while you move it closer and closer to your face.

Finally, in this unit you might be exposed to **reversible figures** like the well known "old lady/young lady" image, **figure-ground images** like the equally well known "vase or faces?" example and other perceptual illusions and phenomena. The Test Preparation graphic organizer at the end of this chapter contains examples of some of these. It is highly unlikely, however, that you would have to specifically recall the name of an illusion or supply an example of one with the name only as a cue on the AP Exam.

Name Hall of Fame

Just as many colleges and universities have their own sports halls of fame, populated by standouts from that particular school who might or might not be part of an all-inclusive, national hall of fame, so too with names from this unit. Specialists in sensation and perception might consider recognition of them indispensable, but, for an introductory college psychology course and for the authors of the Advanced Placement Exam, they are not. While there could possibly be a multiple choice item on the history of psychology which may refer to names like **Wilhelm Wundt, Gustav Fechner, Edward Titchener or Ernst Weber**, you would not have to pull any of those names out of a hat. Each of them, you may recall, was an early researcher in psychophysics, but their names would likely be used simply as another cue for you in responding to a question of greater breadth.

David Hubel and **Thorsten Wiesel** won a Nobel Prize for identification of feature detector cells in the brain, so that makes them pretty important, but, again, no AP Exam question would be completely dependent on simply recalling their names. The concept of *feature analysis* would be the more likely focus.

Essay Themes

The concepts of **set, expectancy** and **schemas** are very important. They overlap with other units (you will encounter them for sure in the Memory unit in the context of eyewitness recall, in Thought and Language in terms of *mental sets* in problem solving and in Social Psychology under the umbrella of prejudice and stereotyping) and they form the foundation of the entire 'perception' portion of this unit. If you don't understand them, go back and review!

The omnipresent "nature, nurture or both?" debate in psychology is relevant in this unit. Do we *learn* about size and shape constancy, or are we in some way hard wired, perhaps for some evolutionary reasons, to "get" such things? You could ask the same question about our mastery of depth and distance cues, and probably most anything else in this unit!

Test Preparation: Sensation and Perception

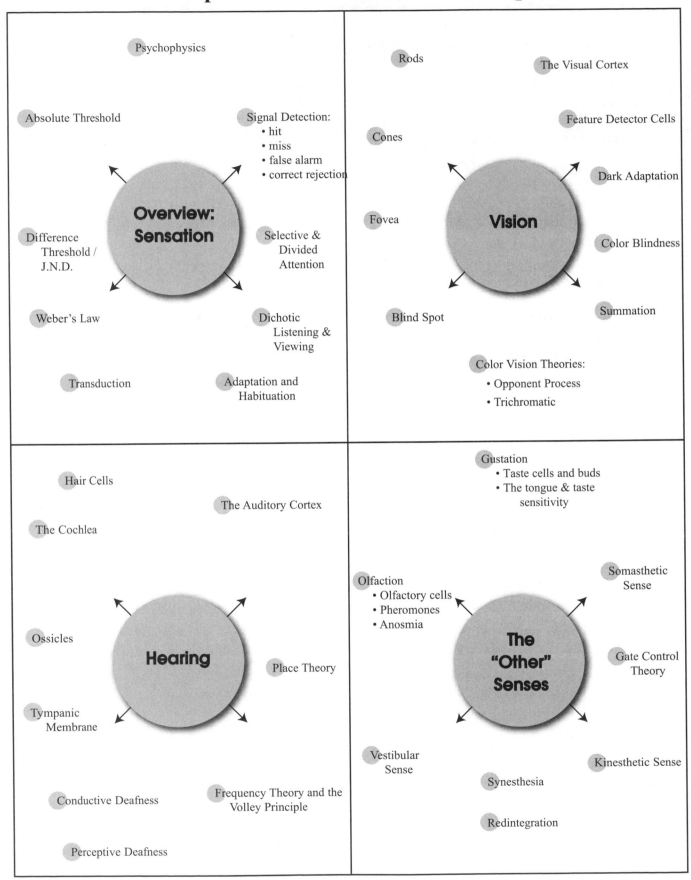

Overview: Sensation

- Psychophysics
- Absolute Threshold
- Signal Detection:
  - hit
  - miss
  - false alarm
  - correct rejection
- Difference Threshold / J.N.D.
- Selective & Divided Attention
- Weber's Law
- Dichotic Listening & Viewing
- Transduction
- Adaptation and Habituation

Vision

- Rods
- The Visual Cortex
- Cones
- Feature Detector Cells
- Fovea
- Dark Adaptation
- Color Blindness
- Blind Spot
- Summation
- Color Vision Theories:
  - Opponent Process
  - Trichromatic

Hearing

- Hair Cells
- The Auditory Cortex
- The Cochlea
- Ossicles
- Place Theory
- Tympanic Membrane
- Conductive Deafness
- Frequency Theory and the Volley Principle
- Perceptive Deafness

The "Other" Senses

- Gustation
  - Taste cells and buds
  - The tongue & taste sensitivity
- Olfaction
  - Olfactory cells
  - Pheromones
  - Anosmia
- Somasthetic Sense
- Gate Control Theory
- Vestibular Sense
- Kinesthetic Sense
- Synesthesia
- Redintegration

38

Test Preparation: Sensation and Perception

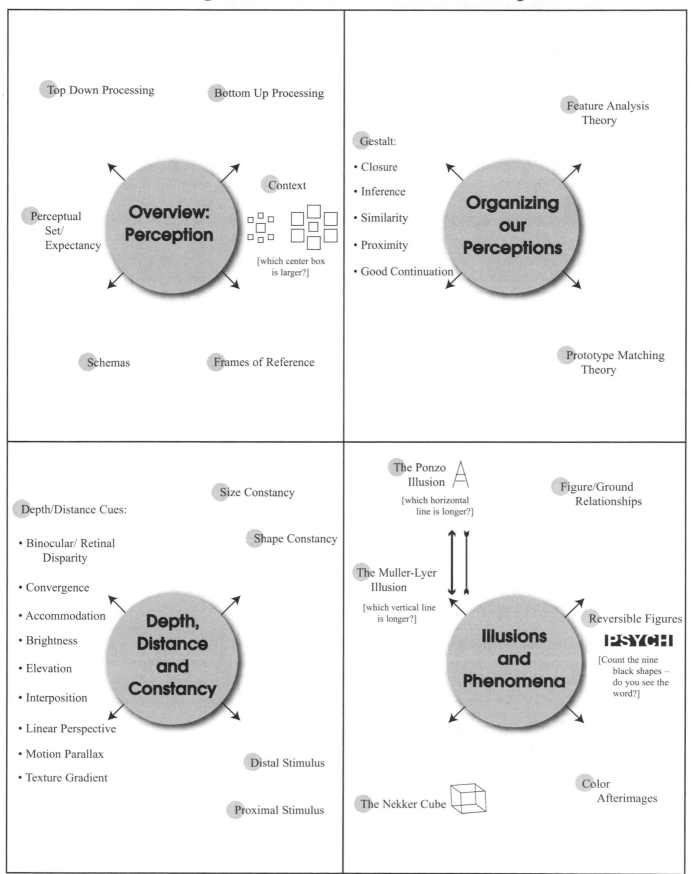

Overview: Perception

Top Down Processing

Bottom Up Processing

Context
[which center box is larger?]

Perceptual Set/ Expectancy

Schemas

Frames of Reference

Organizing our Perceptions

Feature Analysis Theory

Gestalt:
• Closure
• Inference
• Similarity
• Proximity
• Good Continuation

Prototype Matching Theory

Depth, Distance and Constancy

Size Constancy

Shape Constancy

Depth/Distance Cues:
• Binocular/ Retinal Disparity
• Convergence
• Accommodation
• Brightness
• Elevation
• Interposition
• Linear Perspective
• Motion Parallax
• Texture Gradient

Distal Stimulus

Proximal Stimulus

Illusions and Phenomena

The Ponzo Illusion
[which horizontal line is longer?]

Figure/Ground Relationships

The Muller-Lyer Illusion
[which vertical line is longer?]

Reversible Figures

PSYCH
[Count the nine black shapes – do you see the word?]

The Nekker Cube

Color Afterimages

39

Practice Items

- again, time yourself, but don't go too quickly... 8-10 minutes should be about right
- again, remember that these items are *not* in order of difficulty, as they would be on the actual advanced placement examination

1. Perceptive deafness

    (A) is a psychological rather than a physiological phenomenon
    (B) results from damage to the tympanic membrane
    (C) results if the ossicles connected to the ear drum can no longer carry sound waves into the cochlea
    (D) results from damage to the hair cells in the cochlea
    (E) results from damage to the anvil, hammer and stirrups

2. The process by which sound waves are transformed into electrochemical messages is known as

    (A) sensory assimilation
    (B) sensory migration
    (C) energy gradient
    (D) amelioration
    (E) transduction

3. The tendencies of humans to group stimuli by similarity and by physical proximity to each other are illustrative of

    (A) prototype theory
    (B) perceptual inference
    (C) gestalt principles
    (D) the concept of constancy
    (E) good continuation

4. Olfactory communication among animals takes the form of

    (A) pheromones
    (B) feature detection
    (C) somasthesis
    (D) synesthesia
    (E) redintegration

5. Which of the following depth and distance cues are binocular?

    (A) retinal disparity and convergence
    (B) convergence and accommodation
    (C) accommodation and texture gradient
    (D) motion parallax and interposition
    (E) linear perspective and retinal disparity

6. As a train recedes into the distance, the image of the train that falls on your retina grows smaller. That image

    (A) is thus considered dichotic
    (B) is called the distal stimulus
    (C) is called the proximal stimulus
    (D) "fools" your brain into misinterpreting size constancy
    (E) can therefore no longer be processed by the rods and cones

7. Viewing a computer screen, a man identifies the letter 'R' even though it is in a highly impressionistic and unfamiliar font, because he judges that the letter shares the typical characteristics of the models for an 'R' the man has in his head. This is most consistent with

    (A) feature analysis theory
    (B) perceptual constancy
    (C) accommodation
    (D) prototype matching theory
    (E) closure

8. Place theory states that

    (A) the accuracy of recall of a particular event is very much dependent on the physical location in which one attempts to retrieve the memory
    (B) hair cells at particular locations on the basilar membrane respond to incoming sound waves, and the auditory cortex interprets those locations to identify the pitch of a sound
    (C) humans determine depth and distance almost exclusively in terms of the placement of one object in relation to all other objects in the visual field
    (D) humans determine depth and distance almost exclusively in terms of the elevated location of a particular object in the visual field
    (E) rods and cones are located at the back of the retina to increase visual acuity

9. One classic measure of the minimum amount of sound the typical human can detect at least half the time it is present is the tick of a watch under quiet conditions at a distance of 20 feet. This is an example of

   (A) volley principle
   (B) assimilation
   (C) absolute threshold
   (D) the J.N.D.
   (E) gate control

10. Which of the following is the correct progression of visual processing in the human eye?

   (A) rods and cones; bipolar cells; ganglion cells; optic nerve
   (B) rods and cones; ganglion cells; bipolar cells; optic nerve
   (C) bipolar cells; ganglion cells; rods; cones
   (D) bipolar cells; rods and cones; ganglion cells; optic nerve
   (E) optic nerve; rods and cones; ganglion cells; bipolar cells

11. Weber's Law states that

   (A) in humans, adult perception is superior to adolescent perception
   (B) humans tend to grossly underestimate changes in aversive stimuli
   (C) humans tend to grossly overestimate changes in aversive stimuli
   (D) the smallest noticeable change in a stimulus is proportional to the original stimulus
   (E) the J.N.D. is typically illusory

12. In the following representation of signal detection, what would II and III be, respectively?

-SUBJECT RESPONSE-

	"yes"	"no"
present	I	II
absent	III	IV

-TONE-

(A) a false alarm; a correct rejection
(B) a hit; a false alarm
(C) a hit; a miss
(D) a miss; a correct rejection
(E) a miss; a false alarm

13. As a depth and distance cue, texture gradient is characterized by

(A) varying levels of brightness of distant objects
(B) reduced clarity of the distant image(s) in the visual field
(C) differences in the two images received by each retina
(D) parallel lines receding into one single line in the visual field
(E) recognition of proximal stimuli

14. After repeated exposure to a stimulus, an individual no longer attends to it, until it increases or decreases in intensity. This is called

(A) convergence
(B) activation synthesis
(C) decay
(D) lateral inhibition
(E) habituation

15. Which of the following is the correct progression of a sound wave through the human ear?

(A) auditory nerve; semicircular canal; auditory canal; cochlea; oval window

(B) auditory nerve; auditory canal; cochlea; oval window; hair cells

(C) auditory canal; tympanic membrane; ossicles; oval window; cochlea

(D) hair cells; oval window; tympanic membrane; ossicles

(E) oval window; tympanic membrane; auditory nerve; cochlea

Chapter IV

States of Consciousness

This unit carries the least weight of all in the advanced placement curriculum. Only 3 or 4 of the 100 multiple choice items on the AP Exam will be from this area. Many students think that's unfortunate, because this is often one of the most popular topics in introductory psychology. People enjoy learning about dreams and dream interpretation, the nature of hypnosis and the influence of psychoactive drugs. It's quite stimulating to really think about these things as well: just what is hypnosis anyway? is it an "altered state of consciousness" or merely a "relaxed state of suggestibility"? how valid are the various sleep and dream theories? do dreams really mean anything? can we learn from them? do we sleep more than we need, or are we generally sleep deprived? what causes sleep disorders? are they learned, biological, or some combination of the two? why do many individuals actively seek "altered states of consciousness"?

Sleep

In order to understand theories as to why we sleep when we sleep, for example, we must first understand how a typical night's sleep progresses. There are five stages of sleep, four of them conveniently numbered one through four and the fifth called **R.E.M.** (an acronym for **'rapid eye movement'**). **Stages one through four progress from light to deep sleep**. Students, and some teachers, often assume that the R.E.M. period immediately follows the deep sleep of stages three and four, but that is not how it works. The sleeper climbs back up, from stage four to three to two to one, and then enters the R.E.M. period. After it, the sleeper begins a second sleep cycle. From the start of sleep until the end of the R.E.M. period consumes about 90-100 minutes. As the night's sleep goes on, the sleeper spends progressively less time in stages 3 and 4, or deep sleep, and more time in R.E.M., although the complete cycle itself remains at around 90-100 minutes. The extra R.E.M. time is "robbed" from the deepest stages of sleep, stages three and four.

Stage one sleep, light sleep, is characterized by fairly rapid brain wave activity (3 to 7 cycles per second), as recorded on an electroencaphalogram, or EEG. Stage two sleep, in which the largest percentage of your total sleep time is spent, is characterized by **sleep spindles**, small jumbles of very rapid electrical activity. It's still an open question what these mean or what purpose they serve. Stages three and four are thought of as **deep sleep**; this is also sometimes called **delta sleep**, as the longer, slower electrical waves present during these stages are labeled delta waves. In this deeply relaxed state, the sleeper's breathing rate, body temperature and heart rate decrease, and he or she is very difficult to rouse. The individual then retreats back through stages three, two and one and then enters R.E.M. This segment of the sleep cycle, so-called because during it the eyes actually do move beneath the eyelids, is often called **active sleep** or **paradoxical sleep**, because the brain is quite active, and heart rate and blood pressure are elevated, while the major muscle groups of the body are essentially paralyzed. Blood and glucose rush to the brain to facilitate neural activity, and the EEG readout in R.E.M. therefore resembles that of a person who is awake or very lightly asleep, but a naive observer would judge the sleeper to be really "knocked out".

It is in the R.E.M. period that the majority of **dreaming** occurs. If, in a **R.E.M. deprivation** study, an individual is intentionally awakened at the onset of each R.E.M. period for some time, and then later is allowed to sleep normally, the sleeper tends to have longer R.E.M. periods. This is called **R.E.M. rebound**, and suggests that our bodies really need R.E.M. (and thus, perhaps, dreaming?) and will do what is necessary to get it. That idea is supported by the fact that during key periods of development early in life, we need and get more sleep and more R.E.M; it appears to play a major role in that development. Humans seem to have reduced need for sleep as they age, and the percentage of time spent in R.E.M during a typical night's sleep also declines over time.

It seems obvious that we need sleep. Even individuals who go remarkably long periods without "sleep" probably do get what are called **microsleeps**, which are tiny, seconds long periods of sleep that are not necessarily *psychologically* satisfying but do seem to help the person "get through". How much sleep we need and why we seek it when we seek it are questions researchers have frequently investigated. Each of us is governed by an internal biological clock which runs our **circadian rhythms** (in Latin, 'circa' means about, and 'dies' means *day*). Activity in a part of the hypothalamus called *the superchiasmatic nucleus (SCN)* seems to govern this clock. Another factor in these daily rhythms is that when it's dark **the pineal gland** secretes **melatonin** – nowadays some people who have trouble sleeping take synthetic forms of melatonin to deal with the problem. Of course, we live in a world of 24 hour days, but some researchers contend that if our bodies were given free rein they would tend more towards a 25 hour clock. This is suggested by research into **free running rhythms**. The biological clocks of individuals who live in self contained environments with no day and night or man-made time cues seem to want to push to extend the day.

But it is not as if volunteers in free running rhythm studies sleep any more or less, only that they go to sleep an hour later everyday or so for the first weeks in such an environment. So, we're still left with questions about the need for sleep in general. Do we sleep simply to rejuvenate ourselves, to rest and recuperate, as the **restorative theory** of sleep suggests? Or, do we sleep in order to dream? Supporters of **memory consolidation theory** contend that we need to dream in order to sift through the day's events, filing memories which we wish to keep and disposing of those we want to discard (Nobel Prize winner Francis Crick once wrote "we dream to forget..."). Another theory as to why we sleep <u>at night</u> is called the **adaptive non-responding theory**. In it the argument goes that, in evolutionary terms, it has always been safer and more functional for humans to sleep at night. In the distant past, for example, it was adaptive (good for one's survival) to bed down for the evening once it was dark (thus, non-responding), since going out was likely to lead to trouble with unseen tar pits and unfriendly nocturnal creatures.

There are some **sleep disorders** with which you must familiarize yourself. Those you are most likely to encounter on the Advanced Placement Examination are summarized below:

- **insomnia:** dissatisfaction with the amount or quality of one's sleep; an inability to fall asleep, or stay asleep, or at least the subjective judgment of such impairment – some people who complain of having insomnia actually have pretty normal sleep patterns, but don't perceive them as such
- **hypersomnia:** getting or needing too much sleep, perhaps to the point of impairing day to day functioning
- **narcolepsy:** a sudden, involuntary drop into sleep; in many cases, the sufferer quickly enters R.E.M., which makes the condition even more problematic because of the loss of major muscle function which accompanies R.E.M.
- **apnea:** the sufferer frequently stops breathing during the night and must "re-start" themselves, "awakening" to some degree to do so but often without complete awareness, which makes this a disorder that sometimes goes undiagnosed
- **night terrors**: not the same as nightmares; most common in children, although also occurring in adults, this is characterized by a frightened awakening, with high physiological arousal (sweating, increased heart and respiration rates, and so on), but little or no recall of the event in the morning; these are non-R.E.M. occurrences, unlike the typical nightmares all of us experience – they seem to occur during the deepest part of sleep, in stage four, and thus early in the night's sleep, for as you may recall, most stage three and four "delta sleep" occurs during the first two ninety minute sleep cycles of the night
- **somnambulism:** walking in one's sleep; perhaps a result of dreaming in a non-R.E.M. period, when one's body is able to "act out" parts of a dream
- **somniloquy:** talking in one's sleep, with no subsequent recall of doing so

Dreams

As we saw above, **memory consolidation theory** of sleep is also essentially a **dream theory**. The theory envisions dreams as a kind of **information processing mechanism**. Research which indicates that there is a correlation between R.E.M. sleep and memory supports this view. J. Allan Hobson and Robert McCarley have forwarded the **activation-synthesis theory** of dreams. They recognize how active the brain is during R.E.M. periods, when the majority of dreaming takes place, and they postulate that we take what is essentially random neural stimulation (thus, 'activation') and then try to make sense of it by superimposing a story line onto it. We 'synthesize', or combine, random elements into a "dream". You may see a connection here to gestalt psychology which we looked at in the unit on Sensation and Perception. Recall that this school of thought is based on the notion that humans have a strong tendency to seek to organize information into meaningful wholes.

The most well known dream theory comes from the **Freudian psychoanalytic school of thought**. In 1900, Sigmund Freud proposed that **"dreams (are) the royal road to a knowledge of the unconscious activities of the mind"**, and that statement reveals the core of the theory. Freud argued that there was the **manifest content**, the obvious, superficial "plot" of the dream, and the more important **latent content**, which he deemed to be the unconscious, symbolic underlying meaning of the dream. As we will see later in our study of Personality Theory, Freud believed that the unconscious mind was a storehouse of wishes and desires which we were not willing or able to express in the real world but which might reveal themselves in our dreams. Freud's theory remains controversial, and it warrants critical discussion in class and critical analysis in your own head. There are many popular books on dream interpretation which are interesting to explore but should be read with a healthy skepticism. Even Freud himself was known for warning people not to overanalyze dream content, especially without training.

One final area of interest in regard to dreams is the concept of **lucid dreaming**. If you've ever been dreaming and had a sense that you were indeed in a dream, then you recognize the roots of lucid dreaming. If you can at times have awareness that you are in a dream, perhaps you can even control some aspects of the dream. Research has indicated that individuals can teach themselves to influence events in their dreams – some small children have learned to do so in order to control or even stop recurring nightmares.

Hypnosis

Yet another topic from this unit which is worthy of (and probably *requires*) critical analysis is **hypnosis**. There are at least two competing interpretations as to just what hypnosis is: one argues that it is a **very relaxed state** in which the subject is simply more **open to suggestion**, while others contend it is truly an **altered state of consciousness**. The successful use of hypnosis in pain management and addiction control supports that latter hypothesis to an extent, but the debate continues. **Ernest Hilgard**, the name you should probably most associate with the "altered state" side of the debate in preparation for the AP Exam, identified what he called the **hidden observer** in hypnotic subjects. If an individual was hypnotized and told to *dissociate* from some painful stimulus, a highly hypnotizable subject could do so and report low or nonexistent levels of pain, but a second part of their consciousness can report that there was pain. It's as if part of the subject is hypnotized while another part watches the hypnosis session. But the mere idea of some people being "highly hypnotizable" while others are not is a point of interest to those who support the "hypnosis is merely a relaxed state of suggestibility" school of thought; if someone is "highly hypnotizable", maybe that just means they're "highly suggestible" whether they are hypnotized or not.

More on States of Consciousness

Finally, familiarize yourself with the major classes of **psychoactive** (you may also see this as *psychogenic* or *psychotropic*) **drugs**. A psychoactive drug is a chemical substance that impacts behavior, perceptions, moods or mental processes. You should be able to recognize and identify:

- **hallucinogens** such as LSD, peyote and PCP, which alter one's perceptions, sometimes very dramatically
- **opiates** such as morphine or heroin which can suppress pain while also inducing states of euphoria

- **stimulants** like caffeine, nicotine and amphetamines which activate the nervous system and essentially speed up levels of arousal and activity
- **depressants** like alcohol, barbiturates and the benzodiazepines (anti-anxiety drugs) which slow nervous system activity

It's possible you'll be asked about tolerance or withdrawal on the AP Exam. With repetitive use of a psychoactive drug one can build a **tolerance** which results in the need for greater and greater amounts of the drug to duplicate the original effects. And, if one stops taking a substance suddenly after long term usage, there can be distressing side effects collectively referred to as **withdrawal**.

Name Hall of Fame

On the exam you may well see names like **Hobson and McCarley**, in reference to activation-synthesis dream theory, and **Ernest Hilgard's** name is a good bet to show up amongst the multiple choice items, but in both cases they will be given to you and will serve as cues in the stem of an item – it is very unlikely that you would have to identify either as the answer to a question. **Martin Orne** is another name, linked to the study of hypnosis, that might appear, but he would fit into the same category.

Sigmund Freud is a Babe Ruth/ Willie Mays/ Hank Aaron sort of name in psychology – that is, everyone would have him in the hall of fame, even those many psychologists who don't even think his work is 'psychology' (some would label it as an interesting 'philosophy' but would not consider it 'science'). If nothing else, he is significant in the history of psychology, and his ideas have had a profound impact on the way humans think about and talk about themselves. His is a name you have to know or you can't say you "know" psychology.

Wilhelm Wundt is often thought of as the founder of 'psychology', as he set up the first psych lab in Germany in the late 1870's. He's considered a **structuralist**, and that fits in with this unit on States of Consciousness. Structuralists examined the *mental structures* of consciousness, so their name cues you as to their focus. They often used **introspection** to do their work – simply stated, they asked subjects to look inside themselves and report on their cognitive experiences. Another early area of exploration into human consciousness came to be called **functionalism**. There's no surprise here; functionalists were more interested in what our consciousness and cognitions were *for*. They wondered about the *uses* of our sensations and mental processes. **William James**, usually considered the first great American psychologist, was a functionalist.

Essay Themes

Remember that the percentages given to you by the Educational Testing Service and the College Board for each unit in the Advanced Placement Psychology curriculum refer to the multiple choice only. In this case, that percentage is 2-4%, which means 2 to 4 items of the 100 multiple choice questions will involve states of consciousness. The percentage doesn't say anything about essay coverage, but it is very unlikely that an essay would focus on this unit. The more you know about **Freud and psychoanalysis** the better, as that is a prime candidate for at least part of an essay, and this is your first of several exposures to it in the curriculum, but otherwise you needn't worry about an essay asking you to trace the development of a typical night's sleep or to expound on two or three sleep and dream theories. Such an essay proposal would probably be rejected as too narrow in terms of content coverage.

There are topics in this unit which naturally invite critical thinking. For example: what is the evidence regarding hypnosis? What is the evidence about the purposes of sleep? of dreams? What do we make of the fact that people sleep less, with less R.E.M., as they age? babies spend huge amounts of time in R.E.M sleep – are they dreaming at that time? If not, why not? If yes, what form do their dreams take? Reflecting on these issues in class or on your own will deepen your grasp of any specific related concept that might show up on the examination.

Test Preparation: States of Consciousness

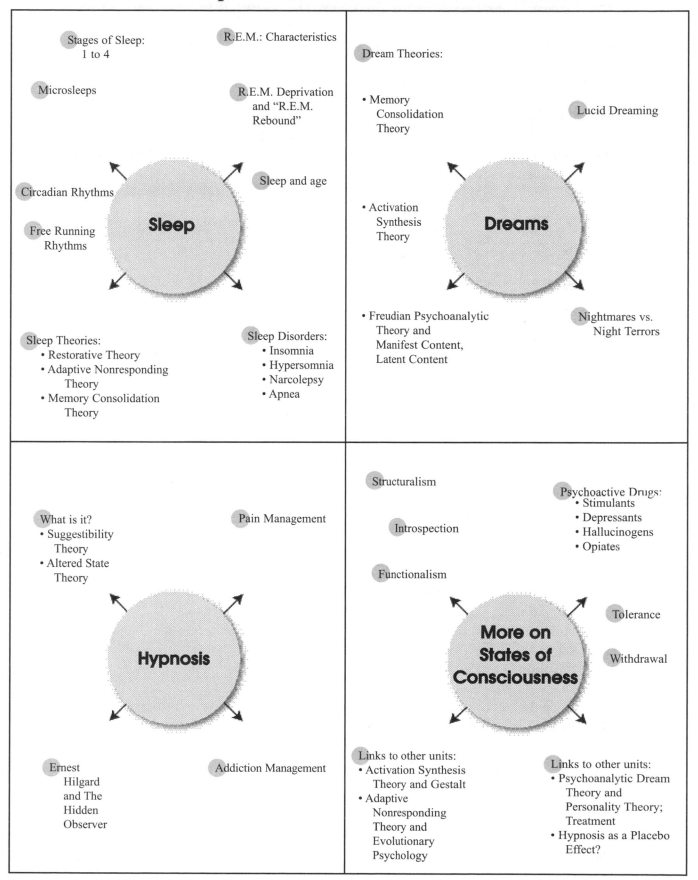

Stages of Sleep:
1 to 4

R.E.M.: Characteristics

Microsleeps

R.E.M. Deprivation
and "R.E.M.
Rebound"

Circadian Rhythms

Sleep and age

Free Running
Rhythms

Sleep

Sleep Theories:
• Restorative Theory
• Adaptive Nonresponding
  Theory
• Memory Consolidation
  Theory

Sleep Disorders:
• Insomnia
• Hypersomnia
• Narcolepsy
• Apnea

Dream Theories:

• Memory
  Consolidation
  Theory

Lucid Dreaming

• Activation
  Synthesis
  Theory

Dreams

• Freudian Psychoanalytic
  Theory and
  Manifest Content,
  Latent Content

Nightmares vs.
Night Terrors

What is it?
• Suggestibility
  Theory
• Altered State
  Theory

Pain Management

Hypnosis

Ernest
Hilgard
and The
Hidden
Observer

Addiction Management

Structuralism

Psychoactive Drugs:
• Stimulants
• Depressants
• Hallucinogens
• Opiates

Introspection

Functionalism

Tolerance

**More on
States of
Consciousness**

Withdrawal

Links to other units:
• Activation Synthesis
  Theory and Gestalt
• Adaptive
  Nonresponding
  Theory and
  Evolutionary
  Psychology

Links to other units:
• Psychoanalytic Dream
  Theory and
  Personality Theory;
  Treatment
• Hypnosis as a Placebo
  Effect?

Practice Items

- **TIME YOURSELF** – there are only ten items in this section, so allow for **seven minutes** maximum. If you take less than three minutes to complete the section, fine, unless you make errors!! If you make <u>any</u> errors, then slow down! Slowing down won't guarantee that you will eliminate mistakes, but the mistakes *do* tell you that you are less than perfect, and one factor you can control on the spot to improve your performance is to take a bit more time.

1. The sleep disorder characterized by spontaneous, involuntary drops into R.E.M. sleep is called

   (A) somnambulism
   (B) apnea
   (C) maintenance insomnia
   (D) bruxism
   (E) narcolepsy

2. The phenomenon of R.E.M. rebound supports the notion that

   (A) we require more R.E.M. sleep as we age
   (B) human infants are not yet developed enough to experience R.E.M sleep
   (C) R.E.M sleep is essential for growth and functioning
   (D) the latent content of dreams is meaningful
   (E) the latent content of dreams is not meaningful

3. Adaptive non-responding theory suggests that

   (A) "dreaming" is really the individual's attempt to make sense of random neural activation
   (B) humans sleep in one phase at night because doing so enhances the chances for survival
   (C) the brain is essentially unresponsive to outside stimulation during most stages of sleep
   (D) sleeping and dreaming are essential for memory formation and storage
   (E) heart rates and brain wave activity rates are positively correlated during sleep

4. As a typical night's sleep progresses, the sleeper experiences less and less

   (A) delta wave sleep
   (B) alpha wave sleep
   (C) theta wave sleep
   (D) R.E.M. sleep
   (E) dreaming

5. Felicia finds she consistently awakens only seconds before her alarm sounds each morning. This is evidence for the existence of

   (A) R.E.M. rebound
   (B) R.E.M. sleep disorder
   (C) the hidden observer
   (D) circadian rhythms
   (E) enuresis

6. The "paradox" of R.E.M. sleep is that

   (A) during it the brain is quite active but the major muscle groups are essentially paralyzed
   (B) there is no evidence which suggests it has a purpose
   (C) adults experience it, but newborns do not
   (D) newborns experience it, but the elderly do not
   (E) the sleeper is not actually "asleep" for most of it

7. These classes of psychoactive drug respectively depress and stimulate the central nervous system:

   (A) opiates and barbiturates
   (B) amphetamines and hallucinogens
   (C) amphetamines and barbiturates
   (D) barbiturates and narcotic analgesics
   (E) barbiturates and amphetamines

8. As age increases

   (A) sleep need increases
   (B) the percentage of the total night's sleep spent in R.E.M. increases
   (C) the percentage of the total night's sleep spent in R.E.M decreases
   (D) sleep spindles in stage two sleep disappear
   (E) rates of night terror episodes increase

9. Which of the following would best support Ernest Hilgard's view of hypnosis as dissociation?

   (A) a hypnotized subject reports that he felt unusually open to suggestion during the hypnotic session
   (B) a hypnotized subject reports awareness of an intensely unpleasant smell but is not directly responsive to it
   (C) a hypnotized subject voluntarily discontinues participation in a hypnotic session
   (D) for some time a hypnotist is unable to rouse a subject from a hypnotic state
   (E) a long term cigarette smoker stops smoking after a series of hypnotic sessions

10. E.E.G. measurements during R.E.M. sleep most resemble measurements from

    (A) delta sleep
    (B) k complexes
    (C) wakefulness
    (D) stage two sleep
    (E) stages three and four sleep

Chapter V

Learning Theory

You will undoubtedly find much that is relevant to your own life experience in this unit which outlines how we learn through conditioning, observation and cognition. We can readily break this unit down into four sub-topics: classical conditioning, operant conditioning, observational or social learning and cognitive learning.

Classical Conditioning

Classical conditioning is based on the making of **associations**. If you ever got excited upon hearing the music of an ice cream truck as a child (or now!), you know about classical conditioning. If you have a pet who comes running out to the kitchen as soon as he or she hears the can opener or the rustling of the bag of food, you know about classical conditioning. Learning the labels used in classical conditioning can be a struggle, but the basic mechanism is familiar to most of us. Simply speaking, the learner associates something that naturally leads to a response with something new, that didn't previously lead to that response. The sound of a can opener by itself doesn't mean anything to a kitten, but when she comes to associate that particular sound with the imminent arrival of food (which *does* naturally interest the kitten), she will respond to that sound. It is now pretty clear that the sound of the can opener must have **reliably predicted** the arrival of food in the past, or the kitten is unlikely to make a strong connection between the two events. In a learning theory course, you would learn more about the Rescorla-Wagner Model, a mathematical formula which demonstrates this concept of **contingency**, but for the AP Exam you need only know that the **conditioned stimulus** (in this case, the sound of the can opener), must reliably predict the presentation of the **unconditioned stimulus** (in this case, the cat food) in order for strong conditioning to occur.

Ivan Pavlov has become the name to associate with classical conditioning in psychology, although he was a not a psychologist and there <u>had</u> been work with such conditioning mechanisms done before his time. Pavlov, a physiologist, was studying the digestive systems of dogs when he made note of how the animals seemed to respond to previously neutral stimuli in much the same way as the kitten we spoke of above. To test this, Pavlov began to pair the presentation of meat powder, which naturally makes a dog salivate, with a previously neutral stimulus. Most people remember this as a bell, but Pavlov actually used metronomes and other tones at first. He presented the sound of a metronome, followed immediately by the arrival of the meat powder, which led to a salivation response in the dogs (in a learning theory course, you would study in more detail the timing of this pairing and encounter terms like temporal conditioning, trace conditioning, simultaneous conditioning and backward conditioning, but you will not be held accountable for them on the AP Examination). After repeated pairings of the metronome and the food, the dogs began to salivate at the sound of the metronome. When the dogs salivated at the playing of the

55

metronome, without the presentation of the food, Pavlov saw there'd been **acquisition** of conditioning. If the dogs were to then salivate upon hearing similar but not identical tones, we would say the dogs had **generalized**. If the dogs salivated only at the metronome and did *not* generalize, we'd say they **discriminated**.

Pavlov would likely have argued that as long as the sound of the metronome and the presentation of the food were paired together in the same rough space and time, the dogs would make the association and conditioning to the metronome would occur. It was in questioning this idea of **contiguity** that Robert Rescorla extended Pavlovian theory with his concept of contingency, mentioned above. Learning theorists today favor Rescorla's model.

Students sometimes struggle with the terminology of Pavlov's classical conditioning, but it's not so difficult to reason most of it out from the terms themselves, although the English versions of those terms are somewhat different than what Pavlov intended in his Russian language descriptions of them. A summary follows:

- **the unconditioned stimulus (or UCS):** this is the thing the organism naturally, reflexively responds to. In trying to break down a classical conditioning example into the appropriate terms, it may be useful to start with the UCS by simply asking yourself, "what naturally caused a response in the learner, without any apparent need for learning?" – that's the UCS. In the kitten example above, the UCS is the cat food – in the case of Pavlov's dogs, it was the meat powder.

- **the conditioned stimulus (or CS):** in identifying this, ask yourself "what is the learner now responding to that they did not previously respond to in this way?" or "what have we now conditioned the learner to respond to?". In the kitten example above, the kitten had learned to respond to the sound of the can opener, which is therefore the CS, while in the Pavlov example, the dogs had been conditioned to salivate upon hearing the metronome, the sound of which had not originally elicited any such response.

- **the unconditioned response (or UCR):** the natural, unlearned, largely reflexive response to the UCS. In the kitten example, it is excitement or anticipation at the presentation of cat food (as manifested by the cat's running into the kitchen), while with Pavlov's dogs it was salivation at the presentation of meat powder.

- **the conditioned response (or CR):** the new, learned response to the CS. For the kitten, it is running into the kitchen in response to the can opener, while for Pavlov's dogs it is salivation at the sound of the metronome.

It can sometimes be a bit trickier to identify the UCR and the CR in the case of classically conditioned **taste aversions**. In the examples above, the UCR and the CR were actually identical, but not so in the example of taste aversions. For example, if you had contracted a virus which had not yet manifested itself at lunch time, you would likely eat a normal meal at that time. Let's say that at around 6 p.m., you begin to vomit, as a result of this virus. You might very well associate the illness with something you had eaten at noontime. In fact, many would argue that we have a **biological predisposition** to make such a connection, as it would be useful for our survival to be able to identify foods that might be harmful to us. Even if it was the virus that caused the illness, you might well connect that unpleasant outcome with the fried clams you had at lunch, and avoid them forevermore. In this case, the unconditioned response (to the unconditioned stimulus of a virus) is vomiting (you didn't learn or become conditioned to vomit in response to a virus – it just happened!), but the conditioned response (to the conditioned stimulus of fried clams) is *aversion*. You probably won't actually vomit at the idea of eating fried clams, but you will avoid eating them.

John B. Watson, who wrote the definitive stuff on **behaviorism** in the first part of the twentieth century, conducted memorable research into classical conditioning of a fear response in 1920, using an orphan who has come to be known as **Little Albert** as his subject. Albert was around a year old when Watson introduced him to a white rat, which Albert liked. He then paired the arrival of the rat with the striking of a very loud gong near Albert's ear, which, quite naturally, Albert did *not* enjoy. Indeed, he cried and tried to escape from the area. After a very few such pairings **(white rat – loud noise = fearful response)**, Albert began to exhibit signs of aversion immediately upon seeing the white rat. Remember, he had originally frolicked happily in the company of the rat, but was now classically conditioned to fear it. Further, Watson argued that Albert then generalized his fear to all white, furry things. Worst of all, later Watson apparently lost track of Albert and never **de-conditioned** him. In order to **extinguish** this classically conditioned response, Watson might have repeatedly presented the CS (again, in this case, it was the white rat) alone. It's presence would not again be paired with the sound of the loud gong. After several trials, the CR would weaken and eventually reach **extinction**. Even after extinction trials are conducted, there are sometimes cases of **spontaneous recovery**, a kind of flashback to the previous conditioning even after it had been de-conditioned. This is usually only a brief recurrence however.

Watson did not conduct extinction trials with Little Albert, which would be considered highly unethical today. This sad ending to the story therefore serves as a link to the **ethical principles** in psychological research that you studied in the first unit of this course. It also makes learning theorists wonder if Albert's conditioning would've been extinguished over time on its own. In effect, later in life, anytime Albert was exposed to a white rat or a white furry object and it was not paired with an aversive stimulus such as a loud noise, that would serve as a kind of naturalistic extinction trial. But what actually happened to Albert remains a mystery.

You might encounter a couple of other terms on the AP Exam, although it is unlikely. Just in case, they are summarized below:

* **blocking:** if your kitten was classically conditioned to come running when she heard the can opener, that learning could then interfere with conditioning to some other stimulus. For example, if you switched to a hand-held can opener that made a distinctly different sound from the first opener, it may take even longer than before for the kitten to connect the sound of it with dinnertime. In essence, the first CS blocks the learning of a new CS, or at least slows it down.

- **second or higher order conditioning:** assume Pavlov's dogs are now salivating at the sound of a metronome, which serves as the conditioned stimulus. Could we now pair the sound of the metronome with some new stimulus, say a red light, and get conditioning to *it*? The red light would *not* be paired with the original unconditioned stimulus, the meat powder. The answer seems to be yes, although the conditioning is generally weaker and requires more trials. Researchers trying to go to a *third* level of conditioning have not been successful.

Operant Conditioning

Operant conditioning also involves making associations, but in this case it is a matter of **connecting behaviors with their consequences**. The learner chooses a response and it is either reinforced or punished. According to early theorist Edward Thorndike, if the result of some chosen response is pleasant or desirable, the organism is likely to repeat that behavior. If the consequence of some act is undesirable, the organism is less likely to act in that way again. This simple principle is called the **law of effect**, and it is the basis of what **B. F. Skinner** later called operant conditioning. You may also see it referred to as **instrumental conditioning**, but Skinner's term would always accompany that usage on the AP Exam.

What is desirable or reinforcing to one potential learner is not necessarily reinforcing to another. Indeed, something that serves as a reinforcer for one individual could actually be a punishment to another. This helps us understand what is called the **Premack Principle**, named after David Premack. It states that one ought to identify what is reinforcing for a subject and then use it to reinforce desired behaviors that the subject is not so likely to perform on his or her own. It is sometimes thought of as **the grandmother clause**, because a grandmother may apply such a principle when she promises her grandchild that he can play in the sandbox if he finishes his asparagus. This would be a successful ploy, of course, only if the grandson enjoys playing in the sandbox. If playing there inevitably leads to painful interactions with his older sister, he may actually be *less* likely to eat his asparagus. In that case, a behaviorist would argue not that operant conditioning doesn't "work", but that one must choose reinforcers and punishers carefully and deliver them promptly so the learner can make the connection between the response and an individually meaningful consequence (this is an example of **contingency in operant conditioning** in that the performance of the behavior must reliably predict that the consequence <u>will</u> occur in order for learning to take place).

Another important point in the application of consequences involves **overjustification**. This predicts that if you begin to reinforce a behavior that the individual is already disposed to perform it may actually discourage the subject from continuing to do it. There is some evidence, for example, that reading programs for schoolchildren can have this effect. If students are promised a reward for reading a certain number of books, they will indeed read more to earn the reward, but often will stop completely once the reward is discontinued. Further, those who already read a lot before the reinforcement program often *read less* while the promise of the reward is in force (although they may still read enough to obtain the reward) and then *continue* to read less after the reward is discontinued.

The important types of consequences you might encounter on the AP Examination are summarized below:

- **positive reinforcement:** this encourages a behavior; it is a pleasurable consequence which is delivered upon completion of some desirable action by the subject. A researcher might **shape** a complex behavior in an animal by positively reinforcing it as it took *successive steps toward the goal behavior*

- **negative reinforcement:** this too encourages a behavior. Think of 'negative' in terms of <u>subtraction</u>, in that an unpleasant condition is REMOVED when a desired behavior is completed; the taking of aspirin is negatively reinforcing in that it removes the pain of a headache. Be careful – this is not the same as punishment, although you will sometimes wrongly hear them used as if they are identical

- **punishment:** this discourages a behavior. It is an aversive (that is, you want to avoid it) consequence which is delivered when a subject does what you do <u>not</u> want him to do

- **primary reinforcers:** reinforcers which are unlearned and are inherently reinforcing to most if not all members of a species. The list of them is short – food and water are definitely on the list, and some would say that love/attachment and sex are primary reinforcers too. Intuitively, some students in our culture think of money as a "primary" reinforcer, because it has become so much desired and in many ways is <u>the</u> reinforcer for industrialized westerners, but its value as a reinforcer is still learned and is largely (though not exclusively at this point) a result of its role as the currency with which you obtain primary reinforcers

- **secondary reinforcers:** we learn to value these, as an animal could be trained to value a poker chip as a reinforcer if poker chips can be used to trade for food; the poker chip has no inherent value to most animals

Finally, you must familiarize yourself with some basic approaches as to how and when consequences are delivered in operant conditioning. In general, there are **continuous schedules** of reinforcement (in which the consequence is delivered after every instance of the goal behavior) and **intermittent (or partial) schedules** of reinforcement, but summaries of four specific types follow:

- **a fixed ratio schedule (FR):** reinforcement will be delivered after a specified number of desired <u>responses</u>. Examples include receiving frequent flyer rewards for some set amount of miles already flown or being paid a certain amount by your employer for every 7 toys you assemble (an "FR = 7" schedule)

- **a variable ratio schedule (VR):** reinforcement will be delivered after some number of <u>responses</u>, but the amount is not specified for the learner. A "VR = 5" schedule means that <u>on the average</u> of every fifth response would be reinforced, but not necessarily every five. Examples include playing the lottery (there will be payoffs but you don't know how many times you have to play to receive one) or repeatedly casting a fishing line into the water in hopes of catching a fish – you do not know how many repetitions of that action you will have to perform before receiving the "reinforcement" of catching a fish

- **a fixed interval schedule (FI):** reinforcement is delivered based on a specified <u>passage of time</u> – the first desired response after that passage of time is reinforced. If you are anxiously awaiting a piece of mail due on Friday and you know what time the mail carrier always arrives, you will check for the mail then but not before; your checking is then reinforced when you find the desired piece of mail

- **a variable interval schedule (VI):** reinforcement is delivered after some established <u>period of time</u> but it changes from one reinforcement to the next. If you are awaiting an important piece of mail due on Friday but the daily delivery time is highly variable, you might be likely to check more often to see if it has arrived, since you do not know exactly when it might get there

Social Learning

Albert Bandura and others would contend that much of what we learn comes from observation. If, for instance, an adult is **modeling** a behavior a child is likely to imitate that model, especially if the adult's behavior is **reinforced** in some way. The child would also have to have a sense that they could successfully and safely carry out the act and control its outcomes to some extent. Bandura called this a sense of **self-efficacy**.

Bandura's famous 1963 study in **social or observational learning** involved the use of adult models, who were videotaped punching and kicking a doll named Bobo. Children who first watched the video were then placed in the same room as depicted in the video, with the same array of toy choices, and promptly imitated the adult models, beating on Bobo. Children in a control group, who did not first view the video and were given a chance to play in the same environment did not behave in such ways. It may be interesting to debate in your classes whether the results would be similar if we replicated Bandura's work today, and if kids are just as likely to imitate pro-social behavior (kind, helping acts) as hurtful behavior.

Cognitive Learning

Some kinds of learning are placed under the heading of **cognitive learning**, even though classical and operant conditioning and observational learning all involve their share of cognitions (that is, thinking and mental processes) as well. Two types you should know about are summarized below:

- **insight learning:** sometimes an organism ruminates on a problem and then has a relatively sudden solution come to mind; picture old cartoons in which a light bulb would turn on over the head of a character who suddenly came upon an idea. Wolfgang Kohler noticed such insights in chimps in the 1920's – he placed bananas in a variety of hard-to-reach locations and watched how the chimps got at them. After a period of simple trial and error, Kohler argues that the chimps would stop and reflect on the problem and then appear to just "get" a solution

- **latent learning:** Edward Tolman coined this term for learning that is not demonstrated until the subject is reinforced for doing so. In his research with rats and maze completion tasks, he found that rats who had been exposed to a maze several times were more likely to run it efficiently and with few errors if there was a reinforcement in the goal box. Many rats apparently learned the maze (Tolman said they had a **'cognitive map'** of it in their heads) on trial runs, but still made errors when tested if they were not rewarded – they immediately navigated the maze however, once there was a reward available.

Finally, familiarize yourself with the concept of **learned helplessness**. It will come up again in your studies, and may also have relevance to your personal experience. Martin Seligman coined the term for a process in which, simply stated, one tries to do something, continually fails, and then quits trying altogether. If an individual believes that, no matter what they do, they cannot control outcomes, they will conclude that they are helpless to effect change. They've learned that they are helpless. This concept is a major foundation of cognitive explanations for depression, and has other applications in psychology which you will encounter in the unit on Personality Theory.

Name Hall of Fame

Ivan Pavlov and **B.F. Skinner** are first ballot inductees into the psychology name hall of fame. Even though there is a lot of evidence that something like classical conditioning had been done before (by men named Sechenov and Twitmyer, for example), Pavlov is still considered its father. Likewise, **Edward Thorndike's** Law of Effect came well before Skinner did his work, and it is the basis of operant conditioning, but Skinner's is the name to know for the Advanced Placement Exam. **John B. Watson** would also probably get into the hall without much argument from anyone. He is usually considered the father of behaviorism, although many introductory psychology students seem to remember him most for questionable ethical practices in his work with **Little Albert** and for losing his university teaching position because of an affair with a research assistant.

Many students of psychology would also have **Albert Bandura's** name on a "top ten list" of who ought to be in the hall of fame; you need to recognize his work in observational learning and modeling and his name. **Martin Seligman** is very well known and still quite active, but you would not likely have to regurgitate his name on its own, although you may well see it linked with the concept of learned helplessness or with cognitive explanations for depression on the examination. **John Garcia's** name might be linked in a question stem or in a response choice to study of classically conditioned taste aversions, and you might have similar cues in regard to latent learning (the name: **Edward Tolman**), insight learning (the name: **Wolfgang Kohler**) and contingency in classical conditioning (the name: **Robert Rescorla**). However, you should not worry about having to pull the names Garcia, Tolman, Kohler or Rescorla by themselves out of your memory. You may, however, have to know **David Premack's** name, but it would be in relation to the Premack Principle in operant conditioning, so that's more a matter of concept recognition than name recognition.

Essay Themes

The very first free response question ever used on an Advanced Placement Psychology Examination was on the **similarities and differences between classical conditioning and operant conditioning**. Such a question would probably not make it to an exam nowadays as it would be ruled out as being too narrowly focused on just one unit. Still, it does tell you that this stuff is pretty important in the minds of those who create the test. If you don't have a pretty good grip on what classical and operant conditioning are, you don't really know learning theory anyhow.

A solid critical thinking question in this unit revolves around observational learning. Specifically, what is the evidence regarding violence in the media and it's impact on human behavior? If you explore this issue in a lively class discussion, it will deepen your grasp of the fundamental concepts in social learning, and learning theory in general.

This whole unit is about **behaviorism**, and that school of thought has made a frequent showing on free response AP Exam items. By the end of the advanced placement course, you ought to be able to write a succinct paragraph or so outlining the central thrust of each of the major schools of thought in psychology (behaviorist, psychoanalytic/psychodynamic, cognitive, biomedical, humanist). That by itself would've gotten you through more than one essay on previous AP tests. As the course progresses, **you will see much overlap between this unit and others** (like Development, Motivation, Personality, Abnormal Psych and Treatment), so, while it isn't particularly large, it could be quite important.

Test Preparation: Learning Theory

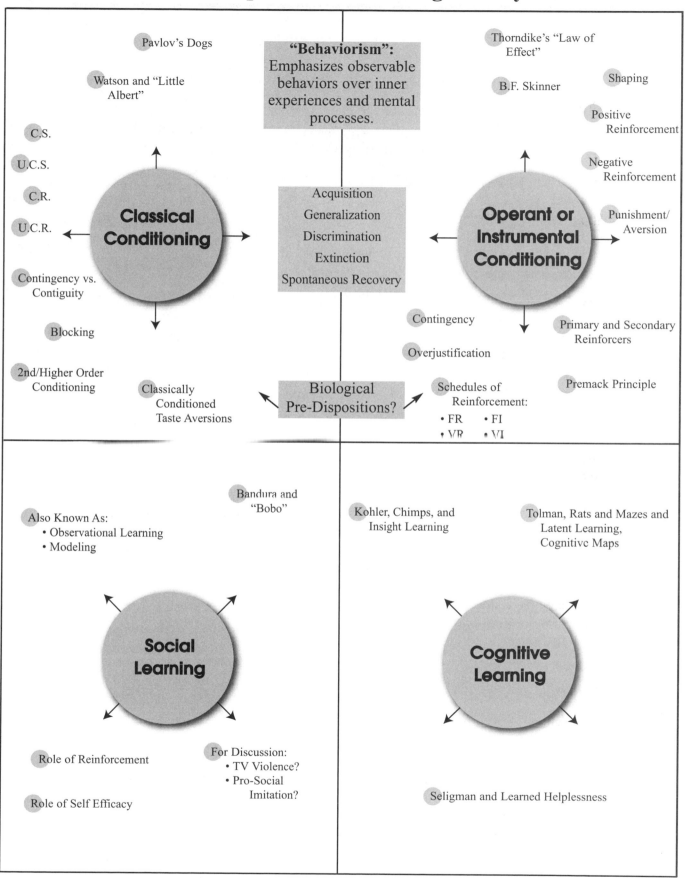

Pavlov's Dogs

Watson and "Little Albert"

C.S.

U.C.S.

C.R.

U.C.R.

Contingency vs. Contiguity

Blocking

2nd/Higher Order Conditioning

Classically Conditioned Taste Aversions

Classical Conditioning

"Behaviorism": Emphasizes observable behaviors over inner experiences and mental processes.

Acquisition
Generalization
Discrimination
Extinction
Spontaneous Recovery

Biological Pre-Dispositions?

Thorndike's "Law of Effect"

B.F. Skinner

Shaping

Positive Reinforcement

Negative Reinforcement

Punishment/ Aversion

Operant or Instrumental Conditioning

Contingency

Overjustification

Primary and Secondary Reinforcers

Premack Principle

Schedules of Reinforcement:
• FR   • FI
• VR   • VI

Bandura and "Bobo"

Also Known As:
• Observational Learning
• Modeling

Kohler, Chimps, and Insight Learning

Tolman, Rats and Mazes and Latent Learning, Cognitive Maps

Social Learning

Role of Reinforcement

Role of Self Efficacy

For Discussion:
• TV Violence?
• Pro-Social Imitation?

Cognitive Learning

Seligman and Learned Helplessness

Practice Items

  * The first two items are in reference to the following scenario:

A group of ranchers attempt to discourage coyotes from raiding their sheep by lacing the wool of their flock with a substance that makes sheep violently ill if they eat it. Very quickly, the wolves in that pack avoid that flock altogether.

1. In this scenario, what are the UCS, CS and CR, respectively?

   (A) the substance, the sheep's wool, aversion to the flock
   (B) the sheep's wool, the substance, aversion to the flock
   (C) aversion to the flock, violent illness, the substance
   (D) the substance, the sheep's wool, violent illness
   (E) the wolves, the sheep, aversion to the flock

2. The ranchers discover that wolves from this pack will not raid the treated flock, but do continue to raid other nearby flocks. This is an example of

   (A) stimulus generalization
   (B) response generalization
   (C) chaining
   (D) spontaneous recovery
   (E) discrimination

3. A rat learns to escape an electric shock as soon as it is administered by running through a small opening in an operant chamber. This is an example of

   (A) primary reinforcement
   (B) secondary reinforcement
   (C) negative reinforcement
   (D) omission training
   (E) vicarious conditioning

4. In operant conditioning, the Premack Principle states that

   (A) primary reinforcers have more intrinsic reinforcing value than secondary reinforcers
   (B) a previously learned response can block the learning of a later, similar response
   (C) one can pair a conditioned stimulus with a second conditioned stimulus and acquire conditioning to that second stimulus
   (D) a desired behavior for a particular individual can be effectively used as a reinforcer for another, less preferred activity
   (E) punishment is ineffective

5. In a language laboratory, a language teacher tunes into her students at varying, unpredictable times and awards bonus points if a student is continuing to engage in the oral lesson. This is an example of

    (A) a variable interval schedule of reinforcement
    (B) a variable ratio schedule of reinforcement
    (C) progressive reinforcement
    (D) regressive reinforcement
    (E) trace conditioning

6. How would Ivan Pavlov have conducted extinction trials after his classical conditioning of a salivation response in dogs?

    (A) by repeatedly presenting the CS without ever again pairing it with the UCS
    (B) by reinforcing the behavior he wished to extinguish
    (C) through the use of temporal conditioning
    (D) by administering a placebo to the dogs immediately after conditioning
    (E) through modeling

7. Which of the following is the best evidence in support of biological predispositions in learning?

    (A) a child imitates what he sees on television
    (B) a man associates a bright yellow light with sickness
    (C) an infant monkey is more likely to imitate a videotaped fear response of an adult responding to the presence of a snake than a model responding fearfully to the presence of a worm
    (D) a rat learns a chain of behaviors in order to earn a food reward
    (E) a dog barks as a request for food

8. According to Edward Tolman, a rat might assimilate the details of a maze almost by happenstance through simple exposure, although it may not demonstrate that knowledge in the absence of reinforcement. He called this

    (A) overlearning
    (B) overjustification
    (C) self efficacy
    (D) latent learning
    (E) insight learning

9. The theories of B.F. Skinner are best summarized in which of the following quotes?

    (A) "Dreams are the royal road to the unconscious"
    (B) "Operant conditioning shapes behavior as a sculptor shapes a lump of clay"
    (C) "To my mind, empathy in itself is a healing agent"
    (D) "Nothing exists from whose nature some effect does not follow"
    (E) "Most human behavior is learned by observation through modeling"

10. According to Robert Rescorla, the strength of a classically conditioned response decreases as the predictive value of the CS-UCS pairing decreases. He argued that this is so because classical conditioning requires

    (A) contiguity
    (B) contingency
    (C) acquisition
    (D) systematic shaping
    (E) immediate reinforcement

Chapter VI

Cognition Part I: Memory

Introduction

Seven to nine of the one hundred multiple choice items on the AP Psychology Exam will involve "Cognition", which in turn is broken into two parts: "Memory" and "Thought and Language". Many of the concepts you will encounter in studying Memory can be demonstrated for you, and they'll thus be easy to retain. This topic also contains reference to the use of **mnemonic devices**. Learning about such memory aids will help you in this unit and also in retaining information from future chapters and other courses.

The **information processing model of memory** is built on a three phase flow in human memory: first, we **encode** information, then we must **store** it, and finally we must be able to **retrieve** what we have stored. Some liken this model to the workings of a library. When a librarian receives a new book, he first identifies and catalogues it and then he places it on a shelf, from which it can be readily retrieved. Books can be "lost" at any step along the way. If, for example, a catalogued book was borrowed and returned but then replaced on the wrong shelf, it would essentially be "lost" even though it is in the library. This would be especially true in a library with a very large capacity; a book that ought to have been placed on shelf number one on the first floor of the library which was instead placed on shelf number five on the seventh floor of the library might just as well have been burned, as its retrieval would require a book-by-book review of the entire inventory.

A more commonly used analogy for this information processing model is drawn with computers. You could not pass in the research paper you have typed on your word processor (encoding) unless you have saved your work (storage) and also remembered its file name so that you can retrieve it.

Another model for memory, the Atkinson-Shiffrin model, overlaps in many ways with the information processing model. It does, however, differentiate between different types of storage mechanisms, postulating the existence of a **sensory register, short term memory (STM) and long term memory (LTM)**. The sensory register, or simply **sensory memory**, allows us to take in the plethora of sensory inputs which are available at any moment. Its functioning is very brief – most of what "hits" the sensory register receives no further attention or processing from the observer. In effect, such information is not encoded and is then lost.

Encoding

Before we explore STM and LTM further, let's look at how we <u>do</u> encode material. It's pretty clear that the **more deeply you process incoming information**, the more likely it is that you will retain it for future reference. We can attribute much of our inability to remember to **shallow processing** when we first encountered the material. In school, for instance, we often use simple **rehearsal** as a means to encode what we are taught. This is a relatively shallow way to encode the information if we fail to attach any **meaning** to it or place it in some relevant **context**. It's interesting to note that many students who claim they cannot remember, say, the last ten U.S. presidents, can remember numerous details about the last ten CD'S put out by their favorite musical group. They may even spend more time rehearsing the list of presidents in preparation for a test than they ever spent "rehearsing" the names of the CD titles or band members, but the latter has meaning to them and is thus more readily stored and retrieved.

Phone numbers, social security numbers and bank card numbers are all examples of how encoding can be facilitated through **chunking**. Rather than remembering 11 digits in a string, we can group the digits into more manageable segments. Thus, 14325581212 becomes 1-432-558-1212; 1776186519181945 can be chunked into 1776, 1865, 1918, 1945, and NFLCIAFBINASA can be read as NFL, CIA, FBI, NASA. In the latter two examples, the chunking method is combined with the attachment of meaning or context to the groupings, which increases ease of recall.

Our encoding can also be effected by **schemas** which impact our memory for people, places and situations. <u>A schema is a cognitive framework based on our previous experience</u>, a set of expectations which can help us fill in the gaps in our memories. Of course, such schemas can also lead us to build things into memories that fit our expectations but not the reality of the circumstance. This is called **constructive memory** or **<u>confabulation</u>**.

Have you ever had difficulty recalling a specific word but had a sense that it was a long word or that it had three syllables? If so, it may be that when you first learned the word you encoded it **structurally** or **visually**. If you cannot pull the word out of your memory but you do remember that it rhymes with something else or have a feel for the rhythm or sound of the word, it could be because you encoded it **acoustically**. If you can recall that a word is synonymous with another word, even though you cannot at the moment recall the actual word, this might be attributed to earlier **semantic encoding**. A commonly used illustration of these types of encoding involves analyzing the errors individuals make in attempting to recall the names of the seven dwarves from the "Snow White" fairy tale (of course, one cannot remember something to which they have not been exposed, and there may well be a cultural or generational bias in this example; there are many other such examples one could utilize instead):

- an example of a *semantic encoding error*: remembering a dwarf who was "really smart" without specific name recall; there was an intelligent character named Doc
- an example of an *acoustic encoding error*: remembering a character called Dumpy or Bumpy instead of the actual character, Grumpy

- an example of a *visual encoding error*: remembering how characters appeared, that most had beards although one did not (Bashful), and so on
- an example of a *structural encoding error*: remembering characters with names ending in an "ey" sound, since many of the actual character names are built in that way

The aforementioned **mnemonic devices** rely on our ability to make mental images like some of those above. In order to remember something using mnemonics, one links some part of it (a visual image, the way the word or a part of the word sounds, etc.) to something one already knows. Some mnemonic techniques for name recall work by making a connection between the name you hear and the face you see – for instance, if introduced to a man named Cliff you might picture his face or head as a high, steep cliff. Later, upon seeing his face, the image of a cliff comes back to you. The key is to first attend to and hear the name. Many people who argue that they're "not good with names" probably never really encode the name when introduced to someone.

In other mnemonic approaches, you tie a set of images to a familiar place (like your bedroom) and then simply mentally walk your way through that familiar scene, retrieving the images as you go. This is called the *method of loci*. Or you create an image using "peg words" which you have memorized; you then simply recall the already memorized peg words and the image you associated with it comes back to you (the classic *peg word mnemonic* requires that you memorize the number one as a bun, two as a shoe, three as a tree, four as a door, five as a hive, six as sticks, seven as heaven, eight as gate, nine as line and ten as hen; each peg word rhymes with its corresponding number; if you wish to remember a list of things to get at the store, you "hang an image" on those pegs, imagining biting into a hamburger *bun* which is filled with MILK, then picturing a *shoe* with a huge head of LETTUCE stuffed into it, etc.). Many memory experts would contend that the images or techniques one uses are less important than the effort it takes in even trying to use a mnemonic. That effort alone encourages deeper, more meaningful processing.

Before we move onto storage, here is a quick summary of the brain structures involved in memory that you are most likely to see on the AP Exam:

the **hippocampus:** considered part of the limbic system, it seems responsible for the formation of new memories; damage to the neurons in the hippocampus which release *acetylcholine* (you may recall our discussion of that neurotransmitter's role in memory in our unit on the Biological Bases of Behavior) would likely not effect retrieval of previously stored memories but might prevent storage of any new material

- **the cerebellum:** located in the old, hind brain, it seems involved in memory for conditioned responses, such as a classically conditioned eye blink response; procedural memories may also be stored here and in the *putamen*, which is part of the limbic system

- **the prefrontal cortex:** seems at least partly involved in "habit" learning; a person with damage to the hippocampus might well retain the ability to perform some "habit-based" behavior even though he or she has no explicit memory of having learned that behavior because of the hippocampal damage; another part of the limbic system, the *caudate nucleus*, also appears to play a role in storage of habit memories; the entire cortex, especially the temporal and frontal lobes, seem involved in the retrieval of various types of memories

- **the amygdala:** this important structure in the emotional limbic system appears to play a big role in the formation and storage of unconscious memories, especially highly stressful ones

Storage

When we try to store information that enters our sensory memory in short term memory, it quickly becomes apparent that **STM has a rather limited capacity**. In general, that is deemed to be **about 20-30 seconds** and about **7 +/– 2 unrelated items** (the latter was identified by researcher George Miller and is often called the **"magic number"** of short term memory capacity). If no deeper processing is done in order to enter material into longer term storage, it will fade pretty rapidly, and, if we try to hold more than 8 or 9 items in STM, we tend to start knocking out earlier items. Often, you will hear STM linked to a term called working memory, as if they are synonymous, but that's not exactly true. **Working memory** seems to be a phase between STM and LTM, which allows for information that is already stored to be brought to conscious awareness, while also juggling new material as it enters short term memory. Some people think of working memory as a desktop, where you array the files you have and the newer stuff you're being exposed to in order to understand and process it all. You will not need to concern yourself with this "STM vs. working memory vs. LTM" distinction in terms of your AP Exam preparation however.

Long term memory is thought by many to have no limits in terms of capacity. Theoretically, we cannot "run out of room" in LTM. If we "do something" with incoming material through rehearsal, chunking, mnemonic elaboration or some other processing strategy, it can enter relatively permanent storage. Later, we'll look at how we still manage to "forget" things that are in LTM.

There are a few other types of memory you should know about for the advanced placement course. They are summarized below:

- **episodic memory:** memory for specific events in one's life
- **flashbulb memory:** an especially vivid episodic memory for a major event; although research has indicated that the vividness of the memory does not necessarily predict well for its accuracy, in a prototypical flashbulb memory individuals feel they can recall exactly what they were doing when they heard the verdict at the O.J. Simpson trial or that Princess Diana had passed away in an accident; memory for the events of September 11, 2001 will undoubtedly become a classic example of flashbulb memory

- **procedural memory:** recall for specific actions, such as riding a bicycle or tying one's shoes or swimming; these are the most enduring types of memories; it is essentially true that "once you learn to ride a bike you never forget"
- **semantic memory:** memory for information; your school work is largely a matter of semantic memory
- **state dependent memory:** the theory that one is more likely to recall details of something if one is in a similar emotional and physical state as when exposed to the events one is trying to recall; a person who witnessed a scenario in a highly excited emotional state would recall details of that scenario better if in a similarly excited state
- **context dependent memory:** the theory that one is more likely to recall information if one is in the same physical space or a similar physical context as when one encountered the material; theoretically, the best place to be tested on your knowledge of advanced placement psychology material would be in the room where you were taught the material
- **eidetic imagery/memory:** the official term for photographic memory; in its true form this is quite rare, as it involves very precise and long lasting memory as if one has an actual photograph to "look at" in their head

Retrieval

Many of the memory problems we all have involve **retrieval issues**; that is, the memory is "in there" but we just can't seem to pull it out. Thus we have the common **tip of the tongue phenomenon**, which is usually seen as a retrieval problem. Also, while we sometimes cannot precisely <u>recall</u> details stored in our memories, we can <u>recognize</u> them when cued in some way. An item on a test that asked you to give a definition of a term is assessing your **recall** of that concept, while a multiple choice item is assessing **recognition**. Further, at times it appears we "remember" something without knowing that we do. This is called **implicit memory**, as opposed to **explicit memories** which you can consciously declare (explicit memory is sometimes called *declarative memory*). An implicit memory may need to be *primed* or cued in order for you to recall it. For example, in research done with patients who had damage to the hippocampus, the patients were unable to declare any explicit recall of items in a word list they were shown. However, if cued by, say, letter combinations like 'ch' and asked to think of the first word that came to mind beginning with 'ch', they were more likely to come up with words that they had seen on the list they'd been shown earlier (in this example, perhaps the word 'charter'), even though they had no conscious recollection of having seen the words.

When individuals with healthy memory systems are given a list of words to remember, we often see evidence of an interesting set of phenomena known collectively as the **serial position effect**. If given a series of fifteen words describing behaviors in a baseball game (such as hit, pitch, bunt, and so on), individuals are more likely to recall items presented at the beginning of the list (called the **primacy effect**) and the end of the list (the **recency effect**). Recall is also better for words that stand out for their **semantic distinctiveness** (that is, they have meanings that catch one's attention or do not fit the schema of the list). Further, some individuals might "remember" words that in fact were never presented. In their attempts to reconstruct the list they may then confabulate items that meet their expectancy of what *might* be on such a list.

Expectancy or set can also greatly influence one's **eyewitness recall**. An eyewitness to a crime might unknowingly apply gender, racial or place schemas in trying to reconstruct the events they witnessed. Thus, it is possible to add details to a memory just as it is easy to forget (or **"level"**) details. Researcher Elizabeth Loftus has also discovered that how one is asked to recall events (the **framing** of the questions) can influence how those events are then recalled. This is similar in a sense to the idea of posing "leading questions" in a courtroom. If a witness to a robbery is asked "which hand was the gun in?" before it is even established that there *was* a gun, this can elicit responses quite different from more open ended questioning techniques.

Forgetting

Some memories are omitted simply because they never get beyond the limitations of short term memory or because they are not well processed or because they **decay** over time with diminishing reference to them (although early memory researcher Hermann Ebbinghaus postulated in his **"forgetting curve"** that there is rapid decay of memory for nonsense syllables but that decay will flatten out at approximately 20-30% in long term retention – thus, it doesn't ALL fade). Others are forgotten because of interference from other information. In **proactive interference**, something from the past inhibits your attempts to recall more recent material. For instance, your locker combination from sophomore year is still in your mind the first few times you try to open your new locker in junior year. Soon, you will see evidence of **retroactive interference**, in which new information works backward to erase or inhibit older memories – your junior year combination now interferes with recall of the previous year's combination.

The terms above may help you in sorting out two labels for different types of memory dysfunction: retrograde amnesia and anterograde amnesia. In retroactive interference, new information works backward (just as a "retro fashion trend" moves us backward in time to an earlier style), interfering with recall of older information. In **retrograde amnesia**, some trauma or damage works backward, erasing memories from the period before the damage occurred. If you were in a car accident and suffered retrograde amnesia, you would have memory loss for events which came *before* the accident. Knowing that, you can then reason out **anterograde amnesia** – if you were in a car accident and suffered from anterograde amnesia, you would have memory loss for information *since* the accident. Damage to the hippocampus would likely lead to anterograde amnesia. Memories stored before the damage occurred would remain in place, but you would be unable to form new memories.

The related concepts of **positive and negative transfer** may help you understand the 'interferences' mentioned above. If you can throw a softball or baseball well, will there be positive transfer of that skill in learning to throw a javelin in track and field? Does being a good skier have positive or negative transfer in terms of learning to snowboard? If you did well in biology last year, will that help you in chemistry this year? That is, will the previous learning help you with the new learning, or might it actually hinder your performance on the new task, at least at first?

Finally, sometimes we are motivated to forget. Indeed, few of us would choose to have the capability to remember everything that happens to us. There are many things we choose to **suppress**; we consciously push them out of our heads, at least for the time being. We might also **repress** especially painful memories; we bury them so deeply in our unconscious mind that we are no longer aware of their existence.

Name Hall of Fame

You don't have much to worry about in terms of name recall in this unit. **Elizabeth Loftus** would be a serious candidate for inclusion into a psychology hall of fame, but you still probably will not have to "know" her name in order to get a multiple choice item correct. You certainly ought to know about her work in eyewitness recall however. It's possible you will encounter the name **Hermann Ebbinghaus**, although it would more likely appear in an item about the history of psychology. Your grasp of his "forgetting curve" is much more likely to be assessed than is recall of his name. **Endel Tulving** is credited with coining the terms procedural, semantic and episodic memory, but, again, his name would be supplied for you on the exam. Likewise with **Richard Atkinson** and **Richard Shiffrin** of the Atkinson-Shiffrin model.

Essay Themes

Eyewitness recall is a major area of study in this unit, and exploration of it covers a lot of other ground in memory, so it may be a valuable focus point for you in your preparation. You certainly must have a basic understanding of the workings of **short term memory** and **long term memory**. Finally, it is relatively easy to envision an essay item which asks about phenomena in **"forgetting"** while overlapping with **Freudian theory** in terms of repression and suppression, cognitive changes in **development over the lifespan**, and perhaps units on **testing and individual differences** and **thought/language**. Remember, the Advanced Placement Psychology test development committee tries hard to come up with free response questions which cut across multiple content areas.

Test Preparation: Cognition Part I: Memory

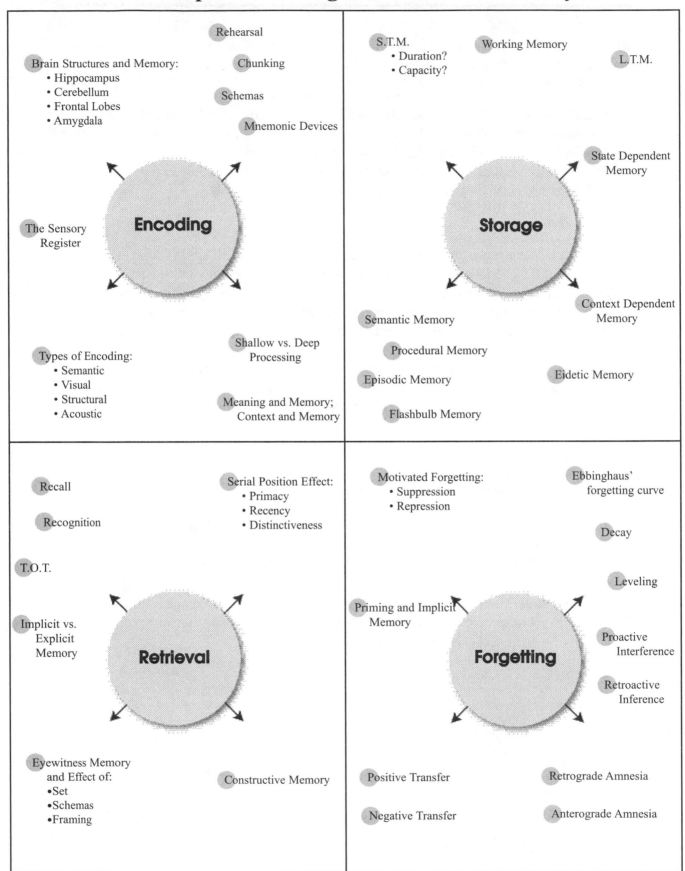

Rehearsal

Chunking

Schemas

Mnemonic Devices

Brain Structures and Memory:
• Hippocampus
• Cerebellum
• Frontal Lobes
• Amygdala

Encoding

The Sensory Register

Types of Encoding:
• Semantic
• Visual
• Structural
• Acoustic

Shallow vs. Deep Processing

Meaning and Memory; Context and Memory

S.T.M.
• Duration?
• Capacity?

Working Memory

L.T.M.

Storage

State Dependent Memory

Context Dependent Memory

Semantic Memory

Procedural Memory

Episodic Memory

Eidetic Memory

Flashbulb Memory

Recall

Recognition

T.O.T.

Implicit vs. Explicit Memory

Retrieval

Serial Position Effect:
• Primacy
• Recency
• Distinctiveness

Eyewitness Memory and Effect of:
•Set
•Schemas
•Framing

Constructive Memory

Motivated Forgetting:
• Suppression
• Repression

Ebbinghaus' forgetting curve

Decay

Leveling

Priming and Implicit Memory

Forgetting

Proactive Interference

Retroactive Inference

Positive Transfer

Retrograde Amnesia

Negative Transfer

Anterograde Amnesia

Practice Items

1. In the late 19th century, Hermann Ebbinghaus tested his own recall of lists of nonsense syllables he had previously learned through rehearsal. From this work, he proposed the concept of a forgetting curve, which suggests

   (A) new material will quickly interfere with recall of old material
   (B) material already stored in long term memory takes precedence over new material, especially if that material is relatively meaningless
   (C) there is no long term retention of nonsensical information
   (D) recall of meaningless items drops very quickly after initial learning but then tapers and levels off
   (E) memory for nonsensical information is explicit but not implicit

2. Which of the following is the best argument to account for the primacy effect in recalling a series of items?

   (A) the items you recall were presented more recently than other items
   (B) you tend to recall the most important items on a list
   (C) the first items on the list are likely to be more effectively rehearsed than other items
   (D) there has not been adequate time for retroactive interference to occur
   (E) you tend to recall items that stand out as having unique or surprising meanings

3. The rare ability to exactly maintain detailed visual memories over a significant period of time is called

   (A) flashbulb memory
   (B) eidetic imagery
   (C) semantic memory
   (D) hyperphasia
   (E) aphasia

4. The amygdala is associated with which of the following types of memory?

   (A) emotionally charged unconscious memories
   (B) procedural memory
   (C) flashbulb memory
   (D) state dependent memory for recent events
   (E) state dependent memory for semantic knowledge

5. On the first day of a study, an individual is classically conditioned to blink at the sound of a buzzer. On day two of the study, that same individual is somewhat slower to acquire the blink response at the sound of a bell. This "blocking" effect is an example of

   (A) lesioning
   (B) regression
   (C) repression
   (D) retroactive interference
   (E) proactive interference

6. During class a student is asked to recall the name of the artist who painted the ceiling of the Sistine Chapel. The student is being assessed on

   (A) constructive memory
   (B) reconstructive memory
   (C) episodic memory
   (D) working memory
   (E) semantic memory

7. The portion of the limbic system which seems to be responsible for the formation of new memories is

   (A) the caudate nucleus
   (B) the septum
   (C) the basal ganglia
   (D) the hippocampus
   (E) the hypothalamus

8. A seventy year old man successfully rides a bicycle for the first time since he was twelve years old. This is an example of:

   (A) working memory
   (B) semantic memory
   (C) iconic memory
   (D) primary memory
   (E) procedural memory

9. Which of the following is the best illustration of the effect of framing in memory?

   (A) subjects report different speeds of the cars involved in a videotaped automobile accident depending on whether they were asked how fast the cars were traveling when they "made contact" with each other vs. "smashed into" each other

   (B) an eyewitness to a crime "fills in the gaps" of his account by relying on his expectations of what might typically have happened in such a case

   (C) an eyewitness to a crime recalls fewer and fewer details of the events as time passes

   (D) police officers choose members of a line-up who bear no physical resemblance to their suspect

   (E) an individual can only recall details which match the frame of reference he had prior to exposure to those details

10. Which of the following is the best example of context dependent memory?

   (A) a potential eyewitness to a crime tells two different stories to two different questioners

   (B) students who learn a vocabulary list while in a particular classroom do better at recalling the words when in that same room

   (C) individuals with damage to the cerebellum are unable to form short term memories

   (D) a rat cannot retain memory of a learned response if it is learned in an unfamiliar environment

   (E) a man who learned several complicated definitions while in a joyful mood does better in recalling the definitions when again in a joyful mood

GO ON TO THE NEXT PAGE

Chapter VII

Cognition Part II: Thought and Language

Introduction

You might expect to encounter anywhere from four to eight items on thinking, problem solving and language acquisition on the AP Exam. This topic also has clear connections to Developmental Psychology and to the chapter on Intelligence, Assessment and Individual Differences.

We will begin with a look at how humans solve problems, followed by examination of some of the typical errors people make in decision making and judgment. Next, we will explore the basics of language acquisition and some general theories about how we so readily learn language at an early age and how language interacts with thought and culture.

Thinking and Solving Problems

Experts on thinking and problem solving make frequent reference to 'concepts' and 'prototypes', so to start with you need to know what psychologists mean when they use those terms. **Concepts** are ideas that we group together because of some shared properties or characteristics. Husky, collie and poodle are examples of the concept category 'dog'. On the AP Exam you may encounter different types of such categories: superordinate, basic and subordinate. With the

> **superordinate category** MUSICAL INSTRUMENTS, we could have the
> **basic category** GUITARS, and the
> **subordinate category** ELECTRIC GUITARS; we could also have the

> **superordinate category** GUITARS, and the
> **basic category** ELECTRIC GUITARS, and the
> **subordinate category** FENDER (or GIBSON, LES PAUL and other types of electric guitar)

A **prototype** is a model, a "best example" of a particular thing. If you were asked to think of the prototypical 'bird', you'd be more likely to mention robin or eagle or sparrow than thrush or pterodactyl.

On the other hand, if you were being tested on your ability to think divergently, you would want to generate an answer like "warbler" to the question "can you supply me with the names of as many birds as you can?" Most of your thinking in school is **convergent thinking**; that is, there is an "answer" the teacher is seeking and he or she wants the students to converge on it, just as cars converge at a four way stop sign. The "right answer" is in the intersection! In **divergent thinking**, you are asked to think creatively, to generate as many possible answers to a question or problem as you can. In true "brainstorming" sessions, participants are encouraged to offer any possible solution to a problem that comes to mind. No editing or judgment is allowed during this period. Sometimes participants find it useful to stop when creativity has seemingly been exhausted to allow **incubation** to occur. They leave the problem for a time, allowing their minds to "work on it" without conscious effort. This can lead to further insights when they return to the problem. Only <u>after</u> such steps are taken does the creative thinking group edit or eliminate some ideas, while many are combined and recombined with others.

Humans seem to be unique among animals in that they can take part in a process like that described above and then reflect on their thoughts and methods. This thinking about one's own problem solving strategies is called **metacognition**. It allows people to evaluate the success of their approaches, which fall into two general categories: algorithms and heuristics.

An **algorithm** is a sure fire way to solve a problem. It is a step by step method which guarantees a solution as long as each step is properly executed. **Heuristics** are short cuts in problem solving. You will sometimes see them referred to as "rules of thumb". Each has strengths and weaknesses. If you quickly know the answer to the question "what is 79 times 10?", then you see the potential value of heuristics. Long ago you probably learned the heuristic that suggests you simply add a zero to any number which is multiplied by ten. This saves you the trouble of "doing it all the way out" algorithmically.

Variables, Errors and Fallacies in Problem Solving

Use of heuristics can also lead to trouble. In the 1970's, researchers Richard <u>Kahneman</u> and Amos Tversky identified two common heuristic errors that you must know for this course; the **availability heuristic** and the **representativeness heuristic**. In the case of the former, we judge the probability of some event based on what comes most readily to mind (what is most readily <u>available</u> in the mind). The example Kahneman and Tversky used (that has become so well known that now people are rarely guilty of using the availability heuristic in answering it) involved the dangers of airplane travel vs. roadway travel. While any individual is statistically much more likely to be hurt or killed in a car accident than in a plane crash (it's about ten times more likely!), they often predicted the reverse, because the relatively rare plane crashes get so much attention and thus come more easily to mind than the all too common car crashes which occur every day.

In the <u>representativeness heuris</u>tic we judge the likelihood of some event based on how well it matches some picture or expectation we already have in our head. Kahneman and Tversky asked questions like this: is the following individual more likely to be an Ivy League psychology professor or a truck driver? – *a man, 5' 7", 155 pounds, wears glasses, attends poetry readings, enjoys classical music*. Most people reported that such a person was more likely to be an Ivy League professor, even though Kahneman and Tversky argued that it is far more likely to be a truck driver, if only because there are hundreds of thousands of truck drivers and probably only 100 to 200 Ivy League psychology professors all told. Even if fully 50% of those professors fit the schema they described, it'd still be far more likely statistically that such a man was a truck driver.

In attempting to solve problems humans are sometimes limited by **functional fixedness**; that is, they are trapped in seeing only certain, prescribed uses for some object. A potato is for eating, not to be used as a temporary emergency gas cap. A paper clip is for attaching things to each other, not for making "earrings" or "chains". This in turn is related to the concept of **mental set**, which is a kind of fixation on one particular way to solve a problem. The best teachers of mathematics are able to teach students to understand a problem and to see solutions from perspectives the student can handle. Often, students can solve problems using certain formulaic methods, but then are trapped into approaching all problems in that one way, even when that strategy simply won't work any longer.

We often fall victim to **implicit assumptions** in problem solving. That is, we assume there are rules limiting what we can do even when such rules do not exist. The classic example of this, contained in most introductory psychology textbooks, is the "nine dot problem". Problem solvers are asked to connect nine dots, arranged in three rows of three, without picking up pen or pencil, using four lines (or fewer) which must be straight. Because the dots are arranged in a box-like configuration,

people assume that they must work "within the box" which is suggested by the dots. In fact, avoiding this implicit assumption is the key to solving the problem, as one must "break out of the box" in order to reach a solution.

Take no more than 5 seconds to respond to the following:

"What is 8 times 7 times 6 times 5 times 4 times 3 times 2 times 1?"

The answer is 40,320. Few people get that in five seconds of course, but they DO give higher estimates than those asked

"What is 1 times 2 times 3 times 4 times 5 times 6 times 7 times 8?"

The questions are the same, but the **framing** of them influences responses, as is often true in problem solving.

A concept that is under-represented in introductory psychology textbooks but which quite commonly hinders humans in thinking and problem solving is **confirmation bias**. In it, individuals tend to look for and attend to evidence that supports what they already believe, and disregard or "explain away" evidence to the contrary. Once a person becomes convinced that most UFO sightings are indeed cases of extraterrestrial visitation, they are less likely to pay attention to arguments which offer alternative hypotheses. They will, however, latch onto stories which might confirm their previous conviction. This may also be linked to the tendency of people to be overconfident in their judgments and decisions, a consistent finding among researchers. We tend to want to be "right", and to believe that we already are!

Language

The study of language, how we acquire it and how it interacts with behavior and cognition is sometimes called **psycholinguistics**. There is ongoing discussion as to just how much we are pre-programmed at birth to acquire language. Case studies of children living in extreme social isolation for the first years of their lives, as **in the "Genie" case study** and the case of **"The Wild Child of Aveyron"**, add complexity to this debate. Genie was discovered in 1971 living in what appeared to be a "normal" middle class home in California. In fact, her parents had essentially imprisoned her in her bedroom for most of the first 13 years of her life, for reasons that remain unclear. She had little sensory input in the room, no appropriate social interaction and was apparently punished for making sounds. When she was removed from this wretched situation, she made some significant strides at first in acquiring spoken language, but then pretty much stopped progressing. Some contend she could've continued to develop if the people who worked with her had a more systematic approach to helping her. Indeed, there was a fair amount of "competition" between various people involved with her case, and some would say the tensions that arose as a result might've blocked Genie's potential. Another question that arose early on: were Genie's language deficits a result of Genie's social isolation, or had she been born mentally handicapped? Remarkably, Genie was quite engaging socially, and she demonstrated awareness of what had happened to her, and that further complicated the "was she born mentally retarded?" issue. Genie is still living in California but authorities are now very protective of her privacy. It does seem clear that she made no dramatic improvement since the "Genie Project" was discontinued.

Some of these same themes permeated the case of "Victor", who was discovered living in the woods near Aveyron, France around 1800. It appeared he was about the same age as Genie was when she was discovered. He too was brought into civilized society and efforts were made to teach him language. He too stopped progressing after some early success, and the project to help him learn was abandoned. He died some 20 years later, possessing only rudimentary language skills.

Linguist Noam Chomsky argues that language acquisition is native to humans, given a reasonable environment. He theorizes that we have a kind of **language acquisition device** (or L.A.D.) in our brains which allow us to soak up language, especially during critical periods in early childhood. If we miss those **critical periods**, it might be too late to make up for the loss (others prefer to think of these as *sensitive*, rather than *critical* periods; this suggests that the "window" for learning is not completely closed at any particular time). This natural predisposition to learn language helps to explain, he argues, why we can understand the many different possible **deep structures** of a sentence drawn from one basic arrangement of words (its **surface structure**). No one ever "teaches" us that the sentence "The artist painted me on his front porch", which has a simple eight word surface structure, has many different potential meanings, yet we somehow know it.

Children generally progress from **cooing** to a **babbling** stage (which at first sounds similar in babies no matter what the language they're born into but then begins to include the basic sounds, or **phonemes**, of the language they're immersed in) to a **holophrastic stage** (in which children essentially express complete thoughts with one word, as in saying "juice" to mean "pardon me, I would very much like something to drink if you don't mind") to a stage of **telegraphic speech** (the two or three word sentence stage, as in "me walk" or "mommy give toy") and finally to acquisition of proper **syntax** (appropriate word order).

Very generally speaking, a child will be cooing, gurgling and squealing at around two months old, and then babble at around six months. These two stages are sometimes thought of as *pre-linguistic stages*. Soon the child begins to use the sounds of the language, phonemes, to form morphemes, which have meaning (you might think 'm' for 'morpheme', 'm' for meaning). A **morpheme** can be a word or a piece of a word, as long as it adds meaning. For instance, 'ch' is a phoneme, a sound of the English language, while 'ed' is both a phoneme and a morpheme, as 'ed' at the end of a word adds the concept of past tense to that word. It is typical for a child to move to single words by around one year old. Estimates are that the typical child may have 50 or so words in their vocabulary by 18 months of age.

In forming sentences, children often make mistakes such as **overregularization**. An example is "Yesterday, I goed to the store". Apparently, they have learned that 'ed' adds past tense to a word but have not yet learned the exceptions to that rule. They are thus overusing the regulation (you may see this referred to as **overgeneralization** as well). Of course, a child who says "Yesterday I goed to the store" has still gotten her point across even if the grammar is incorrect. This illustrates the distinction between **descriptive grammar** and **prescriptive grammar**. If an adult has ever corrected you for saying something like "I ain't going" and you replied "oh, you know what I mean", you are basically arguing for descriptive grammar while the adult is holding you to the proper, prescribed way of expressing yourself.

Almost any introductory psychology text will have a section on **ape language**, a fascinating subject. It is unlikely that you will encounter the topic on the Advanced Placement Examination, but this is an area worth exploring, especially in regards to the major questions that arise from it, such as; what *is* 'language'? are apes who learn to use words and sentences using them in the same way that humans use them? do they understand that a word is essentially a symbol for something else? if apes have difficulty with syntax, and research suggests they do, is that evidence that they really aren't using 'language' but have merely been conditioned to respond in certain ways to certain sounds, much as they might to a bell or horn?

Finally, you should familiarize yourself with the **Whorfian Hypothesis** or the **Linguistic Relativity Theory** (you may also see this called the **Whorf-Sapir Hypothesis**). It states that one's language influences the ways one thinks. The classic example which was once very commonly used refers to Alaskan Eskimo words for 'snow'; allegedly, Eskimos have far more such words than do other, less snow-laden cultures, and this leads them to think differently about their world. This "fact" by itself is in dispute, as is the question of whether language influences cognition and culture or vice versa. Because the Whorfian Hypothesis is not really accepted in its entirety any longer, you are not very likely to see it on the AP Psychology test, but it certainly does make for a fine discussion topic in any case.

Name Hall of Fame

Noam Chomsky is likely to show up on a typical AP Exam, although the item would be more along the lines of a "Chomsky's theory of the L.A.D. refers to _____" type question than a "Who forwarded the theory of the L.A.D.?" type question. In other words, you will probably not have to recall his name specifically. **Richard Kahneman** and **Amos Tversky** are leading researchers in problem solving, but they too would not be "the answer" to a question. **The "Genie" case study** and the case of **Victor, The Wild Child of Aveyron** are both important and could be used by your teacher to highlight issues of language acquisition in this unit or in a discussion of nature vs. nurture and critical period debates in developmental psychology, so you should have a basic familiarity with one or both of those stories.

Essay Themes

The **"nature, nurture or false dichotomy?"** argument lends itself to free response formats, although it may fall more neatly into the units on Developmental Psychology and Personality Theory. **Critical period theory**, which proposes a window of time during which a child is especially ready to learn language and which further suggests that if that opportunity is missed that it might be too late to catch up, is clearly intertwined with nature/nurture themes. Any proposed free response item asking you to summarize the flow and timetable of typical language acquisition in children would likely be rejected as too narrowly confined to one unit. An essay proposal focusing exclusively on problem solving strategies and common errors would probably meet the same fate during the test development process.

Test Preparation: Cognition Part II: Thought and Language

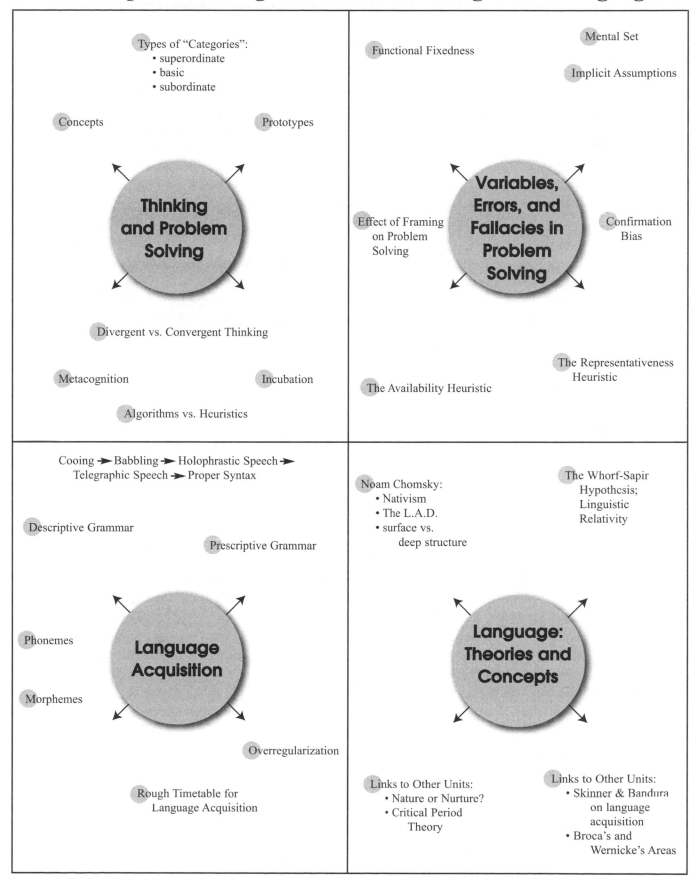

Types of "Categories":
• superordinate
• basic
• subordinate

Concepts

Prototypes

Thinking and Problem Solving

Divergent vs. Convergent Thinking

Metacognition

Incubation

Algorithms vs. Heuristics

Functional Fixedness

Mental Set

Implicit Assumptions

Variables, Errors, and Fallacies in Problem Solving

Effect of Framing on Problem Solving

Confirmation Bias

The Representativeness Heuristic

The Availability Heuristic

Cooing ➤ Babbling ➤ Holophrastic Speech ➤ Telegraphic Speech ➤ Proper Syntax

Descriptive Grammar

Prescriptive Grammar

Phonemes

Language Acquisition

Morphemes

Overregularization

Rough Timetable for Language Acquisition

Noam Chomsky:
• Nativism
• The L.A.D.
• surface vs. deep structure

The Whorf-Sapir Hypothesis; Linguistic Relativity

Language: Theories and Concepts

Links to Other Units:
• Nature or Nurture?
• Critical Period Theory

Links to Other Units:
• Skinner & Bandura on language acquisition
• Broca's and Wernicke's Areas

85

Practice Items

1. Which of the following would serve as the best argument AGAINST the Whorf-Sapir Linguistic Relativity Theory?

   (A) the fact that a culture has different specific words to express the same thing doesn't necessarily mean that an individual who knows those words thinks differently about that thing
   (B) there is cross cultural evidence which supports the idea that few cultural difference exist in terms of when children acquire language
   (C) there is evidence which supports the idea that there is such a thing as an inborn tendency to absorb language
   (D) there is evidence to suggest that holophrastic speech develops before telegraphic speech even cross culturally
   (E) the fact that apes seem able to learn human language to some extent does not mean that they can, with proper training, learn language as well as humans do

2. A mathematics teacher consistently attempts the same solution to a problem, and seems unable to generate other possible approaches when the original one fails to work. This is an example of

   (A) a mental set
   (B) overgeneralization
   (C) an algorithm
   (D) framing
   (E) a prescriptive error

3. "A great many people think they are thinking when they are merely rearranging their prejudices". This quote from psychologist William James illustrates the tendency to ignore or rationalize information that refutes what one already believes, called

   (A) perceptual set
   (B) confirmation bias
   (C) linguistic relativity
   (D) algorithmic reasoning
   (E) functional fixedness

4. A child's use of a single word like 'up' to convey a more complex idea or desire is called

   (A) lexical simplicity
   (B) lexical ambiguity
   (C) automaticity
   (D) telegraphic speech
   (E) holophrastic speech

5. Which of the following is the best example of a heuristic in problem solving?

   (A) a researcher unwittingly stumbles onto a discovery that has little to do with her original topic of study
   (B) a police officer decides that a suspect is guilty because the suspect fits a profile the officer is familiar with
   (C) a student is asked "what is 17 times 10?" and quickly responds '170' by adding a zero to the number '17'
   (D) a man tries to fix his car but quickly quits trying when he doesn't meet with immediate success
   (E) a group of elementary school students generate several different possible solutions to an in-class "bridge building" project

6. Reflecting upon one's own thoughts and problem solving strategies is called

   (A) prototyping
   (B) cognitive mapping
   (C) cognitive consistency
   (D) cognitive dissonance
   (E) metacognition

7. The fundamental sounds of a language are called

   (A) semantics
   (B) morphemes
   (C) phonemes
   (D) holophrastics
   (E) pragmatics

8. One error humans sometimes make in judging the probable occurrence of some event involves the ease in which previous occurrences come to mind. This is called

   (A) the representativeness heuristic
   (B) the availability heuristic
   (C) deduction
   (D) induction
   (E) overregularization

9. Cooing and babbling are considered to be

    (A) holophrastic utterances
    (B) pre-linguistic events in human development
    (C) syntactically correct
    (D) examples of overextension
    (E) prescriptive applications of semantics

10. Which of the following is the best example of poor syntax?

    (A) "We go"
    (B) "Run here"
    (C) "I drinked the milk"
    (D) "This a fun game is"
    (E) "I enjoy what happened yesterday"

Chapter VIII

Developmental Psychology

Introduction

Although this unit will have the typical seven to nine percent of the multiple choice items on the AP Exam, there is more than the typical amount of information in it. It covers a broad range of material, examining physical, cognitive, social, emotional and moral development across the life span. There are a multitude of connections with other units as well, which makes this a valuable topic indeed in your overall test preparation.

Themes in Development

In general, developmental theories can be broken into two categories: continuous and discontinuous. **Continuity theories** propose that development is very gradual and that it is difficult at any one time to notice the changes that are occurring. **Discontinuity theories** are more stage-like, in that changes occur more dramatically and obviously; one "makes a jump" to another level. Such stage theories also suggest that development through the stages is largely unchanging and universal. Everyone goes through the same steps in the same order. As you look at various stage theories in this chapter, you will see this is a nice topic for discussion and critique.

You've probably encountered the famed **nature vs. nurture** debate elsewhere in your schooling, perhaps in English or History classes. Most developmental psychologists would argue that it is a *"false dichotomy"*; that is, it isn't an either/or question at all. A wonderful analogy for this is offered by psychologists who contend that engaging in the nature vs. nurture debate is much like asking "what is more important on a soccer field, the length or the width?" Of course you need both to have a soccer field, just as it is impossible to completely separate out the influences of biology and environment on human development.

Twin studies are a powerful and fascinating way to explore the question of what makes us develop as we do. The most dramatic of these involve identical twins separated at birth or soon after. When reunited decades later, they often display remarkable similarities in habit, lifestyle, intelligence and personality. This seems to support those who favor "nature" in the nature/nurture debate, although some critics argue that we need to focus as much on possible differences between reunited identical twins as we do on whether they smoke the same brand of cigarette or work in similar occupations.

As part of the nature vs. nurture issue it's important to recognize the terms maturation and socialization. **Maturation** refers to development that largely unfolds on its own, as if according to a biological program, as long as the individual is in a reasonably supportive environment. Most children will simply progress to walking "when they're ready ", and they don't require intensive training to do so. If you recall the **Genie** and **Wild Child of Aveyron**

89

case studies from the unit on Thought and Language, you will see that those are cases in which the child was in such a restrictive environment that maturation in many ways was blocked (that is, of course, if the two children were cognitively and physically healthy in the first place, which is a question still open to debate). While in that less than supportive environment, they missed the theoretical **critical period** for language acquisition, and could therefore never fully gain the skills a healthy child in a healthy setting would have acquired.

Socialization refers to the impact of the social environment on development. It is an ongoing process in which skills, attitudes, and behaviors are shaped by society. A child may begin to babble as a result of simple maturation, but then is socialized into the particular language of the society in which he or she lives.

Prenatal Development; Reflexes; Physical Development

While in the womb, a child-to-be progresses through *zygotic* (the first two weeks or so) to *embryonic* (from 2 weeks to about 2 months) to *fetal* stages. At any point along the way, exposure to **teratogens** can impair normal development. A teratogen is anything that harms the organism prenatally. Alcohol is a teratogen; if the mother drinks during pregnancy, it can injure the child. Children born with *fetal alcohol syndrome* have distinctive facial features (such as a wider than normal set of the eyes), behavioral impairment and often serious mental retardation. Cigarette smoking, x-rays and lead exposure can also function as teratogens.

You might encounter **imprinting** on the AP Exam, even though it is questionable whether it applies to human infants. The term refers to a newborn's tendency to respond to an active stimulus in its environment as if it is its mother. In most "natural" cases, such a stimulus *is* the mother, and it would be a healthy, adaptive response for the newborn to attach to the mom quickly. Critical period theory may apply to imprinting as well; the time immediately after birth seems particularly important for such attachment in many animals. In the 1930's, **Konrad Lorenz** tinkered with this natural mechanism by replacing a mother duck with a surrogate: namely, Konrad Lorenz. The baby ducklings imprinted on him, and followed him around as mother-figure. It is generally believed that human attachment is more complex and ongoing, and is not subject to a single critical period as described above.

While human newborns may not attach, literally or figuratively, to whatever stimulus presents itself after birth, it is clear that human newborns and infants do need physical touch and nurturance. **Harry Harlow** refers to this as **contact comfort**. He conducted research with infant monkeys who were separated from their biological mothers and placed with artificial, surrogate parents. Harlow found that the baby monkeys sought comfort and support from soft, terry cloth "mothers" rather than hard, wire "mothers", even when it was the wire mother that had provided the child nourishment, through a bottle attached to the surrogate's body. Since then research has shown, for example, that premature human babies grow faster and healthier if given daily massages, and it has become accepted wisdom that frequent, nurturing physical touch is essential for healthy development in humans. If, as a youngster, you had a favorite blanket or doll to which you were attached, it may be this **transitional object** was giving you some of that desired physical contact.

Human babies don't come with directions but they do come with some built in reflexes. Those you might encounter on the AP Examination are summarized below:

- **the sucking reflex:** just what you would think it is – put something in the mouth of a child and he or she will reflexively suck on it
- **the grasping reflex:** also self explanatory – place your finger in the palm of a newborn (or *neonate*) and his or her tiny hand will close around it
- **the rooting reflex:** touch a baby on the cheek and he or she will turn the head in that direction, "rooting" for a food source
- **the stepping reflex:** support a newborn under the arms and it will simulate walking strides
- **the moro reflex:** sometimes called the *startle reflex*; an unexpected and intrusive stimulus, such as a loud noise, elicits a response in which the child pulls the arms and legs into the body then extends them out again, often accompanied by a quivering or shaking of the body

Are breathing, blinking, crying, swallowing and smiling "reflexes"? Some would place them in the category and others would not, although all manifest themselves very early in neonates. If reflexes are an intuitive, programmed, involuntary response to a stimulus, then blinking and swallowing seem to qualify. Breathing isn't a response to a stimulus per se, but it probably belongs on the list as well. Do babies cry and smile directly in response to stimuli? Perhaps not, but crying and smiling too are included on many lists of inborn reflexes.

One thing human babies certainly do very early on is imitate. Your textbook may even have photos depicting babies just a few days old **mimicking facial expressions**.

There is evidence that while human babies are not born with **depth perception** that they acquire some degree of it fairly early in life. **Eleanor Gibson** and her colleagues used a **visual cliff apparatus** to study the depth perception of children before they could walk. A baby was placed on a surface and encouraged to crawl across what appeared to be a rather large drop. Even with their own mothers coaxing them, babies as young as six months old would not cross the drop (they were safe at all times; the "cliff" was merely an illusion created by a checkerboard pattern under a glass surface). Gibson concluded that this was because the babies could indeed perceive that there was a potentially dangerous drop. Of course, it's difficult to know what's <u>really</u> going on in the mind of an infant. You learned about *habituation* in the chapter on Sensation and Perception, and that tendency in humans to stop attending to something after repetitive exposure to it is often used by developmental psychologists to explore what prelinguistic children are experiencing. Theoretically, we can guess that a child who has stopped looking at something has lost interest in it, but that remains only an educated guess.

Cognitive Development

The big theory in cognitive development is that of Swiss psychologist **Jean Piaget**. He studied the thinking of youngsters, paying special attention to the errors that they made. From his observations, he developed a stage theory of cognitive development that is still very much embraced today, although many argue that Piaget underestimated the abilities of children at many points in their growth.

Piaget believed that children handled the new information they constantly encountered by means of **assimilation and accommodation**. In the former, the child attempts to fit new experiences into the cognitive frameworks they already possess. In the latter, they actually change their schemas or behaviors to fit the new information. A classic example used by many teachers involves a child's identification of animals: a youngster who has learned the word 'doggie' sees a coyote at the zoo and identifies it as 'doggie'; the child is attempting to assimilate this new thing, a coyote, into a previously formed 'doggie' schema. Soon, the child will accommodate by creating a new, 'coyote' schema.

Piaget argued that we all progress through four stages of cognitive development, assimilating and accommodating as we go. A summary of those stages follows:

- **the sensorimotor stage** (birth to around 2 years old): the cognitive task of the child here is to explore and learn about the environment, through the use of the senses and one's developing motor abilities; during this period a child grasps the concept of **object permanence** (understanding that a ball that rolls out of sight into a closet still exists, even though unseen).

- **the preoperational stage** (two to around seven years old): in this stage, children begin pretend play, which demonstrates that they are beginning to be able to **think symbolically** – that is, that one thing can represent something else; this also indicates that something no longer needs to be physically present in order for the child to know about it and think about it; children in this period are highly **egocentric** – for Piaget, this means they are cognitively unable to take the perspective of another

- **the concrete operational stage** (about 7 to 11 years old): this is often identified as the stage in which the child becomes capable of **logical thinking**, although this may be an area in which Piaget underestimated kids – many would say preoperational children think logically as well. Children in this period are not yet able to think abstractly although they are quite comfortable with **use of mental representations**; a key Piagetian milestone in this stage involves mastery of **conservation**, the idea that the amount of something doesn't change with changes in its appearance or arrangement. You may have heard about children who are disappointed because they wanted dad to cut the pizza into eight pieces and he only cut it into four; they feel he's cheated them out of a substantial amount of pizza! Some theorists argue that mastery of conservation of number comes earlier than mastery of conservation of volume and mass, but the AP Examination will not assess you on such a distinction. In general, children master conservation by eight or nine years old.

- **the formal operational stage** (11 years of age or so onward): one critique of Piaget's theory is that he focused only on younger children and then inappropriately lumped everyone over the age of twelve together in one cognitive group; it is in this stage that people **think abstractly and hypothetically**, able to consider future possibilities and imaginary scenarios

The work of Russian theorist **Lev Vygotsky** has recently garnered renewed interest. Vygotsky passed away in 1934 but his views on the impact of the **social context** on a child's cognitive growth were revisited beginning in the 1970's. Vygotsky differs from Piaget in that he clearly believed that cognitive development was less a matter of biological maturation than of social interaction. For example, Vygotsky argued that children internalize the instructions and warnings of those around them into *private or inner speech*. The child thus develops the ability to have internal conversations with him or herself which help to govern behavior. Vygotsky also proposed the idea of a *zone of proximal development or Z.P.D.* This describes the divide between what a child knows and can do and what they *might have the potential to do* given a supportive enough environment.

Social Development

It is unlikely that you will run into items on **birth order theory** on the Advanced Placement Examination, but you might find it interesting to explore the possible effect of your birth order on the development of your personality. **Alfred Adler** was the first to postulate that birth order may have such effects (arguing, for example, that a first born child may be more achievement oriented than a later born child), and his name will come up again in your study of personality theory, so his theory is certainly worth a look. In your own experience for example, you might have felt a sense of *dethronement* as a child when a new sibling arrived in the household. Your parents might have some interesting stories about your reactions to losing some of the attention you had become used to receiving!

You may well expect, however, to encounter questions on attachment styles and parenting styles under the umbrella of social development. **Mary Ainsworth** placed young children in **"strange situations"**, separated for a time from their mothers, and then monitored the children when the mother returned. Ainsworth evaluated their behaviors to measure the level of security and insecurity in the bond between mother and child. A summary of her **attachment styles** follows:

- **avoidant:** the child generally ignores the mother when she returns; in this style the child often appears to "attach" just as much to a stranger as to the mother

- **secure:** the child is somewhat distressed when the mother leaves but is relatively easy to calm and greets the mother warmly upon her return, using her, in Ainsworth's words, as a "secure base of operations"

- **resistant/ambivalent/anxious:** the child sends mixed messages to the mother upon her return, seemingly wanting to be held but then resisting attempts by the mother to do so

- **disorganized:** a newer category in which children appear confused, disoriented and even fearful with their mothers; some postulate a correlation with this style and abusive home environments

Most developmental psychologists agree that these early attachment styles *can predict well for future social functioning*, although there is conflicting evidence as to whether the attachment style one has at one age remains stable over time and across situations.

Separation anxiety and stranger anxiety are two related terms you need to know; they were first discussed in detail in the 1950's and 60's by **John Bowlby**. **Separation anxiety**, which often begins at between six and nine months old, is characterized by distress at being separated from parents or a primary and familiar caregiver (some theorists would contend that there is a correlation between the end of the most intense levels of separation anxiety and mastery of object permanence, which would allow the child to know that dad is not "gone" even though he may temporarily be out of sight). Many theorists believe that by about eight months old children have begun to form schemas for faces that are familiar to them, and can therefore recognize when faces are <u>not</u> familiar. This can lead to **stranger anxiety**, which is characterized by distress upon encountering new, unfamiliar people. There is evidence that separation and stranger anxiety unfold in about the same ways and at about the same times cross culturally, with separation anxiety peaking at about 15 months old, and stranger anxiety peaking sometime late in the first year of life.

In the early 1970's, **Diana Baumrind** described a set of **parenting styles** which would obviously have an impact on a child's social development. A summary of those follows:

- **authoritarian:** this is a top-down parenting approach in which the parents establish the rules, expect obedience and strictly punish transgressions

- **authoritative:** parents are the authority figures but they are willing to listen to input from the children, respect their basic rights and explain the rules and decisions they set down; this is often seen as the most "successful" style in terms of the long term social functioning of the children

- **permissive:** parents give children considerable freedom to make their own decisions, either because they are more tolerant and trusting of their children's abilities or because they are less engaged in the upbringing of the children

Baumrind believed that over ¾ of families operated in one of these three styles. You may encounter a couple of other types, offered by other theorists, on the AP Exam, although it is doubtful:

neglectful: the parents have essentially abrogated responsibility for the raising and control of their children

- **democratic:** a "let's have a vote" approach in which everyone has an equal say in family rule building and decision making; it's doubtful that such a "pure democracy" really exists as a consistent system in families

Your teacher may spend a fair amount of time on the development of gender identity and roles, as this is a highly engaging topic. To discuss this intelligently, it's important to differentiate between some different terms that some people wrongly use interchangeably:

- **sex:** biologically determined (you are biologically a male or a female)

- **gender:** learned behaviors or attitudes associated with one's biological sex

- **gender identity:** the sense of being a boy or a girl

- **gender constancy:** the sense that one is a boy or a girl and, barring very dramatic intervention, will remain so

- **gender role:** the behaviors considered appropriate for males and females in a given social setting

- **gender typing:** the process of learning the roles associated with the distinctions between males and females in a culture

- **androgyny:** the presence of both "male" and "female" behaviors or characteristics in the same person

Adolescence

When individuals enter **puberty**, the point at which they are sexually mature and can reproduce, they acquire primary and secondary sex characteristics. **Primary sex characteristics** are directly involved with reproduction, while **secondary sex characteristics** are, for example the deepening of the voice and growth of pubic and body hair in males, breast and pubic hair development in females. More and more research of late has involved adolescence, adulthood and aging, so you might anticipate more and more emphasis on those areas on the Advanced Placement Exam. In regard to adolescence, you will find it interestingly relevant to learn about theories of the personal fable and the imaginary audience.

David Elkind contends that adolescents tend to create a story of "specialness" about themselves, a **personal fable** in which the teenager invulnerable in the sense that the "rules" of safety don't really apply to them. This is why teenagers seem so much more likely than others to engage in high risk, potentially destructive behaviors.

One might interpret the personal fable as a sort of *egocentrism*. Some make the same connection to the adolescent sense of an **imaginary audience**, the notion that others are always monitoring the adolescent, watching for mistakes, moments of embarrassment, and so on. Of course, many would argue that this phenomenon is not exclusive to the teenage years.

Development Over the Lifespan

The **social clock** is an intriguing concept in development that definitely cuts across "age group" lines. If you feel there is a strong expectation for you to go to college next year and that taking a year off to find out more about yourself would be discouraged, then you have a sense of social clock expectations. If you are 35 years old and single and people consistently ask you why you are not yet married, you will have another sense of the social clock.

The **empty nest syndrome** refers to the adjustments parents make to the last of their children leaving home. For some parents this can be a liberating experience, for others a period of establishing re-acquaintance with each other, for still others a time to find another focus for their efforts and attentions.

Erik Erikson postulated a stage theory of **psychosocial development across the life span**. He contended that people face various crises in their lives that they must resolve in order to continue healthy development. He breaks these periods of crisis into eight stages:

- **trust vs. mistrust** (birth to approximately 18 months): the child learns what to trust in the environment, thus learning also what to trust in him or her self

- **autonomy vs. shame and doubt** (approx. 18 months to 3 years old): the child seeks a sense of internal control and independence

- **initiative vs. guilt** (about 3 to 6 years old): the child seeks a balance between what he or she wants to do and a sense of what is right and wrong, good and bad

- **industry vs. inferiority** (about 6 to 12 years old): the child seeks to master the basic skills required for successful participation in the society, which will give the child a sense of basic competence

- **identity vs. role confusion** (adolescence): the teenager seeks to answer the questions "who am I?" , "what do I want to do and be?"

- **intimacy vs. isolation** (early adulthood): the young adult either successfully establishes strong, committed relationships or faces the task of dealing with some level of isolation

- **generativity vs. stagnation** (middle adulthood): adults, now in their 40's or 50's, either engage in the sharing of their wisdom and experience with members of younger generations or are resentful and even antagonistic toward younger people

- **integrity vs. despair:** (late adulthood): the older adult reflects back on his or her life, feeling either a sense of accomplishment and pride or a sense of missed opportunities and thus, sadness

These stages have been the focus of much research and are subject to much debate. Many people see significant overlap between stages two, three and four, while others argue that the adolescent identity crisis is not specific to adolescence and recurs throughout the life span. Erikson's theory is also nearly three decades old, and the simple fact of increased life expectancy changes how people view different periods of life, not to mention the vast number of sociocultural phenomena which would effect this hierarchy of stages as time passes.

Adulthood and Aging

While one's first impulse might be to believe that contemplation of death and dying is reserved for Erikson's "late adulthood", in fact any of us can face loss, grief and imminent death at any time. **Elisabeth Kubler-Ross** formulated a stage theory addressing our encounters with grief. She argues that we go through five stages (you may see variations and additions to this theory elsewhere, but for the purposes of the advanced placement examination these five stages are the key) in dealing with loss: **denial, anger, bargaining, depression and acceptance**. Kubler-Ross did not envision this as strictly hierarchical, and in your own experience with loss you might have found that you revisit certain stages repeatedly and don't necessarily progress in an orderly fashion through the steps from start to finish.

The **hospice movement** is heavily influenced by work like that of Kubler-Ross, in that it is essentially a philosophy of treatment of the dying that is warm, personalized and informed about the psychological processes which impact those facing relatively imminent death.

Development of Moral Reasoning

Finally, we need to take a quick look at the development of a moral sense. The most well known work in this area was conducted by **Lawrence Kohlberg**, who used a fictional story called **"The Heinz Dilemma"** to evaluate levels of **moral reasoning** in children. The dilemma posed the basic question "would you steal a drug in order to save a life?". Based on his evaluations of the responses children offered to this question, Kohlberg devised yet another stage theory, this with **three levels of moral reasoning:**

- **the preconventional level** (characteristic of children aged 4 to about 10) in which the focus is reward and punishment; the responses are self interested ("I wouldn't steal the drug because I would get into trouble")

- **the conventional level** (characteristic of children aged about 10 to 13) which, as its name suggests, focuses on social conventions; responses center on issues like "what will others think of me?" and "what are the rules we've all agreed to follow?"

- **the postconventional level** (not typically reached until age 13, if it is reached at all) in which moral decisions are based on personal, internal judgments of right and wrong; thus, this is sometimes referred to as *the principled level*

In some ways Kohlberg's theory became most famous when it was criticized, especially by **Carol Gilligan**, who argued that Kohlberg generalized a theory of moral reasoning for all people even though his original participants were all males. She thought that Kohlberg missed the fact that males and females tend to view moral dilemmas differently; men look at such judgments in a more absolute and *justice-based* way, women with a more relative, relationship-based, *caring orientation*.

One useful way to review your grasp of some key concepts in this unit while also exploring an intriguing line of thought is to discuss the relationship between cognitive development and moral development. As one becomes more cognitively advanced, does moral reasoning deepen as well? If so, does that translate into more advanced moral *behavior*? Or is there relatively little connection between intellect and morality?

Name Hall of Fame

Jean Piaget would be a lock for inclusion in anyone's psychology name hall of fame. After him, things get a little more complicated. There are several names in this unit that almost certainly will show up on the AP Exam, but will you have to "know" the <u>name</u> of these individuals who have contributed so much to the field but may not be absolute, no-doubt-about-it candidates for the hall of fame? To be safe, answer 'yes' to this question and look again at **Mary Ainsworth** and her theory of attachment, **Erik Erikson** and his stage theory of psychosocial development across the life span, **Elisabeth Kubler-Ross** and her work on the grieving process and **Lawrence Kohlberg** and **Carol Gilligan** in regard to moral development.

You may also see the names **Lev Vygotsky**, **Diana Baumrind**, **Eleanor Gibson**, **Alfred Adler**, **John Bowlby** and **David Elkind**, but those would appear only in connection with another cue in a multiple choice stem.

Essay Themes

The **nature vs. nurture debate** seems to be a natural candidate for a free response item that could cut across content areas. In the Advanced Placement Psychology program there has yet to be a free response question on a **specific stage theory** or on **stage theories in general**. Such discontinuity theories play a big role in this chapter. Piaget's theory of cognitive development might be the most likely candidate for an essay, although it is even more likely that the test development committee would target stage theories as a whole, again attempting to incorporate elements of other units in the question as well. There are some pretty basic **links between this unit and others**, as suggested by the "test prep" graphic organizer which follows; revisit those in your mind when you begin final preparations for the AP Exam.

Test Preparation: Development

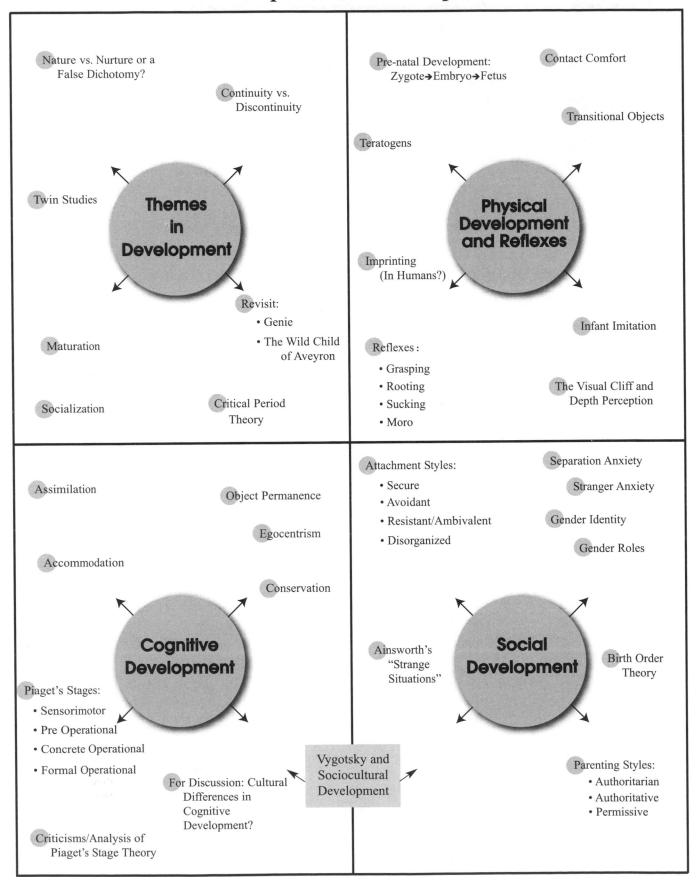

Themes in Development
- Nature vs. Nurture or a False Dichotomy?
- Continuity vs. Discontinuity
- Twin Studies
- Maturation
- Socialization
- Critical Period Theory
- Revisit:
  - Genie
  - The Wild Child of Aveyron

Physical Development and Reflexes
- Pre-natal Development: Zygote→Embryo→Fetus
- Contact Comfort
- Transitional Objects
- Teratogens
- Imprinting (In Humans?)
- Infant Imitation
- Reflexes:
  - Grasping
  - Rooting
  - Sucking
  - Moro
- The Visual Cliff and Depth Perception

Cognitive Development
- Assimilation
- Object Permanence
- Egocentrism
- Accommodation
- Conservation
- Piaget's Stages:
  - Sensorimotor
  - Pre Operational
  - Concrete Operational
  - Formal Operational
- For Discussion: Cultural Differences in Cognitive Development?
- Criticisms/Analysis of Piaget's Stage Theory

Social Development
- Attachment Styles:
  - Secure
  - Avoidant
  - Resistant/Ambivalent
  - Disorganized
- Separation Anxiety
- Stranger Anxiety
- Gender Identity
- Gender Roles
- Ainsworth's "Strange Situations"
- Birth Order Theory
- Parenting Styles:
  - Authoritarian
  - Authoritative
  - Permissive

Vygotsky and Sociocultural Development

100

Test Preparation: Development

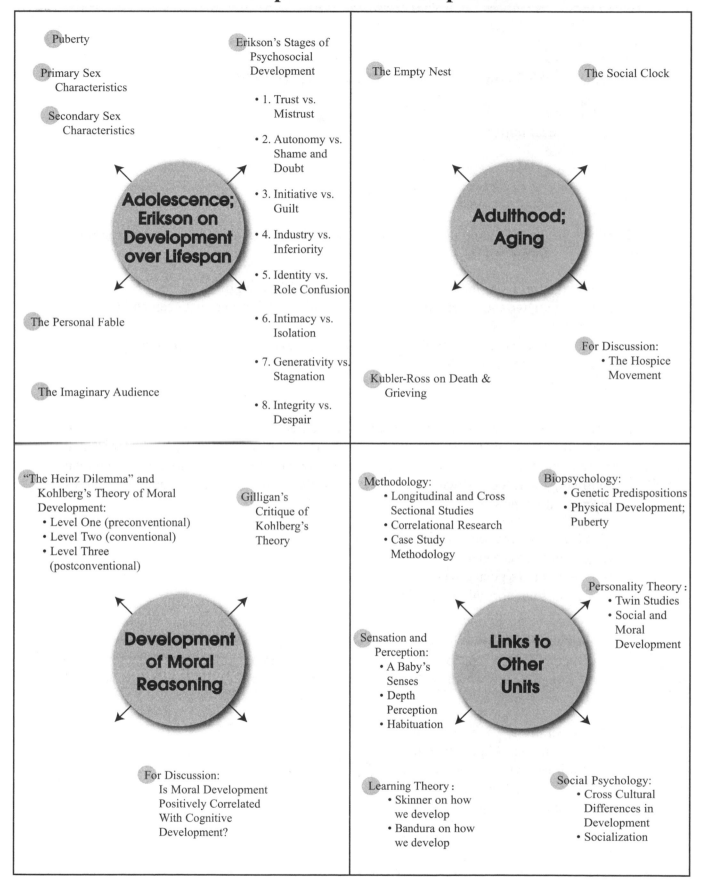

Puberty

Primary Sex Characteristics

Secondary Sex Characteristics

Erikson's Stages of Psychosocial Development

- 1. Trust vs. Mistrust
- 2. Autonomy vs. Shame and Doubt
- 3. Initiative vs. Guilt
- 4. Industry vs. Inferiority
- 5. Identity vs. Role Confusion
- 6. Intimacy vs. Isolation
- 7. Generativity vs. Stagnation
- 8. Integrity vs. Despair

The Personal Fable

The Imaginary Audience

Adolescence; Erikson on Development over Lifespan

The Empty Nest

The Social Clock

Adulthood; Aging

Kubler-Ross on Death & Grieving

For Discussion:
- The Hospice Movement

"The Heinz Dilemma" and Kohlberg's Theory of Moral Development:
- Level One (preconventional)
- Level Two (conventional)
- Level Three (postconventional)

Gilligan's Critique of Kohlberg's Theory

Development of Moral Reasoning

For Discussion:
Is Moral Development Positively Correlated With Cognitive Development?

Methodology:
- Longitudinal and Cross Sectional Studies
- Correlational Research
- Case Study Methodology

Biopsychology:
- Genetic Predispositions
- Physical Development; Puberty

Personality Theory:
- Twin Studies
- Social and Moral Development

Sensation and Perception:
- A Baby's Senses
- Depth Perception
- Habituation

Links to Other Units

Learning Theory:
- Skinner on how we develop
- Bandura on how we develop

Social Psychology:
- Cross Cultural Differences in Development
- Socialization

Practice Items

1. Which of the following would be most likely to potentially act as a teratogen?

    (A) candy
    (B) physical nurturance
    (C) music
    (D) alcohol
    (E) anger

2. Which of the following is a central criticism of Jean Piaget's stage theory of cognitive development?

    (A) Piaget failed to include clear age delineations for each of his stages
    (B) Piaget gave too much attention to the cognitive differences between children and adults
    (C) Piaget chose a test sample that was too large to examine appropriately
    (D) Piaget often overestimated the cognitive abilities of children
    (E) Piaget often underestimated the cognitive abilities of children

3. Lawrence Kohlberg used the fictional "Heinz Dilemma" to assess the development of moral reasoning in children. One child is asked "would you steal a drug in order to save a life?" and the child responds "yes, because a person's life is even more important than following the rules". At which point would Kohlberg likely place such an answer in his theoretical framework?

    (A) level one: preconventional
    (B) level two: conventional
    (C) level three: postconventional
    (D) level four: formal operational
    (E) level five: abstract

4. One theme in Shakespeare's "MacBeth" revolves around an older man reflecting upon and evaluating the worth of his life. Erik Erikson referred to this as a psychosocial conflict between

    (A) generativity vs. stagnation
    (B) identity vs. role confusion
    (C) intimacy vs. isolation
    (D) integrity vs. despair
    (E) autonomy vs. doubt

5. In girls, breast development at puberty is an example of

   (A) accommodation
   (B) assimilation
   (C) a primary sex characteristic
   (D) a secondary sex characteristic
   (E) androgyny

6. Which of the following is the best example of a "continuity" theory in development?

   (A) identical twins raised together score identically on measures of intelligence
   (B) a deaf child misses a sensitive period for language acquisition but still learns sign language
   (C) a caterpillar is suddenly transformed into a butterfly
   (D) an individual's personality remains stable across situations
   (E) a seed gradually grows to become a giant oak tree

7. Maturation

   (A) is a less powerful mechanism in humans than in other primates
   (B) is the systematic development of the body and nervous system which unfolds naturally if a child is in a reasonably supportive environment
   (C) is governed by adult agents of socialization
   (D) differs significantly from culture to culture
   (E) is the direct result of influences such as social learning, classical and operant conditioning, latent learning and insight learning

8. When stimulated on one side of the mouth, a healthy human newborn will automatically turn its head in that direction, searching with its mouth for a food source. This is called

   (A) the Babinski reflex
   (B) the rooting reflex
   (C) the Moro reflex
   (D) habituation
   (E) the palmar grasp

9. A young adult moving through Erik Erikson's sixth stage of development over the lifespan wrestles with the conflict between

   (A) trust and mistrust
   (B) identity and role confusion
   (C) generativity and stagnation
   (D) intimacy and isolation
   (E) industry and inferiority

10. During a classroom discussion on cheating in schools, a student argues "students shouldn't cheat because it's important to follow the rules". For Lawrence Kohlberg, this would be most representative of

    (A) ambivalent attachment
    (B) formal operations
    (C) generativity
    (D) postconventional moral reasoning
    (E) conventional moral reasoning

11. Developmentally, object permanence and conservation are typically mastered in which two of Jean Piaget's stages of cognitive development, respectively?

    (A) formal operational; preoperational
    (B) concrete operational; formal operational
    (C) concrete operational; sensorimotor
    (D) sensorimotor; concrete operational
    (E) sensorimotor; preoperational

12. Mary Ainsworth used a "strange situations" scenario to examine attachment in young children, and found that the majority of children have _____ attachment to their mothers

    (A) secure
    (B) anxious
    (C) ambivalent
    (D) avoidant
    (E) disorganized

13. Which of the following best summarizes Carol Gilligan's central criticism of Lawrence Kohlberg's theory of moral development?

    (A) Kohlberg proposed three primary levels of moral reasoning while Gilligan argued for a fourth which Kohlberg had not accounted for
    (B) responses from a large percentage of volunteers indicated a lack of understanding of the questions they were being asked
    (C) males and females tend to view moral situations in different ways
    (D) Kohlberg's theory was based only on the responses of females
    (E) Kohlberg's levels of moral development were too broadly defined

14. Harry Harlow's work with infant monkeys and surrogate mothers suggests that

    (A) infants seek not simply a food source but also a source of contact comfort
    (B) inborn reflexes in primates are more limited than was once thought
    (C) when distressed, an infant will turn reflexively to a caregiver that has to that point been its primary food source
    (D) even the simplest primates learn through observation
    (E) infants tend to avoid attachment to surrogate parents

15. One theory of adolescent development proposes that individuals in that age range tend to have an exaggerated sense of their own uniqueness and invulnerability. This is called

    (A) preoperational thinking
    (B) concrete operational thinking
    (C) the personal fable
    (D) the looking glass self
    (E) the self serving bias

NO TESTING MATERIAL ON THIS PAGE

GO ON TO THE NEXT PAGE

Chapter IX

Motivation and Emotion

Introduction

In the official advanced placement psychology curriculum progression, this unit comes <u>before</u> the unit on development, but the order used in this book is easily defensible as well. Indeed, the biggest variability in college level textbooks is probably in the placement of developmental psychology. Those textbooks also sometimes break *this* topic into two separate chapters, one specifically on motivation and the other focusing on emotion. In a sense, then, this is another "two in one" chapter, but you probably won't find it overwhelming in terms of total volume of material.

Motivation

We'll begin with a summary of some major perspectives, which endeavor to explain why we do what we do:

- **Ethology:** This view focuses on the biological bases for behavior, especially as regards instincts. Some people don't like the term **'instinct'** partly because in the past it has been used in a kind of circular argument explaining behavior ("he did what he did out of instinct"... "but why does he have this instinct?"... "he was born with it"). An 'instinct' is an innate, preprogrammed behavior in response to some stimulus – it is thus unlearned. A true 'instinct' is present in most all healthy members of the species. These **fixed action patterns** manifest themselves in response to some particular environmental stimulus (**a trigger feature or sign stimulus**). For example, some types of small birds instinctively hide from hawks; they appear to recognize the hawk as a dangerous predator by the hawk's *eyes*. The eyes are thus the trigger feature releasing the fixed action pattern of flight.

- **Sociobiology:** This controversial perspective is based on the contention that people behave in ways that are most likely to **perpetuate their own genes**. A once classic example of this referred to nomadic extended family groups of indigenous peoples. When such a group faced especially difficult environmental conditions and short supplies, older members of the band might voluntarily leave the group to die, apparently committing a kind of *altruistic suicide* in order to assure the survival of the others. A sociobiologist would argue that this was not so much a pro-social act as an attempt to keep ones own genes alive through the survival of one's offspring. Some have questioned just how often such events actually occur, and many wonder in any case just how well this theory explains more mundane human motivations.

- **Drive Theory:** You may also see this referred to as *drive reduction theory*. It is based on the notion that we all have needs which must be fulfilled. If we are deprived of them we will be driven to act in ways to meet those needs and return to **homeostasis**, an ideal internal state of balance or equilibrium. If an individual is exceptionally cold, he will be driven to seek warmth in order to become internally steady again. This theory is often criticized because it implies that humans are always doing things to <u>reduce tension</u>, when it seems clear that sometimes people actually go out of their way to seek stimulation.

- **Arousal Theory:** The argument here is that we each have our own sense of appropriate arousal and we act in ways to remain at a comfortable arousal level. For some people, a lazy Saturday on the couch in front of the television is perfectly stimulating, while others would find such a day intensely uncomfortable and would be motivated to "do" more. Some individuals are highly motivated to seek stimulation, others feel comfortably "stimulated" even when relatively inactive. Historically, some individuals have looked out at the ocean from a safe harbor and felt a great pull to explore "what's out there", while another person standing right by their side might have had no such feeling. **Yerkes-Dodson Law** is a prediction about the relationship between arousal levels and performance; it suggests that there is an interaction between aroused states, the difficulty of the task to be carried out, and eventual performance on that task. For example, a moderate level of stimulation (in the form of nervousness, anxiety, etc.) is best for performance on a difficult task, while one might be able to handle a much higher level of arousal in performing a well learned or "easy" task.

- **Cognitive Dissonance Theory:** This theory postulates that we strive to bring our thoughts, attitudes and behaviors into agreement with each other. In a sense, we are thus seeking a kind of cognitive homeostasis, more commonly referred to as **cognitive consistency**. If you belong to a group in school that speaks out against drunk driving but then drink heavily at a party and attempt to drive home (please do not do such a dangerous thing), you will undoubtedly feel tension and anxiety. A cognitive dissonance theorist would argue that your previously stated attitude and current behavior are in conflict, and that you will thus be motivated either to modify your attitude or adjust your behavior in order to return to a comfortable internal state.

- **Incentive Theory:** This theory suggests that **we are pulled toward behaviors by rewards** or incentives. These can be external (**extrinsic motivation**), as in the payment of cash bonuses to employees who do exceptional work, or internal (**intrinsic motivation**), as in training for a marathon because finishing such a race would give you a sense of satisfaction. Incentives could also be negative; an individual may be motivated to behave in a certain way **to avoid an unpleasant outcome**. You can see the obvious connection here between incentive theory and **behavioral** concepts of positive and negative reinforcement and punishment, which you studied in the unit on Learning Theory.

- **Abraham Maslow's Hierarchy of Needs:** Humanists like Abraham Maslow are very optimistic about human nature and motivation. Maslow theorized that we all have needs which we are motivated to satisfy; some are fundamental survival needs, while others are more ambitious, such as the desire to reach one's full potential as a human. Maslow called this the need for **self-actualization**; for him it is the highest goal to which individuals aspire. In order to reach self-actualization one must first meet lower level needs in his hierarchy: in order, they are the **physiological needs** for food and water, the need for **shelter and safety**, the need for **belonging and companionship** and the need for **self esteem**. Even Maslow acknowledged, however, that many people do not reach or even attempt to reach true self-actualization, which is in part characterized by self acceptance, a willingness and desire to consider the needs and wants of others, creativity, spontaneity and healthy nonconformity.

Maslow's theory is very popular, although its worth discussing whether you think it *is* strictly hierarchical – that is, do all people follow this same flow in the same order? What about hunger strikers who deprive themselves of food, one of the most basic physiological needs, in order to meet other goals? What of individuals who seem to value social needs for belonging above a need for self esteem?

There are many different types of specific motivations that psychologists examine, and it is difficult to predict which are most likely to show up on the Advanced Placement Examination. It is safe to say, however, that you should know a bit about the motivations behind *eating, aggression and achievement.*

The hypothalamus, in the limbic system of the brain, seems to play a primary role in the regulation of appetite and satisfaction. **The lateral hypothalamus (the LH) is most** involved in "hunger" messages, while the **ventromedial hypothalamus (the VMH)** sends "stop, I think you've had just about enough!" messages. Thus, some think of the LH as the hunger center of the brain, and the VMH as the satiety center. In terms of the hypothalamus, that's what you will need to know for the AP Exam, but, not surprisingly, there is lots more to the drive to eat then isolated brain function. There are **cultural contributions** (begin with television commercials and cultural "ideals" of beauty which heavily influence individuals' sense of self image), **social contributions** (eating because others are eating or because one is at a "social event", for example), **external cues** (food is readily available, or the school bell rings to signal that it's "time" for lunch) and a host of other physiological mechanisms at work. Those include the **endocrine system** (as in the function of the hormones *insulin* in using blood sugar, and *leptin*, which tells the brain that sufficient fat stores exist, thus signaling satisfaction) and a theory based on the concept of **set point**. This states that our brain and endocrine system essentially act as a thermostat does in a home – if the thermostat is set at 68 degrees, the furnace turns itself on when the temperature drops below that level and turns itself off when the temperature climbs above 68 degrees. In the same way, our body has an individual set point for body weight and adjusts metabolically to keep you at that level. This may help to explain why dieting by itself is often frustratingly unsuccessful in keeping you at some goal weight – your body is apparently battling to get you back to your set point.

You could probably take an entire college course on aggression. It's a big and all too relevant topic, but, in terms of the AP Exam, you only need to know a bit about it. For instance, you may encounter a distinction between **hostile and instrumental aggression**. Hostile aggression is carried out for its own sake, while instrumental aggression at least theoretically is aggression which is working toward some other goal besides the aggression itself. Bumping someone out of the way to get possession of the ball in soccer would be deemed instrumental aggression, while bumping someone into the wall in the school corridor would likely be viewed as hostile aggression. You could likely have a stimulating discussion in class about other examples: is stepping on an ant hostile or instrumental aggression? punching an opponent in a boxing match? yelling out the window at a driver who is about to cut you off in traffic?

Some theorists argue that aggression can be **cathartic**. They contend that the American fondness for football or professional wrestling or violent movies serves as a safety valve for aggression – if people can "get their aggressions out" in such settings , they won't actually act them out in more dangerous ways. Freudian psychoanalytic theory is often associated with this view, which is not surprising when you know that it is based on the importance of the unconscious mind and its influence on behavior. The catharsis theory is an interesting topic for classroom discussion and analysis.

The drive to achieve has been a much studied topic. Various methods have been used to attempt to measure **achievement motivation**. One is called the **Thematic Apperception Test, or T.A.T.**. Used by researchers like David McClelland, this **projective test** (so called because of the expectation that one might "project" something about themselves onto an otherwise ambiguous stimulus) involves presenting a photograph or picture to a volunteer and asking them to tell a story about it. The stories are then rated for levels of achievement motivation. In general, McClelland and others have reported, after analysis of their T.A.T. results, that there is a link between a *desire to achieve* and a *fear of failure*. Individuals with a high drive to succeed and a relatively low fear of failure are most likely to seek challenges which are worthy of their efforts but also reasonably attainable, whereas a person with a high fear of failure might choose to pursue very "safe" paths or nearly impossible ones. In the latter case, they are thus allowed to fail, since no one, including themselves, really expected success in the first place.

Another kind of projective test was used by Matina Horner in 1970. She supplied the first line of a possible story and asked volunteers to take it from there. One such first line was "John has just finished his first year of medical school and is first in his class...", while another read "Jane has just finished her first year of medical school and is first in her class...". She too rated the products for the drive to succeed. At that time one of her conclusions was that some women feared success, that they had a "will to fail". It may be interesting to discuss in class what the results would be if her work was replicated today.

There are some types of "conflict", identified by Kurt Lewin, which you must learn about to prepare for the AP Exam. These might be placed in various spots in an introductory textbook (often linked to study of *stress*, as each can be pretty stress-inducing), but we will handle them here. One is called an approach-approach conflict. If you have ever had two equally attractive options on a Saturday night and couldn't decide which one to choose, then you have experienced an **approach-approach conflict**. Both choices are desirable, but you can only opt for one of them. In an **avoidance-avoidance conflict**, you are compelled to choose between two equally <u>unattractive</u> options. A trip to the dentist is an oft used example. Do you make an appointment even though you'd rather not out of fear and anxiety, or do you allow your teeth to rot out of your head? Neither choice tops your list of priorities, but you must do one or the other. In an **approach-avoidance conflict**, a certain situation has both attractive and unattractive elements which make it difficult for you to decide what to do. For example: you very much like the programs at a certain college that has accepted you, but it is very expensive. Or, you are in love with a person but also fear losing your freedom if you commit to him or her. Or you're playing a sport that you love but the coach drives you crazy. Each of these examples could also become **multiple approach-avoidance conflicts**. You are in love with someone but fear commitment; so far, simple approach-avoidance. That someone also has a lot of money, which would be advantageous, but you know it would make you feel guilty. Further, your parents love your partner and have really "adopted" him or her, but your partner's parents don't like <u>you</u>, and so on.

Emotion

The emotion section of this unit is relatively light on content; much of it is linked with other units, especially BioPsychology. The one difficult area involves the basic theories of emotional response. It can be hard to sort them out, especcially since they are usually referred to by names which do not cue you as to their meaning.

In the **James-Lange Theory**, we first experience physiological changes and then later label those as signs of a certain emotion. First we feel our hearts pounding and our palms sweating as we veer off the highway to avoid an accident, and then, when we come to a stop on the shoulder of the road, we say "I was afraid". The labeling of the emotion follows the bodily responses. It's almost as if the physical creates the emotional. One way to remember this is to link J-L (for James-Lange) with J-L for "jump, then label". In **Cannon-Bard Theory** (sometimes called **Thalamic Theory**, after the thalamus, the relay station in the mid-brain), the recognition of physiological changes and the awareness of the emotion are processed simultaneously by the thalamus. To help your recall with this theory, picture yourself standing next to a cannon which unexpectedly fires, and you leap in the air while simultaneously expressing surprise. In **Schacter-Singer Theory** (also called **Two Factor Theory** and **Cognitive Physiological Theory**), one can interpret the identical physical sensations differently according to the context in which they occur. The same feeling of butterflies in your stomach would tell you that you are <u>nervous</u> before a big game, but might tell you that you are <u>happily excited</u> as you open a huge birthday present. There are thus two factors at work – physical sensation and cognitive labeling, which sounds suspiciously like James-Lange Theory except that the specific *situation* is taken into account as well. That is one way to help you to remember this theory: think 'S' for Schacter-Singer and 'S' for situations.

Study of theories which emphasize the role of cognitions in emotional response leads us to a brief examination of **stress**. While early researcher Hans Selye argued that we all deal with stress in much the same way (his **General Adaptation Syndrome** included steps of **alarm**, **resistance** and finally **exhaustion** – you can remember this with *G.A.S.* is *A.R.E.*), more recent work by theorists such as Richard Lazarus propose that individual cognitive appraisal of the situation is the key in responding to stress. According to Lazarus, we first evaluate whether or not this is a stressful event to us (our **primary appraisal**), and we then judge whether and how we can cope with the stressor (our **secondary appraisal**).

In the earlier unit on sensation and perception you studied opponent process theory as it relates to color afterimages. Some experts contend that opponent processes help to explain emotions as well. You may recall that drive theory suggests we are driven to satisfy needs in order to return to homeostasis. **Opponent process theories** make a similar argument, which has been used to account for why some individuals enjoy bungee jumping or rock climbing or become addicted to certain drugs. When you do your first dangerous rock climb, your initial emotional response will likely be fear and anxiety. After completing the climb, you do not merely return to a homeostatic baseline but instead have an opposing feeling of happiness, even euphoria. The next time you go climbing, according to the theory, the primary emotion of fear is reduced, but the opposing process of elation can be just as great or greater than the first time around. You can see how such a process might also trap you in a pattern of drug abuse. If the primary "high" of taking a drug is less intense on repeated administration, and the opposing "crash" is just as unpleasant, if not more so, than it was at first, sometimes the user falls into taking more of the drug to escape the crash, thus beginning a perilous cycle.

In your review of the biological bases of emotional response, you might also consider how polygraphs, or lie detectors theoretically work. Basically, their job is to measure sympathetic nervous system responses which might be indicative of lying (such as elevated heart rate, increased sweating and so on). You might have fun in class discussing the validity of this approach.

Researcher Paul Ekman has done work in the study of lying, but is even more well known for his **cross cultural research into the facial expression of emotions**. He found that individuals in all cultures tend to recognize and express basic emotions in the same way in terms of facial expression. This suggests that some fundamental kinds of emotional response (researcher Robert Plutchik proposes there are 8 basic human emotions: surprise, disgust, fear, anger, joy, sadness, acceptance and anticipation) are inborn in humans.

But we can also apparently induce some emotions through simple physical manipulations. **Facial feedback hypothesis** states that if one "forces" a smile, it really is more likely that individual will feel happier. Try it – make yourself "look sad" and then see how you feel!

Although it is pretty unlikely to come up on the AP Exam, you can protect yourself against the possibility and end this chapter on an upbeat note by reflecting for a moment on Robert Sternberg's **Triangular Theory of Love**. Sternberg, who also has a well respected *triarchic theory of intelligence* which is discussed in chapter XI, contends that there are three basic possible elements in a "love" relationship: passion, commitment and intimacy. These components are present in different combinations in the various types of love. For instance, in *companionate love*, or friendship, there may be commitment and intimacy (be careful not to equate this with sexual intimacy, a common error in recalling this theory;

Sternberg thinks of intimacy as emotional closeness and sharing) but there is no passion. A relationship which has all three elements he labeled *consummate love*. Again, you will not likely be asked to label one type of love over another on the AP Exam, but this is a very interesting attempt to describe something that many think is indescribable.

Name Hall of Fame

Abraham Maslow is one of the more well known names in psychology, and you must recognize his connection to the humanistic school of thought and to his hierarchy of needs. You might see **Clark Hull's** name when drive theory is mentioned, or **Edmund Wilson's** name in relation to sociobiology. **Konrad Lorenz** is a name to associate with ethology; likewise with **Leon Festinger** and cognitive dissonance theory. Of those, only Maslow's is a name that you might have to know in order to answer a question correctly. In the content outline you saw the names of **David McClelland** and **Matina Horner** in reference to their studies on achievement, but you will not be directly tested on recall of those people, and the same almost certainly applies to **Paul Ekman, Robert Sternberg, Richard Lazarus, Susan Folkman, Kurt Lewin or Hans Selye;** they would be named only in connection to their particular theories and it'd be your knowledge of the <u>theory</u> that would be assessed.

Essay Themes

In this unit you've seen another reference to **opponent process theory**, echoing work you did in the unit on sensation and perception. You could also look at the inhibitory and excitatory action of neurotransmitters, from the chapter on the biology of behavior, as a kind of opposing process. Obviously then, this is the kind of theme that can cut across content areas and is thus a rich area for a possible free response question. Even if it never comes up as an essay item, it will help you across the board on the multiple choice section to know opponent process theories well.

Although such an item may be dismissed by the test development committee as too specific to one unit, it isn't hard to imagine a free response item which asked you to **account for some particular human behavior** from the perspective of an ethologist, sociobiologist, drive theorist, etc. See the upper left quadrant on side one of the "test prep" scheme to remind yourself of those major schools of thought.

Test Preparation: Motivation and Emotion

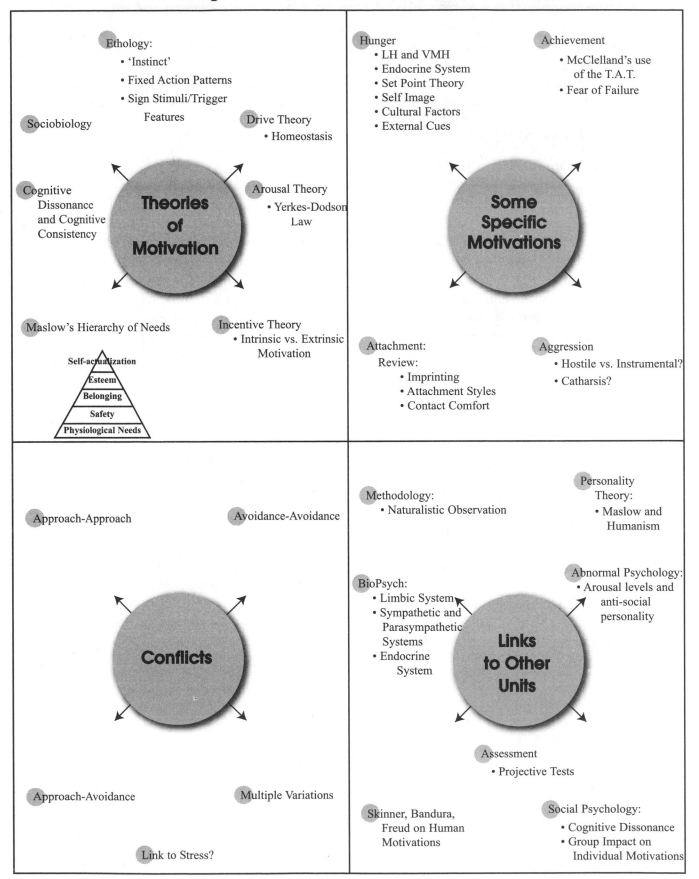

Theories of Motivation

Ethology:
- 'Instinct'
- Fixed Action Patterns
- Sign Stimuli/Trigger Features

Sociobiology

Drive Theory
- Homeostasis

Cognitive Dissonance and Cognitive Consistency

Arousal Theory
- Yerkes-Dodson Law

Maslow's Hierarchy of Needs

Self-actualization
Esteem
Belonging
Safety
Physiological Needs

Incentive Theory
- Intrinsic vs. Extrinsic Motivation

Some Specific Motivations

Hunger
- LH and VMH
- Endocrine System
- Set Point Theory
- Self Image
- Cultural Factors
- External Cues

Achievement
- McClelland's use of the T.A.T.
- Fear of Failure

Attachment:
Review:
- Imprinting
- Attachment Styles
- Contact Comfort

Aggression
- Hostile vs. Instrumental?
- Catharsis?

Conflicts

Approach-Approach

Avoidance-Avoidance

Approach-Avoidance

Multiple Variations

Link to Stress?

Links to Other Units

Methodology:
- Naturalistic Observation

Personality Theory:
- Maslow and Humanism

BioPsych:
- Limbic System
- Sympathetic and Parasympathetic Systems
- Endocrine System

Abnormal Psychology:
- Arousal levels and anti-social personality

Assessment
- Projective Tests

Skinner, Bandura, Freud on Human Motivations

Social Psychology:
- Cognitive Dissonance
- Group Impact on Individual Motivations

114

Test Preparation: Emotion

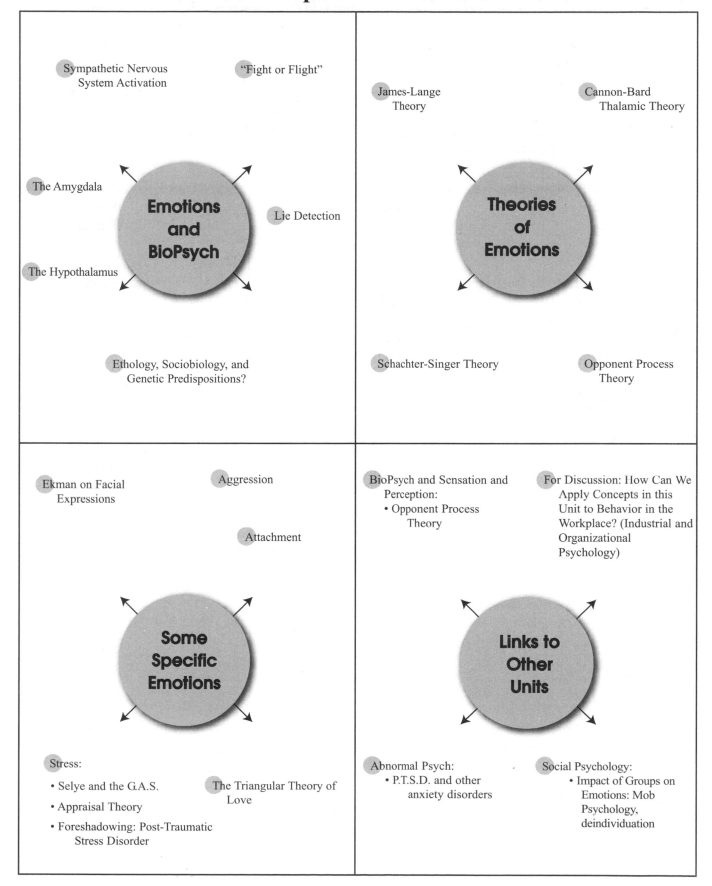

Emotions and BioPsych

- Sympathetic Nervous System Activation
- "Fight or Flight"
- The Amygdala
- Lie Detection
- The Hypothalamus
- Ethology, Sociobiology, and Genetic Predispositions?

Theories of Emotions

- James-Lange Theory
- Cannon-Bard Thalamic Theory
- Schachter-Singer Theory
- Opponent Process Theory

Some Specific Emotions

- Ekman on Facial Expressions
- Aggression
- Attachment
- Stress:
  - Selye and the G.A.S.
  - Appraisal Theory
  - Foreshadowing: Post-Traumatic Stress Disorder
- The Triangular Theory of Love

Links to Other Units

- BioPsych and Sensation and Perception:
  - Opponent Process Theory
- For Discussion: How Can We Apply Concepts in this Unit to Behavior in the Workplace? (Industrial and Organizational Psychology)
- Abnormal Psych:
  - P.T.S.D. and other anxiety disorders
- Social Psychology:
  - Impact of Groups on Emotions: Mob Psychology, deindividuation

115

Practice Items

Here's a review of things to think about when attempting any of these chapter review sets of questions:

* **Time yourself:** shoot to finish a 15 item section within 10 or 11 minutes
* **Cross out those distractors** you've eliminated as you proceed
* **Do not leave any item blank,** especially if you can eliminate even one distractor as clearly incorrect
* These chapter review items are not in **order of difficulty**, although items **will** be on the full length practice examinations at the end of this book and, of course, on the AP Exam itself

1. Which of the following would be the strongest piece of evidence in support of Paul Ekman's research findings into facial expressions of emotions?

   (A) a boy who was born blind covers his face with his hands when embarrassed, even though he has clearly never seen an "embarrassed face"
   (B) a criminology student is confident that she can "read" the facial expressions of suspected criminals
   (C) a criminology student is convinced that it is impossible to "read" the facial expressions of suspected criminals
   (D) a newborn does not appear to utilize a social smile in response to others
   (E) adults in different cultures appear to express joy, despair, surprise and disgust very differently in terms of facial expression

2. A Viking explorer sets out on a journey to unexplored new lands hoping to acquire wealth and admiration from his peers. Which of the following theories of motivation best explains this particular explorer's voyage?

   (A) incentive theory
   (B) drive theory
   (C) sociobiological theory
   (D) cognitive dissonance theory
   (E) ethological theory

3. "To think is easy. To act is difficult. To act as one thinks is the most difficult of all". This statement, attributed to Johann Wolfgang von Goethe is most reflective of which of the following theories?

   (A) arousal theory
   (B) cognitive dissonance theory
   (C) attribution theory
   (D) James – Lange Theory
   (E) cognitive physiological theory

4. An organism's optimal, balanced internal physiological state is called

   (A) reciprocal determinism
   (B) homeostasis
   (C) interventionism
   (D) dissonance
   (E) cognitive consistency

5. Which of the following human brain structures seems most responsible for satiety and feeding, respectively?

   (A) the septum; the amygdala
   (B) the amygdala; the cerebellum
   (C) the cerebellum; the amygdala
   (D) the lateral hypothalamus; the ventromedial hypothalamus
   (E) the ventromedial hypothalamus; the lateral hypothalamus

6. This theory proposes that humans are largely motivated to behave in ways that will keep their genes alive in the future:

   (A) sociobiology
   (B) social resonance theory
   (C) social perpetuation theory
   (D) drive theory
   (E) utilitarianism

7. According to Abraham Maslow's hierarchy of needs, which of the following statements is true?

   (A) individuals who fail to reach self-actualization inevitably feel a sense of despair in later life
   (B) the fundamental need for social affiliation is the first step in the hierarchy
   (C) there are significant cultural differences in the rate at which individuals attain self-actualization
   (D) in western, industrialized cultures, women tend to rely on men to satisfy their safety and esteem needs
   (E) physiological needs must be met before an individual achieves self-actualization

8. Which of the following poses an approach-approach conflict?

   (A) choosing to go out with a set of friends one evening, although you'd also hoped to have a quiet dinner with your romantic partner
   (B) choosing to attend a classical music concert with your aunt simply out of respect for her
   (C) seeking out a close friend who has been anxious to ask you to a party
   (D) choosing to go to the dentist, even though it may be painful or unpleasant
   (E) avoiding the dentist because it may be painful or unpleasant

9. "..(W)e feel sorry because we cry, angry because we strike, afraid because we tremble ...". This quote summarizes which of the following theories of emotional response?

   (A) Plutchick's emotion wheel
   (B) opponent process theory
   (C) Two Factor Theory
   (D) James-Lange Theory
   (E) Cannon-Bard Thalamic Theory

10. A mountaineer claims to want to climb a difficult mountain *because* it is dangerous. This is best accounted for by

   (A) attribution theory
   (B) ethological theory
   (C) arousal theory
   (D) fixed action theory
   (E) cognitive dissonance theory

11. Which of the following is the most accurate criticism of drive theory?

   (A) it does not account for the motivation to satisfy hunger or thirst
   (B) it does not account for the motivation to satisfy the sex drive
   (C) it does not give sufficient attention to homeostatic regulation
   (D) often, humans seek to increase rather than decrease their levels of arousal and stimulation
   (E) individual motivations vary cross-culturally

12. A field mouse instinctively freezes at the sight of a hawk. Studies indicate that it is not the wing span, the talons or the sound of the hawk that cue the mouse's response, but, rather, its eyes. An ethologist would call the hawk's eyes

    (A) an incentive
    (B) a fixed action pattern
    (C) a trigger feature
    (D) a conditioned stimulus
    (E) an engram

13. The cognitive appraisal model of stress forwarded by Richard Lazarus and Susan Folkman proposes that the major factor in the experience of stress is

    (A) the individual's personal assessment of the situation and how stressful it is
    (B) whether or not the stressors involve other individuals in the surrounding environment
    (C) the duration of the stressful event
    (D) the amount of control over the stressful event one has
    (E) whether or not there have been previous stressors in that individual's life

14. In terms of the motivation to eat, which of the following is not an example of an external cue?

    (A) the availability of food
    (B) the interaction of the pituitary gland and the hypothalamus
    (C) the time of day
    (D) a social event in which eating is the centerpiece
    (E) the fact that others around you are eating

15. David McClelland would argue that individuals with a high need to achieve and a low fear of failure would tend to choose tasks

    (A) based on how others are likely to view their choice
    (B) that insure success
    (C) that appear nearly impossible, in order to avoid responsibility for potential failure
    (D) from which it would be relatively easy to extricate oneself
    (E) that supply a reasonable but still challenging chance for success

GO ON TO THE NEXT PAGE

Chapter X

Personality

Introduction

This may be the most important unit in terms of success on the Advanced Placement Examination, because it has substantial overlap with other topics in the AP course, and it also describes the major schools of thought in present day psychology. If you don't know about those in some detail, you simply do not "know" college level introductory psychology.

Before summarizing those major perspectives, we will consider some significant themes which often crop up in the study of personality. One of those is the **nature vs. nurture** debate, which we already touched upon in the unit on Development. There, we learned about **twin studies** and reflected back even further on the concept of **genetic predispositions**, first mentioned in the chapter on BioPsychology.

Many students, when asked to take sides in the nature vs. nurture controversy, are reluctant to do so. They argue that personality and development in general involves "a little bit of both". You might think of that as taking the easy way out, but this is a case where straddling the fence might indeed be the best approach to the problem. Once again, many theorists contend that the nature vs. nurture debate is a "false dichotomy"; that is, we humans cannot attribute our growth solely to either nature or nurture. Remember the oft-quoted question: "what's more important in a soccer field, the length or the width?". Of course, you don't have a soccer field without both.

Another central theme in this unit is that of the **stability of personality across situations**. Does each of us have personality characteristics that are consistent no matter what the circumstance, or is the situation the major determinant in how we behave? Theorists like **Walter Mischel** have argued for the latter, and are thus sometimes called **situationists**.

Many theorists also wonder about the **stability of personality over time**. If we were to conduct a longitudinal study on a group of individuals deemed to be "shy" at age six, would we discover that they are still "shy" at fifty six? This question invites others: how do we operationally define 'shyness'? what measures do we use to assess levels of shyness? and how do we control for variability in situations over time? We will explore some of that in this chapter, and in the next unit on Assessment of Individual Differences.

It's possible that the AP exam will make reference to nomothetic vs. idiographic approaches to the study of personality. **Idiographic methods** involve the evaluation of single case studies *individually* (that word sounds enough like 'idiographic' to perhaps cue your recall if you encounter the term on an examination). That definition may make more sense to you when you compare it to **nomothetic approaches**; in those, researchers assume that all people share pretty much the same traits, merely to different degrees. Therefore, they essentially look at each individual in comparison to others – to some sense of a 'norm' amongst all people. The word 'norm' might sound enough like 'nomothetic' to help you with recall of it in the future.

Trait Theory

The first personality theory we'll look at is **Trait Theory** (sometimes called **Trait/Type Theory**). A **'trait'** is a characteristic tendency toward certain behaviors or emotions no matter what the situation. There are several different theories as to which traits are most basic in humans. **Gordon Allport** was the first to try to list and describe fundamental human personality traits. He is also credited with coining the terms **cardinal trait** (the single characteristic in most people that is most dominant and consistent), **central trait** (a handful of significant tendencies in an individual that are less pervasive than cardinal traits) and **secondary trait** (characteristics that are often present in an individual but are not nearly as "defining" of that individual as a cardinal trait would be).

Raymond Cattell used a complex statistical analysis of abilities or characteristics that seem to "go together", called **factor analysis**, to attempt to catalogue human personality traits. He identified sixteen characteristics as most fundamental in describing all people. These are known as the sixteen personality factors (**16 PF**). He argued that you could describe anyone using these 16 factors (such as assertiveness, conscientiousness and self sufficiency), although the degree to which each is present differs from person to person.

Hans Eysenck contended that there were three essential components of personality: psychoticism, extroversion and neuroticism (you might associate Eysenck's name with the mnemonic **P.E.N.** to help you recall this). Psychoticism refers to the general level of emotional caring and empathy one has (or doesn't have); extroversion (you may also see this spelled as 'extrAversion') refers to how outgoing, friendly and social a person is; and neuroticism is linked to the level of basic emotional stability one possesses, as measured in terms of self esteem, feelings of guilt and so on.

Another attempt to distill the list of core human characteristics manages to cut the number to two: **Type A** personalities and **Type B** personalities. Type A's are driven, competitive, rigid, hostile and intense, while Type B's, well, aren't. They're viewed as more calm, laid back and easy going. The theory was derived from the uncovering of a statistical correlation between the presence of what came to be called Type A characteristics and stress related illness such as heart disease. Critics of this theory point out that placing all people into one of two categories is just not very realistic.

The most popular trait theory at present is called **the Big Five**, or **the Five Factor Model**. Those five personality traits, used to describe everyone to some greater or lesser degree, are openness, conscientiousness, extroversion (perhaps the most studied of all these traits), agreeableness and neuroticism. These are summarized below:

- **openness:** the degree to which one is open to new experiences and learning
- **conscientiousness:** the degree to which one is responsible, hard working and reliable; this is sometimes thought of as *dependability*
- **extroversion/extraversion:** the degree to which one is outgoing, expressive, active and social
- **agreeableness:** the degree to which one is honest, considerate, likable and tolerant
- **neuroticism:** the degree to which one is anxious, self conscious or impulsive; it might be easier to think of this as *emotionality*

To assess and to deepen your grasp of this theory and the others in this unit, it is useful to critique them in classroom discussion. Ask yourself what *you* see as weaknesses of each theory. For example, a central argument against trait theory is that it does not take the power of the situation into account; in fact, it's based on the idea that a 'trait' is only a trait if it is consistent no matter what the situation. Trait theorists are also criticized for stopping at mere description of personality traits; they offer little in the way of explanation as to where those characteristics come from.

Psychoanalytic Theory and the Neo-Freudians

A long standing but much criticized perspective on personality is **Sigmund Freud's psychoanalytic theory**. Its primary focus is on the influence of **unconscious conflict, especially rooted in early childhood**. Because it is based on the existence of something, the unconscious mind, that is impossible to observe or test, many scientists dismiss psychoanalysis as a set of interesting ideas and nothing more. Still, it has had a huge cultural and historical impact, in part, perhaps, because of its emphasis on sexual conflict. This simultaneously catches the attention of the public and disillusions many psychologists who think Freud went overboard with his sex-based interpretations of personality development.

A commonly used metaphor for Freud's conception of the psyche is that of *an iceberg*. Upon viewing an iceberg, some may see it as a slab of ice floating on the surface of the water. They fail to realize that there is a much larger foundation of ice below the water line, without which the tip of the iceberg that we can see would not exist. According to Freud, that tip represents the **conscious mind**, while the submerged portion is the **unconscious mind**. He also postulated the existence of a **preconscious mind**; this is the part of the iceberg that is immediately below the surface, out of sight for the moment but easy to see if one looks. You may recall reference to the unconscious mind in our earlier study of Freudian dream interpretation. Freud claimed that dreams were the "royal road to the unconscious", telling us things we might not be willing to tell ourselves consciously. Sometimes, according to Freud, we also tell others things that we don't consciously wish to tell them but which come out anyway, as in a **Freudian Slip** like "that's a nice mess...uh...I mean DRESS, you're wearing".

Freud also proposed the existence of three components of the psyche, the terms for which have become part of everyday language: id, ego and superego. **The id** is all below the water line, in the unconscious mind. It is based on **the pleasure principle**, essentially looking to meet needs without restriction. It is like a little child who wants what she wants when she wants it. The **ego**, mostly but not entirely situated above the water line, is **the reality principle**, working to balance the id's desire for immediate gratification with **the superego's** harsh judgment of how one ought to behave, while remaining mindful of the demands of the external world. The superego, the last of the three to develop, is mostly under the surface and is often referred to as an internalized mother's voice. Thus the ego is the part of us that we are most aware of, the "referee" of our mind; the id is the powerful but unconscious urge for immediate and complete gratification, while the superego, only part of which is accessible to us consciously, is the exceedingly harsh "conscience".

According to Freud, the ego protects itself from pain and anxiety through the use of unconscious **defense mechanisms**. These often help us through difficult or traumatic periods in our lives, although they can be maladaptive (damaging to your survival or happiness) if carried to excess. Below is a summary of the defense mechanisms you are most likely to encounter on the AP Exam:

- **denial:** rejecting the truth of a painful reality, as in a person's refusal to accept a frightening medical diagnosis

- **displacement:** "taking out" an emotion on a safe or more accessible target than the actual source of the emotion, as in punching a wall rather than confronting the boss who has angered you

- **projection:** attributing something that we don't like about ourselves to someone else, as in accusing your best friends of being controlling and rigid when it is you who unconsciously fear your own tendencies toward such behavior

- **rationalization:** this is basically excuse making, as in telling yourself that you had to cheat on the exam because everyone else was probably going to do it as well

- **reaction formation:** associating the word 'opposite' with this may help in your recall of it. Sometimes we unconsciously protect ourselves from undesirable emotions by behaving in ways that are exactly opposite of how we truly feel, as in showering a person with affection when we really, at heart, resent them

- **regression:** figuratively going back in time to a safer, simpler way of being, as in assuming childlike behaviors when facing stress or trauma

- **repression:** this is essentially unconscious forgetting; something painful is buried so deeply that we no longer even know it is part of us, as sometimes occurs when an individual must deal with physical or sexual abuse in childhood

- **sublimation:** one way to help your recall of this is to associate the term with 'substitution'; an undesirable emotion or drive is unconsciously replaced by a socially acceptable one. Some Freudians might argue, for instance, that a surgeon is sublimating aggressive tendencies; making incisions is a socially acceptable and even heroic way to be aggressive

- **suppression:** this is essentially conscious forgetting, a conscious attempt to push something out of your mind. If you are asked about job prospects for the summer and at the moment you have none despite repeated efforts, you might say "I'm trying not to think about that". In a sense, this is different from a "true" defense mechanism in that it is conscious

Another part of Freud's theory is that of the five **psychosexual stages:** oral, anal, phallic, latency and genital. In each stage, an individual faces certain conflicts. If those conflicts are appropriately resolved, all well and good. If, however, the individual remains fixated on a certain stage, it could have far reaching, lifelong implications.

In the **oral stage** of development (birth to about 2 years old), pleasure is derived from the mouth. In the **anal stage** (2 to 4 years old), the focus is on the anus, especially as regards the control of urination and defecation. During the **phallic stage**, the youngster learns that he can derive pleasure from stimulation of the genitals. It is at this time that the child faces the **Oedipus Complex** (you may also see this as Oedipal Complex, Oedipus Conflict and Oedipal Conflict). Freud theorized that boys at this stage unconsciously feel romantic attraction to their mothers and thus feel in competition with their fathers. A boy resolves this conflict by *identifying* with the father, taking on many of his dad's characteristics and *internalizing* the father's beliefs and morality. The child then sublimates his Oedipal urges, channeling them into socially acceptable activities, which leads him into a long **latency period**, in which sexual energy is submerged ('latent' essentially means 'hidden'). This lasts through the middle of childhood up to adolescence. The final stage of mature adult sexuality which begins at that point is called the **genital stage**.

Freud's theory has certainly had influence on popular culture. If you have ever heard someone referred to as "anal", you have heard a Freudian reference. An "anal" person is basically Type A – uptight, time bound, driven. A Freudian would argue that such a person did not successfully resolve the anal stage of psychosexual development and is thus fixated on the control issues inherent in that stage.

One critique of his theory is that it is too male-centered. For instance, there is a version of the Oedipus Complex for females, usually called the **Electra Complex**, but it was a bit of an afterthought in psychoanalysis. Some also see a male bias in Freud's conception of **penis envy**, the phallic stage phenomenon in which girls notice and are jealous of a boy's penis. Some Freudians contend that this unconscious penis envy contributes to a fundamental sense of inferiority in females.

Of course, it is difficult to argue against Freud, because so much of what he proposes is not really measurable or observable. This, as we've seen, is one of the central criticisms of Freudian theory. Others we've already touched upon are its male bias and its emphasis on sexual conflict. The **neo-Freudians** were leaders in the revision of pure Freudian theory. One leading neo-Freudian was **Carl Jung**, a staunch follower of Freud at one point who added to Freudian theory by postulating the existence of the **collective unconscious**. This is a set of common themes, or archetypes, inherited from the wealth of human experience and shared by all people. These **archetypes** include a sense of "femaleness" in males (**anima**) and a sense of "maleness" in females (**animus**). Jung also introduced archetypes like "the shadow" (the dark side we all have deep inside us), "the hero", "the wise old man" and "the nurturing mother". These archetypes are often expressed through a culture's mythology and folk tales.

Another neo-Freudian was **Karen Horney**, who was a leader in adding a female perspective to psychoanalytic theory. She, for example, argued that males may well be jealous, on an unconscious level, of the female ability to have children. This came to be called **womb envy**. Horney also theorized that we are all driven by an instinctual sense of **basic anxiety**, a kind of unease in a dangerous world, and she also argued that **social and cultural factors** play a much larger role in the growth of personality than Freud had believed.

Alfred Adler was another psychoanalyst who eventually broke with Freud. We made brief reference to his *birth order theory* in the chapter on Developmental Psychology. He's probably best known for his conception of the **inferiority complex**. Adler contended that we all have a drive to be competent, but many of us feel a deep sense of inferiority as well. Thus, our personality is largely based on the pursuit of superiority.

Social Cognitive Theory and Behavioral Theory

Next we turn to **Social Cognitive Theory**, which also overlaps with **Behavioral Theory**. Thus, you might see them referred to separately or in different combinations, such as *Cognitive Behavioral Theory or Social Learning Theory*. Later, in the unit on Treatment of Psychological Disorders, you will learn about the cognitive-behavioral therapeutic approach, which will be easy for you to understand after you've finished this section.

Albert Bandura's theories may best exemplify this **combination of cognitive, social and behavioral elements**. You may remember his "Bobo Doll" study of observational/social learning in the unit on Learning Theory. Bandura believed that we learn and develop through active interaction with the environment. Thus, he went further than the radical behaviorists who would argue that our personalities are *solely* the result of conditioning. Bandura disagreed with the radical behaviorists in recognizing that there is a role for human thought processes and decision making in this learning equation. We develop through watching others in our surroundings, yes, but we also choose which environments to be in, which in turn exposes us to certain types of individuals and situations, which in turn leads us to make other choices, which in turn afford us specific types of experiences which again lead us toward particular choices, and so on. Bandura called this ongoing interaction **reciprocal determinism**. Bandura also thought that an essential piece of this interaction involved **self-efficacy**, the sense that one can control outcomes in one's environment.

Julian Rotter's concepts of **internal and external locus of control** are related to the sense of self-efficacy. Rotter was a behavioral researcher, but he was not a radical behaviorist like B.F. Skinner in that Rotter acknowledged that human cognitions <u>were</u> involved in learning. Individuals with an internal locus of control, for example, have the feeling that to a large extent they can control the consequences of their behaviors. People with an external locus of control tend to see outcomes as being out of their control. A man with such a perspective might view his failure to get a job he desired as "just bad luck" or "all politics", rather than evaluating what he can do to effect a desired outcome in future situations. Rotter is basically talking about the difference between people who believe they can control their own fate and those who believe that there is little they can do to influence what happens to them.

Rotter's proposals are in turn linked to **Fritz Heider's attribution theory**. In it, Heider wonders how individuals account for what happens to them; to what do they attribute their success or failure? A student who does poorly on an exam is making a **dispositional attribution** if she says "I could have and should have tried harder", and is making a **situational attribution** if she says "The classroom was so noisy and the teacher is so bad I couldn't possibly do well". Later, in Social Psychology, we will explore the **fundamental attribution error**, in which people tend to make dispositional attributions for negative behavior by others ("he cut me off in traffic because he's a loser!"), but situational attributions for one's own negative behavior ("the traffic was so crazy I HAD to cut him off or I never would've made my exit").

Another cognitive view of personality comes from **George Kelly**, who proposed the concept of **personal constructs**, which are individual views of good and bad, right and wrong, selfish and unselfish etc. that each of us builds ('constructs') for ourselves.

In the unit on learning theory you learned about **Martin Seligman's** conception of **learned helplessness**. Seligman argues that if a person tries hard to effect some outcome and continually meets with failure, the individual will soon stop trying altogether. In a sense, they've made a cognitive judgment that they are helpless. Seligman also developed a theory of **explanatory styles**, which will play a role in your study of disorders and treatment as well. According to Seligman, an individual with an **optimistic explanatory style** is more likely to tell herself that bad periods will not last and needn't effect one's entire life. The person tends not to blame themselves for bad things that occur. People with a **pessimistic explanatory style** see bad times as stable and unlikely to change. They also see painful events as impacting their entire lives and are more likely to blame themselves for the traumas they experience. It is therefore not surprising that Seligman and others have suggested a correlation between negative explanatory styles and the presence of depression.

Humanistic Theory

The **Humanistic perspective** is probably the most upbeat and optimistic of all the personality theories. Opponents of it in fact argue that the theory is unrealistically positive about human motivations. They also contend that it, like psychoanalysis, is difficult to explore empirically; it's hard to measure humanistic concepts and phenomena.

Humanism is *person-centered* (later, you will learn about *client-centered therapy*, a humanistic approach to treatment of psychological disorders) and very positive about individual human potential. It has been called "The Third Force" in psychology, developing as a kind of response to the rather pessimistic psychoanalytic and behavioral perspectives.

Humanists such as **Carl Rogers** and **Abraham Maslow** believe that people generally strive to reach their fullest potential. As you saw in the last unit on Motivation and Emotion, Maslow called this **self-actualization**. Rogers felt that the a person could reach that goal through relationships characterized by **unconditional positive regard**, or **U.P.R.**. Unfortunately, many relationships are built instead on **conditions of worth**, in which one "loves" another only as long as they meet certain requirements and expectations. Rogers also emphasized the role of *the self* in being happy. He contended that the most contented individuals were those who had the smallest gap between their **ideal self** and their **real self**. Those who see a big disparity between how they would like to be and how they actually are are more likely to have a sense of dissatisfaction with their lives.

Name Hall of Fame

There are LOTS of names in this unit, and many of them would be certain inductees in any psychologist's name hall of fame. Even those who see psychoanalysis only as an interesting philosophy that is not scientifically rigorous enough to be accepted by psychologists would likely still vote **Sigmund Freud** into the hall of fame for his historical and cultural importance. As we saw in learning theory, **B.F. Skinner** easily makes it into the hall of fame as well. You also learned about **Albert Bandura** in that unit. He's a tougher call in terms of hall membership, but here he is in a second unit in the course, so it's best to know his name and not just his theories of observational learning, self-efficacy and reciprocal determinism. **Carl Jung** probably makes it into the hall too, especially since Jungian psychoanalytic approaches are more popular now than strict Freudian methods. It's a good bet that you'll meet the other major neo-Freudians, **Karen Horney** and **Alfred Adler**, on the AP Exam, but it's doubtful that you will have to directly recall their names in order to get an item correct.

Humanists **Abraham Maslow** and **Carl Rogers** would get a majority of votes on the hall of fame ballot. Their names come up in more than one unit of the course, which is reason enough to familiarize yourself with them. Then things get a bit trickier; is **Martin Seligman** in? if he is, then **Fritz Heider** may make it too. You're safe if you only remember personal constructs and locus of control and not the names **George Kelly** and **Julian Rotter**, but what about all the trait theorists – **Gordon Allport, Hans Eysenck** and **Raymond Cattell**? In those cases too, you almost certainly do not need to "know their names" in order to answer questions correctly.

Essay Themes

As you saw in the chapter on development, the **nature/nurture/false dichotomy**? theme is a big one. Since 1992, the first year of the AP psychology examination, the most popular type of free response item has been along the lines of **"explain anxiety/depression/ etc. from each of the following perspectives: psychoanalytic, behavioral, etc."** Having a sound grasp of each of these major schools of psychological thought will serve you very well on the Advanced Placement Exam and in any psychology course you take in the future. On side two of the test prep graphic organizer for this unit, you can see many links to other units, some of which you have not yet studied. That quadrant of the test prep will be useful to you in preparing for free response items on the AP Exam.

Test Preparation: Personality

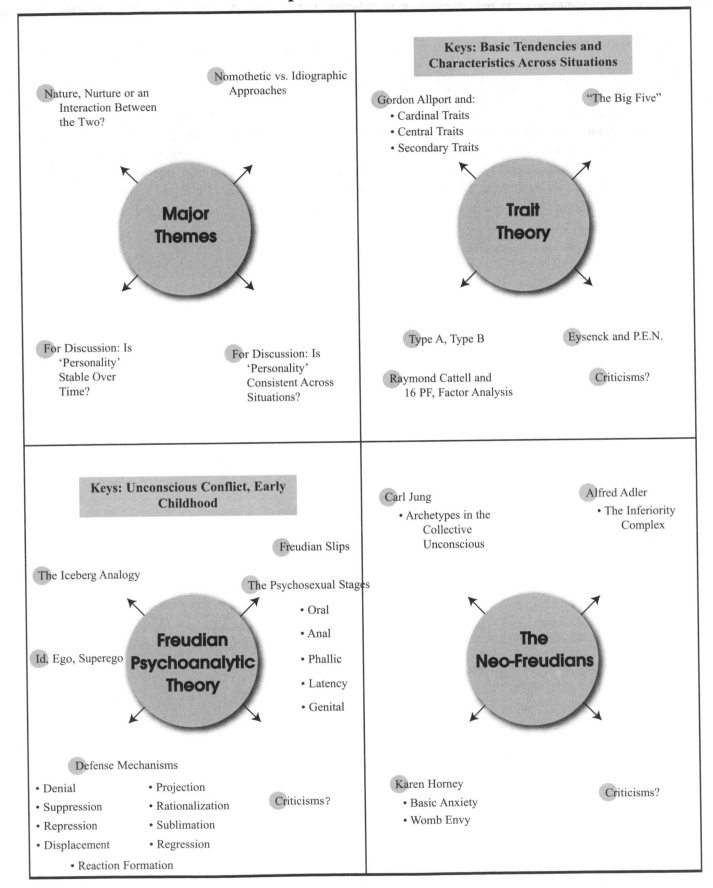

Major Themes

- Nature, Nurture or an Interaction Between the Two?
- Nomothetic vs. Idiographic Approaches
- For Discussion: Is 'Personality' Stable Over Time?
- For Discussion: Is 'Personality' Consistent Across Situations?

Keys: Basic Tendencies and Characteristics Across Situations

Trait Theory

- Gordon Allport and:
  - Cardinal Traits
  - Central Traits
  - Secondary Traits
- "The Big Five"
- Type A, Type B
- Eysenck and P.E.N.
- Raymond Cattell and 16 PF, Factor Analysis
- Criticisms?

Keys: Unconscious Conflict, Early Childhood

Freudian Psychoanalytic Theory

- Freudian Slips
- The Iceberg Analogy
- The Psychosexual Stages
  - Oral
  - Anal
  - Phallic
  - Latency
  - Genital
- Id, Ego, Superego
- Defense Mechanisms
  - Denial
  - Projection
  - Suppression
  - Rationalization
  - Repression
  - Sublimation
  - Displacement
  - Regression
  - Reaction Formation
- Criticisms?

The Neo-Freudians

- Carl Jung
  - Archetypes in the Collective Unconscious
- Alfred Adler
  - The Inferiority Complex
- Karen Horney
  - Basic Anxiety
  - Womb Envy
- Criticisms?

Test Preparation: Personality

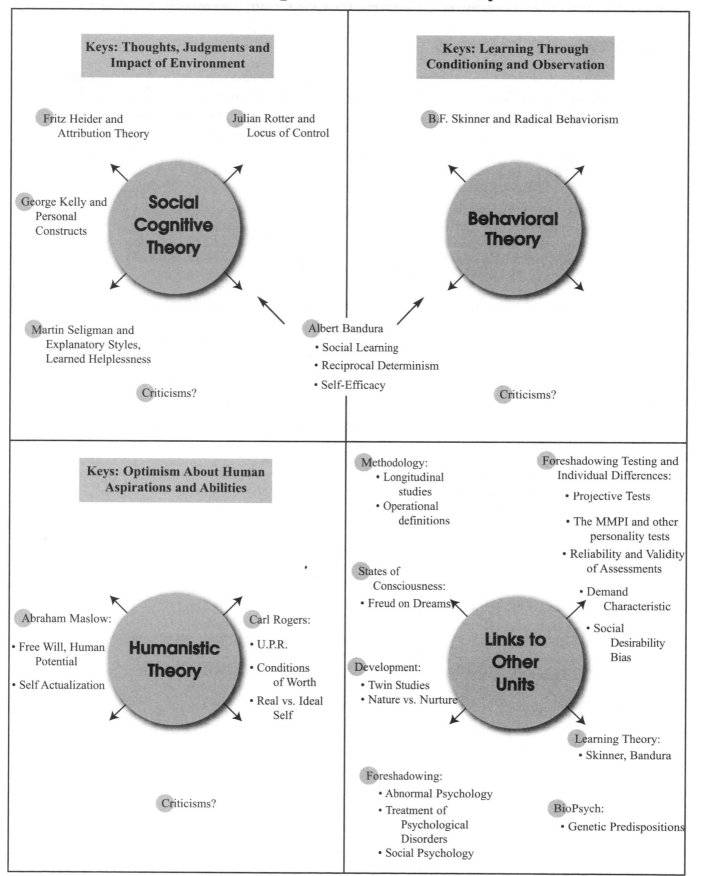

Keys: Thoughts, Judgments and Impact of Environment

Fritz Heider and Attribution Theory

Julian Rotter and Locus of Control

George Kelly and Personal Constructs

Social Cognitive Theory

Martin Seligman and Explanatory Styles, Learned Helplessness

Criticisms?

Albert Bandura
• Social Learning
• Reciprocal Determinism
• Self-Efficacy

Keys: Learning Through Conditioning and Observation

B.F. Skinner and Radical Behaviorism

Behavioral Theory

Criticisms?

Keys: Optimism About Human Aspirations and Abilities

Abraham Maslow:
• Free Will, Human Potential
• Self Actualization

Humanistic Theory

Carl Rogers:
• U.P.R.
• Conditions of Worth
• Real vs. Ideal Self

Criticisms?

Methodology:
• Longitudinal studies
• Operational definitions

States of Consciousness:
• Freud on Dreams

Development:
• Twin Studies
• Nature vs. Nurture

Links to Other Units

Foreshadowing Testing and Individual Differences:
• Projective Tests
• The MMPI and other personality tests
• Reliability and Validity of Assessments
• Demand Characteristic
• Social Desirability Bias

Learning Theory:
• Skinner, Bandura

BioPsych:
• Genetic Predispositions

Foreshadowing:
• Abnormal Psychology
• Treatment of Psychological Disorders
• Social Psychology

131

Practice Items

1. "The only difference between a human and a stone rolling down a hill is that the human thinks he's in charge of his own destiny." This quote from philosopher Baruch Spinoza can serve as a central criticism of which of the following theories of personality?

   (A) Trait Theory
   (B) Type Theory
   (C) Social Learning Theory
   (D) Behaviorist Theory
   (E) Humanistic Theory

2. The "hero", the "shadow", "anima" and "animus" are all

   (A) components of the latency stage of Freudian psychosexual development
   (B) built from early childhood experiences
   (C) elements of the drive for competence and superiority according to Alfred Adler
   (D) roles encouraged by person centered theorists
   (E) archetypes in the collective unconscious according to Carl Jung

3. A four year old boy is rejecting of his father and deeply attached to his mother. Sigmund Freud would contend the boy is in this stage of psychosexual development:

   (A) oral
   (B) anal
   (C) phallic
   (D) latency
   (E) genital

4. One major criticism of Freudian psychoanalytic theory is that it

   (A) describes individual personality characteristics but not their origins
   (B) focuses too much on sexual conflict in adulthood
   (C) assumes that all behaviors are learned through conditioning
   (D) is excessively optimistic about human nature
   (E) is essentially untestable and unmeasurable

5. Which of the following is a criticism a cognitive theorist might level at a behaviorist?

(A) behaviorism focuses too much on the behavior of humans in group situations
(B) behaviorism is too optimistic about the influence individuals can have on the development of their own personalities
(C) behaviorism gives too little credit to human thinking and judgment in the formation of personality
(D) there is little evidence to support the notion that most people seek self-actualization
(E) the concept that one learns through the application of contingencies of reinforcement is nearly impossible to test

6. A proponent of Freudian theory would likely explain an adult's repression of sexual urges as being the result of

(A) negative reinforcement
(B) the law of effect
(C) fixation in the latency stage of psychosexual development
(D) conditions of worth
(E) modeling

7. In Aesop's fable "The Fox and the Grapes", a fox who is unable to reach some attractive looking grapes after repeated attempts claims they would've been sour anyway. This illustrates which of the following unconscious defense mechanisms?

(A) regression
(B) rationalization
(C) internalization
(D) sublimation
(E) identification

8. In Albert Bandura's conception of personality, reciprocal determinism

(A) leads inevitably to a sense of superiority
(B) influences one's sense of the ideal self
(C) contributes to a marked sense of hostility
(D) is marked by a constant interaction between basic elements of personality, the behaviors one chooses, and environmental influences
(E) results in fixation in one or several psychosexual stages of development

9. Which theory of personality would most emphasize the value of unconditional positive regard in relationships?

   (A) Jungian psychoanalytic theory
   (B) Adlerian psychoanalytic theory
   (C) Freudian psychoanalytic theory
   (D) Cognitive Theory
   (E) Humanistic Theory

10. G.K. Chesterton once wrote "It is always the secure who are humble." This quote most supports the existence of

    (A) Alfred Adler's inferiority complex
    (B) the preconscious mind
    (C) archetypes in the collective unconscious
    (D) unconscious defense mechanisms
    (E) the superego

11. The "Big Five" personality characteristics are

    (A) outgoingness, concern, excitability, anxiety, naturalness
    (B) openness, conscientiousness, neuroticism, psychoticism and stability
    (C) openness, conscientiousness, extroversion, agreeableness and neuroticism
    (D) extroversion, neuroticism, psychoticism, anxiety, hostility
    (E) anxiety, hostility, sociability, dependability, emotionality

12. According to Sigmund Freud, deciding whether to return an extra $100 a bank teller accidentally gave you is a conflict between

    (A) conscious and preconscious
    (B) activity and latency
    (C) id and superego
    (D) psychoticism and neuroticism
    (E) prototypes and archetypes

13. Statistically, individuals with characteristics of a Type A personality are more prone to

    (A) introversion
    (B) generosity and empathy
    (C) psychoticism
    (D) cardiac health problems
    (E) sexual promiscuity

14. The famous line from Shakespeare's Hamlet, "Methinks he doth protest too much" expresses the essence of which of the following unconscious defense mechanisms?

   (A) reaction formation
   (B) suppression
   (C) repression
   (D) projection
   (E) displacement

15. According to a psychoanalyst, which of the following would be a probable result of fixation in the anal stage of psychosexual development?

   (A) extreme narcissism
   (B) excessive neatness and obsessiveness
   (C) consistent refusal to eat
   (D) hostile aggression
   (E) feelings of inferiority

NO TESTING MATERIAL ON THIS PAGE

Chapter XI

Testing and Individual Differences

Introduction

This topic is treated differently from textbook to textbook and course to course. Sometimes, theories about 'intelligence', which are a large part of this unit, are handled within the chapter on Thought and Language. In other cases, 'intelligence' is given a separate treatment along with a look at assessments of that elusive concept and other types of assessments used in psychology. Occasionally, part of that assessment section is incorporated into the unit on Personality Theory, as there is much overlap between the two subjects. Here, we will try to tell you what you need to know about all psychological assessments and the many attempts to define 'intelligence' under the Advanced Placement Psychology curriculum umbrella of "Testing and Individual Differences".

Developmental psychologist Jean Piaget once said "intelligence is what you do when you don't know what to do". Some high school psychology students dispute that, placing more emphasis on the acquisition and retention of information in their attempts to define 'intelligence'. How much of 'intelligence' involves memory? How much is it about planning strategies to solve new problems? How much of it is not about 'thinking', per se, at all? (the great American psychologist William James defined 'genius' as ... "little more than the faculty of perceiving in an unhabitual way"). Can we come up with one definition of 'intelligence', or is it so multifaceted that three or four lines in a textbook simply cannot capture its complexity? Are **savants** (individuals with serious cognitive limitations such as mental retardation or autism who possess a remarkable talent in, for example, art or music) 'intelligent'? If not, would you say they are 'unintelligent'? Or does the term not apply at all in such cases? Is intelligence genetically transmitted, or is it more the result of socialization and learning? Many researchers have concluded that intelligence is 50-60% a matter of **heritability**; that is, that 50 to 60 percent of the *difference between individuals* in intelligence is due to genetics (you might recall this concept from our unit on the Biological Bases of Behavior). Do we tend to focus more on the **differences between groups at the expense of differences within groups**? These issues form the crux of the first portion of this unit.

What is Intelligence?

French psychologist **Alfred Binet** is usually considered the father of intelligence testing. He was the first person, working with Theodore Simon, to develop tests to assess one's ability to learn, which some would say is a nice shorthand definition of intelligence. Binet and Simon were working to build a test which could help French officials identify children who might struggle in the public schools. Later, these tests were translated into English and amended by **Lewis Terman** at Stanford University, and the **Stanford-Binet** is still a widely used intelligence test measuring an individual's **"IQ"**, or intelligence quotient. But, before we say more about attempts to measure intelligence, we have to try to define the term.

In 1904 **Charles Spearman** postulated that there is such a thing as general intelligence **("G")** which can be empirically assessed. This "G" is supported, according to Spearman, by specific abilities **("S")** such as skill at mathematical computation, the ability to read and write and much, much more. Other early researchers broadened the scope of the concept by postulating the existence of a wider range of components of intelligence. **Louis Thurstone** contended that there were **eight primary mental abilities. J.P. Guilford** offered a **"cube" model** which included over 200 features of intelligence; his cube resembled a Rubik's Cube, which you may have played with as a youngster. The cube was segmented into blocks, each of which represented a type of intellectual ability.

Raymond Cattell proposed a view that many still accept today. For Cattell, **crystallized intelligence** is the ability to absorb and retain information, while **fluid intelligence** refers to the ability to solve problems one has not seen before. Fluid intelligence also involves speed and flexibility in problem solving. Longitudinal research indicates that such intelligence declines with age, much as one's physical flexibility and speed inevitably declines, even though the older person still "knows" how to do what they could do as a younger person.

Robert Sternberg's triarchic theory features three kinds of intelligence: *creative, practical and analytical.* Another contemporary theory also suggests that there is more than one kind of 'smart'; **Howard Gardner's theory of multiple intelligences** (often abbreviated as "MI") has become enormously popular, especially amongst educators. Gardner proposes eight different types of intelligence: *linguistic, logical-mathematical, musical, spatial* (the ability to accurately perceive, understand and reconstruct visual images – an architect or an interior designer would likely have good spatial intelligence), *bodily-kinesthetic* (accomplished dancers, gymnasts and rock climbers would score well here), *interpersonal* (understanding and empathizing with others), *intrapersonal* (the capacity and willingness to look inside and understand one's own feelings and motivations) and *naturalistic* (the capacity to understand and categorize different elements of the natural world – a farmer or an archeologist would likely possess naturalistic intelligence). He argues that public education's tendency to focus only on verbal and mathematical intelligence obviously does not do justice to other equally valuable kinds of intelligence. Critics of Gardner's theory question his use of the term 'intelligence'. Many ask if the bodily-kinesthetic 'intelligence' of an athlete or craftsman is really a kind of intelligence in the same way verbal reasoning is.

Recently, researchers have also focused much attention on emotional intelligence. In many ways, **'EQ'** (for 'emotional quotient', as compared to 'intelligence quotient', or 'IQ') builds on Gardner's concepts of interpersonal and intrapersonal intelligence. For Gardner, interpersonal intelligence involves awareness of and sensitivity towards others; intrapersonal intelligence features the disposition to look inside oneself, to explore one's own emotions and insights. In combination, that's a fair definition of EQ. Some psychologists would say that emotional intelligence is more valuable and adaptive in our present day world than traditional cognitive views of intelligence.

Intelligence Testing

It is obviously difficult to measure intelligence, in light of the many competing interpretations of what it is. Further, many fear the implications of attempting to assess such an elusive concept. Does a single score on any intelligence test tell us something valuable? Even if it does, how is the score then used? Should a child who has scored poorly on an IQ test be told his or her score? How about a child who has scored exceptionally well? Should a school teacher have access to a student's IQ score? What about the danger of the **self fulfilling prophecy**, in which a teacher's expectations for a student, whatever they may be, actually influences that student's self image and performance? If teachers and students are not given access to IQ scores, who is, and why?

As we saw earlier, the Stanford-Binet (first published in 1905) was the first widely used intelligence test. It was built on the concept of **mental age**. This was a comparison of a child's chronological age to the previously determined average mental ability for that age (often called the **"norm"**). For example, a child of seven years old who scored like the typical seven year old on the intelligence test was said to have a mental age of seven. Since 100 had been normed as the average score for intelligence, this would give the child an IQ of one hundred. The formula for the intelligence quotient was mental age divided by chronological age, multiplied by one hundred (you can now see why it is called IQ, if you recall what a quotient is in mathematics). Thus, a 10 year old child who demonstrated a mental age of 13 on the Stanford-Binet had an IQ of 130 (thirteen divided by ten is 1.3; 100 times 1.3 equals 130).

As you might already have surmised, the concept of mental age soon was viewed as one of the flaws in these early attempts to measure intelligence. It worked well enough for young people, but what happened when you tried to evaluate a 17 year old's intelligence as compared to other 17 year olds? Is there a significant and measurable difference between the mental age of a 17 year old and an 18 year old, for example? The problem only intensifies as the years pass; it seems almost silly to speak of the typical difference in mental ability between a 43 year old and a 45 year old. To remedy this, a more sophisticated statistical attempt to compare one's performance and ability with others developed. This is called the **standard age score, or S.A.S.**

The Stanford-Binet Intelligence Test is still in use today, but an even more commonly used set of intelligence tests is named after their developer, David Wechsler. In the 1930's, Wechsler began to try to address some of the weaknesses in the Stanford-Binet. One of those was the Stanford-Binet's dependence on language. This returns us to the question "what is intelligence?". While most people would agree that intelligence at least in part does involve the ability to communicate, to understand vocabulary and to respond to questions verbally, Wechsler saw that intelligence was more than that as well. He developed task oriented assessments, which were not dependent on the understanding of the language of the tester, or of any language at all. The Wechsler assessments include subtests involving picture completion tasks, object assembly, mazes and more. These sections are in addition to subtests on vocabulary, memory, identifying similarities and differences between objects, and so on.

Wechsler is also credited with being the first to create intelligence tests specific to different age groups. Early versions of the Stanford-Binet fell into the "one size fits all" category. Today, Wechsler's **W.I.S.C.** (the Wechsler Intelligence Scale for Children) and **W.A.I.S.** (the Wechsler Adult Intelligence Scale) are the most commonly used IQ tests.

Early on, individuals deemed to have very high and very low IQ scores were seen as exceptional. We now use the term **"gifted"** for those who score very well (the IQ cutoff today is usually a minimum of 135) and **"retarded"** for those who score on the low end of the scale. The American Psychiatric Association has established the following IQ ranges for various levels of retardation: 55-70 is *mild* retardation, 40 to 55 is *moderate* retardation, 25 to 40 is *severe* retardation and below 25 is *profound* retardation. The term 'retarded' has acquired strongly negative connotations in modern society. It has sadly been used in everyday language as a term of derision, which makes many uncomfortable with its use in any context, but it is still the accepted label in psychology for individuals who have substantial cognitive limitations. Early attempts at similar labeling had met the same fate – 'idiot', 'imbecile' and 'moron' are still commonly used words of insult which were originally used to identify different levels of what we now call retardation.

In the field of education some attention has been given to **exceptional children** at both extremes, with more emphasis historically placed on those who were judged to be retarded or disabled. Some psychologists have argued that gifted children are as "different" in their way as mentally retarded children are in theirs and advocate a strong and perhaps equal commitment to both groups. This might serve as an energizing discussion topic in your class.

You may recall the description of a **normal distribution** in the unit on Statistics and Research Methodology. Below we provide a look at a **perfect normal curve** with percentile distributions and the theoretical examples of perfectly symmetrical curves of IQ and S.A.T. scores. Some theorists would argue that if we could somehow assess the IQ of every human being and then plot each score, we <u>would</u> have a perfectly symmetrical distribution, with the largest percentage of individuals (a little over 68%) falling within one standard deviation away from the mean in either direction. The standard deviation (a statistical measure of the "spread" of scores in relation to the mean) for intelligence scores has been calculated at 15 points, and, as you saw above, the mean IQ score is one hundred; thus, one standard deviation below the mean is $100 - 15$, or 85, two standard deviations below the mean would be $85 - 15$, or 70, and so on. Only a very small percentage of scores on a perfect normal curve would fall at either extreme.

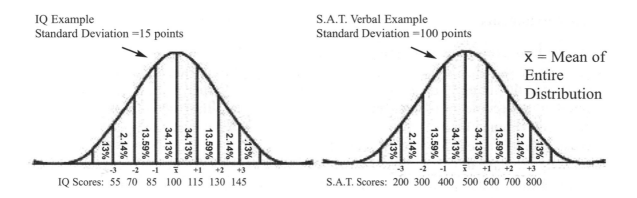

IQ Example
Standard Deviation =15 points

S.A.T. Verbal Example
Standard Deviation =100 points

$\overline{x}$ = Mean of Entire Distribution

IQ Scores: 55 70 85 100 115 130 145

S.A.T. Scores: 200 300 400 500 600 700 800

A quick quiz on the above visual representation:

(A) if you scored three standard deviations above the mean in the S.A.T. Verbal distribution, what was your score?

(B) if you were at the 97th percentile in the IQ distribution, what was your approximate score?

(C) if you earned a 600 on the S.A.T. Verbal, what approximate percentile were you at?

(D) if your IQ score was 85, what approximate percentile were you at?

Answers: (A) 800; (B) 130; (C) 84th; (D) 16th

You might suggest to your teacher that you discuss the concept of **test bias**. You may focus on intelligence tests, but could also easily diverge into biases inherent in the S.A.T., the A.C.T. and other assessments with which you are familiar. Do assessments favor those of certain cultures? Are any commonly used assessments biased against some racial and ethnic groups? Are there gender biases in such standardized tests? Does the language alone in a test often create a biased assessment? Is there, for example, a bias in favor of those who speak certain kinds or dialects of English?

Another discussion topic for your class might revolve around the **Flynn Effect**, a fairly recent finding that IQ scores in America have steadily risen in the last half century even while S.A.T. scores have declined in that same period. What accounts for this seeming contradiction? Is this evidence that our educational systems are falling short in capitalizing on the ever growing talents of young people? Is this a statistical anomaly in that more individuals are now taking the S.A.T. and that we thus have a broader representation of students in that pool of scores? Some would contend that historically only the "cream of the crop" even considered attending college and therefore took the S.A.T. or A.C.T., and that would account for higher scores on such measures at that time.

Other Assessments

Some tests are designed to measure **achievement** (that is, mastery of some body of knowledge or skills), while others purport to measure **aptitude** (the ability to do or learn something in the future). Some assessments strictly rely on **"paper and pencil"** items, with which you've become so familiar in the course of your schooling. Other assessments are more **"performance based"**. You would probably agree that a paper and pencil test for a driver's license is a necessary but not complete method of evaluating whether one can drive well enough to have a license. One still needs to actually demonstrate the ability to drive a car; in this case, actual performance matters most of all in assessing that ability.

Two personality assessments you should be familiar with in preparation for the AP Exam are The **M.M.P.I.** (Minnesota Multiphasic Personality Inventory) and **The Myers-Briggs Inventory**. Both are called "self report inventories" because the subjects are basically identifying for the examiner what is true for themselves. The M.M.P.I. was originally designed to diagnose mental disorders, and it is still the most widely used assessment tool among clinicians. It has over 500 true or false items designed to identify characteristics of personality and behavior. On the Myers-Briggs Inventory you are asked to choose which of three statements is most representative of your thoughts, feelings or behaviors in many given situations.

You may also recall earlier references to **projective tests** of personality, so called because the subject's impression of ambiguous stimuli (such as a set of ink blots) is thought to "say something" about that individual. The theory is that subjects "project" truths about themselves onto the picture, photograph or ink blot they are shown. **The Rorschach Test** offers an array of ink blots for the subject to "identify". **The T.A.T.** (Thematic Apperception Test) requires subjects to tell stories about photographs or drawings. Other projective assessments ask subjects to complete unfinished stories and sentences, or to draw pictures of, for example, themselves or their homes. Such tests have detailed systems for evaluation of responses; it is a misconception to think that those who administer projective tests simply offer a subjective "feel" about what responses represent. Still, questions remain as to their validity – do they really measure what they claim to measure?

Characteristics of all Sound Assessments

Any good assessment must be **standardized**. This means that it is given in the same manner, under the same time limitations and with the identical instructions from administration to administration. Without such standardization, the issue of possible *confounding variables* would arise (you may remember this concept from our first unit on Research Methodology). If, for example, there were no standardized instructions for the S.A.T., some group of students might outperform another not because they were superior on the test but because they were given more extensive directions or more time to complete the assessment.

The establishment of **norms** is another component of standardization. Norms are established by administering an assessment to a representative sample of individuals similar to the population for whom the test is designed. The scores from that sample become the standard to which later test takers can compare their own scores. If there were no norms, you would have no sense of what your "500" on the S.A.T. verbal section or your "22" on the A.C.T. meant.

All legitimate assessments must also be reliable and valid. **Reliability** refers to the consistency of the scoring procedures. **Validity** refers to whether or not the test actually assesses what it claims to assess. For the purposes of the AP Exam, it is probably enough for you to know the basic difference between those two concepts, but a summary of some specific types of reliability and validity follows:

RELIABILITY:

* **test/retest reliability:** does the score you received on a test correlate with your later performance on the same test?

* **equivalent form reliability:** does the score you receive on a test correlate with the score you receive on another test of the same material? For example, if you took the S.A.T. in October and then again in November, you would not have the exact same test, but an equivalent form, and the authors of the S.A.T. contend that in that short period of time your scores on both assessments should be pretty much the same

* **split half reliability:** does your score on the first half of a test correlate with your score on the second half of the test? This type of reliability would not be relevant, for example, to the AP Psychology Examination, since the multiple choice section on that assessment is arranged in order of difficulty; however, on a unit test in your course, this information might tell the teacher a lot about how he or she constructed the test, whether it may be too long, and so on. Another way to calculate split half reliability would be to score odd numbered and even numbered items separately

* **inter-rater reliability:** does the score one grader assigns to your assessment correlate with the score another grader gives on that test? For example, when your AP Psychology free response essays are graded, it is often the case that more than one "reader" scores each of your answers – both readers are "blind" to the score the other gave your work. This is to insure that all readers are scoring similarly according to the rigorous scoring guidelines established at the beginning of the reading session

* **intra-rater reliability:** does the score a grader give on a test match the score they give to the same test when they unknowingly grade it again? Many of your teachers would probably admit that the order in which they read essays, for example, can influence their scoring, even if they have the best intentions regarding fairness. If a teacher read your paper first when starting on a set of 100 essays, would that score correlate with the score the teacher gives if the essay is reinserted into the pile at the very bottom? If, of course, the teacher suspected that they had already scored this essay then you couldn't learn much in terms of intra-rater reliability, but if the scorer graded it anew, as a new essay (which is not an unreasonable expectation in a stack of 100), fatigue and the influence of all the other papers already read might well yield a different score than the first time around

VALIDITY:

* **face validity:** with a quick perusal of the assessment, does the test seem to evaluate what it claims to evaluate? If you were given a test supposedly designed to measure your "musical ability" and the entire first page of the document asked questions about your favorite foods and beverages, you might well question the face validity of the assessment

* **content validity:** does the assessment test the body of material (the content) it is supposed to test? For example: if your history teacher tells you to prepare for a test on the American Revolution and then gives you an exam containing several items on the writing of the Constitution, you might well argue that the test does not have content validity

* **construct validity:** does the assessment accurately test what you have defined as the characteristics you wish to assess? For example: if you developed a test to measure levels of hyperactivity in children, you would have to build (or "construct") an operational definition (again, recall our unit on Research Methodology) of 'hyperactivity' that your test would be designed to evaluate

* **criterion validity:** do the results from the assessment correlate with results from *other* measures designed to assess similar or related things? For example: if you were in charge of acquiring professional football players, and your scouts had identified talented players from watching them in actual competition, you might also look at other criteria (speed in the 40 yard dash, maximum lifts in the weight room, performance in a vertical jump test) to see how much each criteria agrees with the others

* **predictive validity:** does the test accurately forecast the level of some future performance? For example: does performance on the S.A.T. correlate with later college achievement? The authors of the S.A.T. offer much statistical evidence that the test does have predictive validity – you might have an interesting discussion in class as to whether the exam predicts future performance or actually *influences* future performance

It probably goes without saying, especially if you remember our discussion of ethics in psychological research from unit one, that the results of any formal assessment must remain **confidential**.

Name Hall of Fame

Because it is difficult to write multiple choice items about the many theories of intelligence without reliance on the test taker's recall of specific proper names, you are not likely to encounter a lot of items on the topic on the cumulative Advanced Placement Examination. Psychology teachers differ on how much direct recall of proper names should be measured on a test, and so do members of the AP Psychology Test Development Committee. This unit brings that issue to the forefront, because so many of the theories covered here are directly associated with the name of the theorist.

With that said, the names **Howard Gardner** and **Robert Sternberg** are two in this unit that are most likely to be important in and of themselves on the AP Exam. You may remember Sternberg's triangular theory of love, which we looked at in the unit on Emotion. The mere fact that his name arises in more than one unit makes him a solid candidate for induction into our name hall of fame. That earlier reference to his work helps you here as well, as both theories are three pronged, and that can cue you on any 'Sternberg' item in this chapter. Gardner's theory of multiple intelligences has had such a broad cultural impact that you can't really claim to have a good grasp of introductory psychology without recognizing his contributions.

Don't fret too much about the many theories of intelligence and the names of those who forwarded them. The authors of the AP Psychology Examination do not conspire to try to trip students up; they do not wish to confuse you as to whether this item refers to Thurstone's or Guilford's theory for example. The exam will surely assess your knowledge of fluid and crystallized intelligence before it will ask you merely to recall Raymond Cattell's last name.

Alfred Binet's name is an important one in the history of psychology, but his name is associated with his test, which makes things easier for you. Likewise with **David Wechsler**.

Essay Themes

It would be a very difficult task in the time allotted for the AP Psychology Exam to write a free response essay on the different theories of intelligence. For that reason, the test development committee is unlikely to include one. This is not to say that those theories are not worth your study time. Reference to one or two of them could well show up on a free response question, but it's pretty certain that you would not have to deal with more than that.

In the AP Psychology curriculum this unit is entitled "Testing and Individual Differences", and the theme of "difference" (between groups and individuals) is an important one in our ever shrinking world. It would be hard to construct a free response item on the subject that would be manageable for students and "scoreable" for exam readers, but the concepts of **test bias** and **culture fair testing** surely deserve reflection on your part.

Test Preparation: Testing and Individual Differences

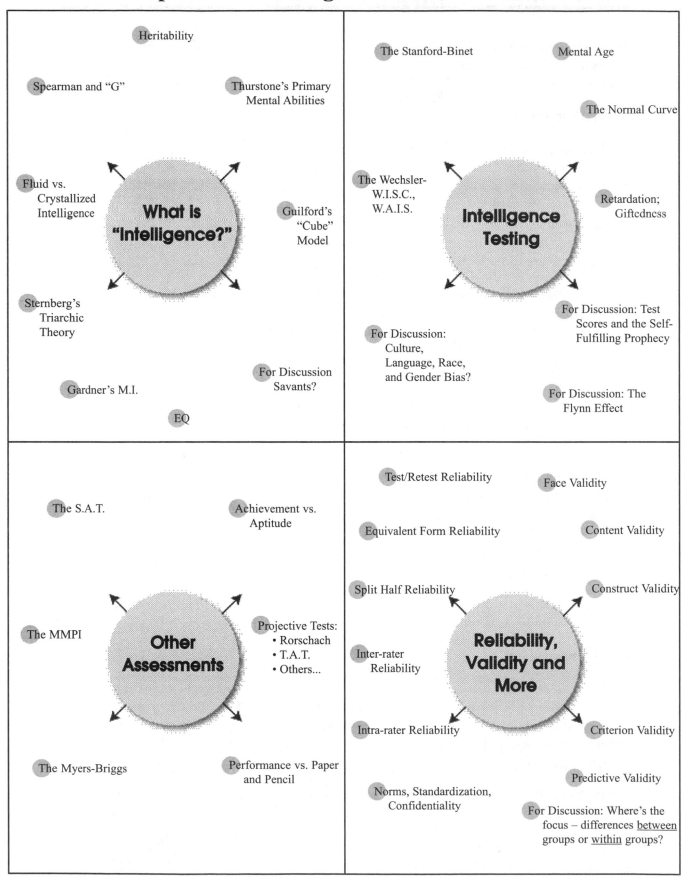

Heritability

Spearman and "G"

Thurstone's Primary Mental Abilities

Fluid vs. Crystallized Intelligence

What is "Intelligence?"

Guilford's "Cube" Model

Sternberg's Triarchic Theory

Gardner's M.I.

EQ

For Discussion Savants?

The Stanford-Binet

Mental Age

The Normal Curve

The Wechsler- W.I.S.C., W.A.I.S.

Intelligence Testing

Retardation; Giftedness

For Discussion: Culture, Language, Race, and Gender Bias?

For Discussion: Test Scores and the Self-Fulfilling Prophecy

For Discussion: The Flynn Effect

The S.A.T.

Achievement vs. Aptitude

The MMPI

Other Assessments

Projective Tests:
• Rorschach
• T.A.T.
• Others...

The Myers-Briggs

Performance vs. Paper and Pencil

Test/Retest Reliability

Face Validity

Equivalent Form Reliability

Content Validity

Split Half Reliability

Construct Validity

Inter-rater Reliability

Reliability, Validity and More

Intra-rater Reliability

Criterion Validity

Predictive Validity

Norms, Standardization, Confidentiality

For Discussion: Where's the focus – differences <u>between</u> groups or <u>within</u> groups?

146

Practice Items

1. On a normal distribution of IQ test scores, with a mean of 100 and a standard deviation of 15 points, a score of 85 would place you in approximately what percentile of the population?

   (A) 3rd
   (B) 16th
   (C) 50th
   (D) 84th
   (E) 97th

2. If you wanted to evaluate the test/retest reliability of a scale in the science laboratory, you would

   (A) weigh a target object on it, then weigh that same object on a scale that you know to be accurate, and compare results
   (B) weigh a target object on it several times in succession
   (C) weigh a target object on it and have a neutral observer record the result
   (D) have an engineer examine a schematic drawing of the scale to determine its reliability
   (E) weigh a container on it, in one condition with material inside, in one condition without

3. Which of the following types of tests is designed to measure an individual's knowledge of a particular subject?

   (A) a self report inventory
   (B) a projective test
   (C) a power test
   (D) an aptitude test
   (E) an achievement test

4. Which of the following best illustrates the concept of content validity?

   (A) an assessment predicts how well you will perform in college
   (B) your performance on the S.A.T. positively correlates with your performance on the Wechsler Intelligence Scale for Children (W.I.S.C.)
   (C) results on the first half of a unit test are almost identical to results on the second half of the test
   (D) a test is determined to accurately assess the learning of material in a particular course
   (E) a test is appropriately administered and confidentiality is maintained

5. The specific term for a mentally handicapped individual who possesses an exceptional ability in mathematical calculation, memory, art or music is

   (A) anosmic
   (B) aphasic
   (C) savant
   (D) autistic
   (E) gifted

6. Which of the following best reflects the concept of heritability?

   (A) your individual height is 90% genetic
   (B) height is entirely inherited
   (C) environment is a big factor in height
   (D) 90% of the difference in height between individuals is the result of genetics
   (E) there are significant cultural differences in average height

7. A major difference between the earliest intelligence tests and Wechsler intelligence tests like the W.I.S.C. and the W.A.I.S. was

   (A) the earliest assessments did not use the concept of mental age
   (B) the earliest assessments were not appropriate for children
   (C) the Wechsler tests were the first English language assessments
   (D) the Wechsler tests were the first to be adequately normed and standardized
   (E) the Wechsler tests had more performance-based rather than purely language-based items

8. Which of the following is NOT a projective test?

   (A) The Myers-Briggs Inventory
   (B) The Rorschach Test
   (C) Draw a Picture tests
   (D) Finish a Story tests
   (E) The Thematic Apperception Test (T.A.T.)

9. Which of the following are theories which suggest the existence of more than one kind of 'intelligence'?

   (A) Gardner's M.I. Theory and Sternberg's Triarchic Theory of Intelligence
   (B) Gardner's M.I. Theory and Spearman's Theory of "G"
   (C) Sternberg's Triarchic Theory of Intelligence and Spearman's Theory of "G"
   (D) Spearman's Theory of "G" and Guilfords "Cube" Model of Intelligence
   (E) the theory of mental age and the theory of fluid intelligence

10. The most widely used assessment in clinical psychology is the

    (A) Strong Preference Test
    (B) W.A.I.S.
    (C) W.I.S.C.
    (D) Stanford-Binet
    (E) M.M.P.I.

GO ON TO THE NEXT PAGE

Chapter XII

Abnormal Psychology

Introduction

Individuals have suffered from mental illnesses since humans have been around. In earlier times, those who suffered from what we now call 'disorders' were thought to be **possessed by witches, demons or evil spirits**. For a very long period, such people were often simply locked away, out of sight of the "healthy" masses. Today, we humans have an entire field of study devoted to the causes, characteristics and treatments of psychological disorders. This is often referred to as "clinical psychology"; we will deal with that discipline in this unit and the next, which covers therapeutic approaches to mental illness.

The sometimes controversial but widely used book which helps clinicians to identify mental disorders is called the "Diagnostic and Statistical Manual". **The DSM-IV-TR** (this revised version of the 4th edition of the manual came out in 2002) contains detailed descriptions of every psychological affliction known today. There are still some who agree with **Thomas Szasz** that such a book serves only to provide us with labels for behaviors that are not "disorders" at all. Szasz argued that such labels could cause as many problems as they solve, in that they demean the individual to whom the tag is applied and that individual might actually feel compelled to live up to the expectations which accompany the "disease" (another example in psychology of the *self fulfilling prophecy*).

In a famous study from the 1970's, **David Rosenhan** explored this issue. He and several compatriots visited different mental institutions and reported that they were hearing voices. They did not report any other symptoms, but, not surprisingly, they were each admitted, most with a preliminary diagnosis of schizophrenia (one of the general symptoms of schizophrenia is auditory or visual hallucinations). One was thought to be possibly suffering from bipolar disorder (once known as manic-depression, this affective disorder is characterized by dramatic shifts in mood). Of course, any responsible physician, nurse or aide would take such symptoms seriously, but it is what happened after these "pseudopatients" were admitted that gets at the heart of the "labeling" debate. Once inside the institution, the pseudopatients returned to their normal behavior, and never again reported experiencing auditory hallucinations. Although they remained as patients for an average of nearly three weeks, no member of the professional staff ever "caught on" that they were really healthy. Rosenhan wrote that several actual patients expressed doubt about the pseudopatients' mental illness, but it seems for most of us that the application of a label like 'schizophrenia' to a person influences how each of their subsequent behaviors is perceived. Imagine, for instance, how *you as a doctor* would react to this scenario: you ask a patient you believe suffers from schizophrenia why they seem to be taking notes on a daily basis, and the patient responds that he is conducting psychological research on institutionalization.

All of the participants in Rosenhan's study were eventually released, of course, but all were told that their condition was "in remission", not cured or absent altogether. Labels do tend to stick.

But it would be nearly impossible to talk about, recognize and treat psychological disorders if we didn't have a commonly agreed upon way of doing so, and the DSM-IV-TR serves that purpose. Its authors try to write **operational definitions of each disorder**, describing their characteristics and the frequency and duration of those symptoms.

Such precise definitions are needed because it can be so hard to distinguish between "unusual" behavior and "disordered" behavior. Of course, one of the criteria for psychological "abnormality" is that the behavior in question is **unusual or atypical**; that is, most people don't do it. But, we all probably do or think things that are atypical without being disordered. So, psychologists and psychiatrists use some **other criteria** to help draw that line more clearly:

- the behavior is **disturbing to others**
- the behavior **violates cultural standards**
- the behavior is **disturbing to self**
- the behavior is **irrational, indefensible or unjustifiable**
- the behavior is **maladaptive** – that is, it hurts one's daily functioning or even one's survival

It isn't necessary for all of these to exist in order to label behavior as' disordered'. For example, it may be hard to tell in many serious mental illnesses whether or not the patient himself is disturbed by his behaviors As you will see, some personality disorders are in part marked by the sufferer's unwillingness or inability to acknowledge that anything is "wrong" with them.

The "cultural standards" criterion is a complicated one. For one thing, some psychological disorders common in one culture or region may be nearly nonexistent in others. Eating disorders are sadly quite common in some western societies but are almost unheard of in many other parts of the world. Dissociative Identity Disorder, once known as multiple personality disorder, also seems peculiar to western cultures, especially America. Also, cultural standards are always subject to debate and to change. Homosexuality was once listed in the DSM, but is no longer. That is just one example of how our societal view of "illness" doesn't necessarily remain constant.

In class, you might further examine that issue in a discussion of **"the insanity defense"**. While 'insanity' is a legal term and not a clinical one, the debate as to when an individual is no longer fully responsible for their behaviors because of mental defect can be a useful way for you to deepen your understanding of the attempt in psychology to clarify the demarcation between 'normal' and 'abnormal'. In the courtroom that line has changed somewhat over time, and the same can be said in psychology as well.

Throughout the rest of this content outline, please keep **"the intern's warning"** in mind – you might discover a tendency to diagnose yourself as you learn more about different disorders. Try to resist that temptation. As you read about Obsessive-Compulsive Disorder, for example, please remember the above criteria for abnormality; the fact that you might be somewhat ritualistic in preparing for a big game or an important recital or in taking your morning shower does not necessarily mean you suffer from O.C.D.

Mood or Affective Disorders

— flat affect — → no emotion → schizophrenic

'Affect' refers to mood or emotion. There are three mood/affective disorders that you are likely to encounter on the AP Examination:

- **major depression:** characterized by deep sadness, feelings of hopelessness and worthlessness, loss of energy, changes in appetite and sleep patterns and suicidal thoughts. You may also see this called **clinical depression** or **unipolar depression** ('uni' means one, so this term refers to the patient's being trapped at one end of the mood spectrum).

- **seasonal affective disorder:** characterized by symptoms similar to major depression but triggered by changes in the seasons. Reduced levels of light during the winter months seem to be the main cause; indeed, intensive exposure to light is a major treatment approach for **S.A.D.**

- **bipolar disorder:** characterized by sudden shifts in mood, from deep depression and listlessness to extreme euphoria, inflated self esteem, a "flight" of ideas and speech and marked distractibility. You might also know it as **manic-depression**. Some sufferers cycle through such changes much more quickly and unexpectedly than others; some often return to a kind of baseline state with relatively no symptoms, while others are either manic or depressed pretty much all the time. You can see why this can be a difficult disorder to diagnose.

Where's the line? issues:

All of us have been depressed at some point or another, perhaps as the result of a trauma or loss, but was it "clinical depression"? One of the criteria for major depression is that it is not necessarily directly associated with a particular stimulus; another is that it has lasted a longer than "normal" amount of time. Likewise, lots of people get "down" in wintertime, because the days are shorter, because the weather precludes involvement in some outdoor activities, and so on, but do not suffer the more serious levels of depression which accompany S.A.D.

The point where extremes of mood are pervasive and damage healthy functioning (are "maladaptive") is certainly important, and so is the self evaluation of the individual – most clinicians would probably consider a person's sense of their own unhappiness as sufficient justification for intervention.

history of...

Etiology of Mood Disorders:

The term 'etiology' refers to the history and possible causes of a disorder. There seems to be a *genetic predisposition* for mood disorders, as evidenced in studies of the occurrence of mood disorders within identical twin pairs. Those who approach this from the **biomedical model** would also focus on *brain chemistry*, especially in regard to serotonin and norepinephrine. There is a correlation between lower than normal activity levels of both those neurotransmitters and the presence of depression, and bipolar disorder may be linked to serotonin activity as well. Further, one common treatment for bipolar disorder, *lithium*, seems to help by operating on the norepinephrine system. There's growing evidence that depression is linked to the stress response, specifically in regard to a stress hormone secreted by the adrenal gland called *cortisol*. It seems as if the brain can be trapped in a kind of stress loop, which can contribute to impaired function in the hippocampus. This in turn may be connected to a kind of breakdown in communication between the prefrontal cortex of the brain and the entire limbic system. Some who suffer with depression have been found to have *lower than normal activity levels* in parts of the frontal lobes.

Psychoanalytic or psychodynamic theorists might trace the roots of depression to unresolved unconscious anger turned inward. **Cognitive psychologists** propose that individuals who suffer from depression may have pessimistic explanatory styles; they tend to blame themselves for bad things that occur, and they believe that such things are more likely to last and impact their entire lives. **Behaviorists** might argue that the symptoms of depression are reinforced in some way, while **humanists** would likely focus on a possible lack of loving interactions and an absence of unconditional acceptance from others in the life of the sufferer. A humanist might also view depression from an *existential perspective* – a depressed individual might be having difficulty finding meaning or purpose in life. A **sociocultural theorist** might well note that depression is statistically more common in females and investigate whether there are societal or environmental factors which lead to this. However, the fact that depression is more prevalent in females across cultures might lead us back to a biomedical explanation – could there be something about female physiology that makes them more vulnerable to depression? Or is it that there are similarities in the ways women are viewed and treated in most cultures? Or does depression result from a complex *interaction* of biological, cultural, cognitive and emotional factors?

Anxiety Disorders

Anxiety disorders are relatively common, but it is important to keep the intern's warning in mind here. All of us have fears, but are we "phobic"? All of us feel anxious or apprehensive or agitated at times, but do we suffer from "generalized anxiety disorder"? All of us may occasionally have unwanted thoughts in our head that we can't dismiss, but does that make us "obsessive"? At what point does an individual cross over into "disordered" behavior?

The anxiety disorders you are most likely to see on the AP Exam are summarized below:

- **generalized anxiety disorder:** marked by ongoing tension, apprehension and nervousness that does not seem to be linked to any specific trigger or stimulus. This may also be referred to by the Freudian term "free floating" anxiety

- **phobia:** not simply a fear, but a deep seated, irrational fear – irrational in the sense that one may feel intense terror even in "safe" conditions. Some are specific phobias (such as fear triggered by certain animals, or by heights or enclosed spaces), some are social phobias (such as intense fear of public speaking) and a third type is *agoraphobia*, an intense fear of public settings or any setting from which there is no ready means of escape in case of a panic attack. Some think of this in terms of it's literal meaning, "fear of the marketplace", while others think of it more as fear of fear – that is, that a sufferer is frightened at the possibility of experiencing panic in an unfamiliar or unsafe environment *Watson – Albert & white rabbit*

- **panic disorder:** marked by "recurrent, unexpected panic attacks" – intense fear, usually accompanied by significant sympathetic nervous system activation, that is not necessarily triggered by any particular event, object or situation. This can also be marked by the concern that one might have a panic attack, or by a general feeling of impending danger

- **obsessive-compulsive disorder:** obsessions are persistent, undesirable thoughts, while compulsions are actions that one feels driven to carry out. One especially disturbing characteristic of this condition is that the sufferer usually recognizes that the obsessions and/or compulsions are irrational or maladaptive, and does not want to have them, but cannot control them

- **posttraumatic stress disorder (P.T.S.D.):** occurring after a deeply troubling event (such as natural disaster, assault or wartime experiences), this is a condition marked by restlessness, irritability, sleep impairment, loss of concentration, nightmares and flashbacks to the traumatic event

Where's the line? issues:

The "maladaptive" criteria is important here. If a compulsion for order has led you to take two or three hours every morning arranging your desk before you can begin work, this will obviously interfere with your functioning on the job. You may well consider yourself an orderly person, but not to such a degree. The "indefensible, irrational or unjustifiable" criteria certainly applies as well. It would be perfectly normal, even healthy, to fear being trapped on the ledge of a tall building. An individual who is phobic about heights might feel genuine agitation, even panic, when merely looking at a photograph of window washers working on a high rise office complex, even though he or she is quite safe.

Etiology of Anxiety Disorders:

Behaviorists offer a powerful learning theory argument for the causes of phobias. They argue such fears are conditioned, perhaps very early in life. Recall the case of Little Albert in the learning theory unit; that is an example of how phobias could be classically conditioned. Such deep seated fears might be operantly conditioned as well – if you innocently approached a dog as a toddler and were bitten, that basic "response resulting in unpleasant consequence" formula might well lead to a life long fear of dogs. You could also develop a phobia through observational learning. If your parents or grandparents demonstrated a powerful fear of mice, you might well imitate that model. Theoretically, compulsive behavior might be operantly reinforced, in that it relieves the anxiety which would come if the behavior was *not* carried out. In fact, some victims of O.C.D. say that, while they do not want to do what they do, it feels better to do it than *not* to.

From the **biomedical viewpoint**, there is pretty strong evidence to support a *genetic predisposition* argument for panic disorder, phobia and O.C.D. You may remember from our work on the biological bases of behavior that G.A.B.A. is the major inhibitory neurotransmitter – think of it as functioning something like the brakes on a car. There is a correlation between the presence of anxiety disorders and *lower than normal levels of G.A.B.A.* It's as if the brakes in the car are not working properly. Some anti-depressants which encourage serotonin activity also help people with O.C.D., so it's reasonable to assume that *malfunctions in the serotonin system* play some role in that disorder. The *amygdala*, in the limbic system, is very much involved in fear and aggression, and dysfunction in it may well play a role in the development of phobias.

Cognitive psychologists contend that panic disorder can result from a misinterpretation of bodily sensations. They argue that sufferers may view relatively normal physiological responses to stress as more dangerous and alarming than others do. In general, cognitive theorists would contend that anxiety disorders are rooted in cycles of self defeating and maladaptive thoughts.

For **a psychoanalyst**, the object of a phobia might symbolically represent an unconscious conflict, perhaps sexual in nature. A *person or client centered therapist*, from the **humanistic** school of thought might trace the origins of anxiety to a gap between one's real self and one's ideal self.

Dissociative Disorders

These disorders are marked by a loss of identity or the sense of self. The victim is disconnected ("dissociated") from who they are and what has happened to them.

The dissociative disorders you should know for the AP test are summarized below: *previous early trauma in childhood*

- **dissociative identity disorder:** also known as multiple personality disorder, this rare condition involves the existence of two or more separate personalties housed in one body. It's important not to confuse this with schizophrenia, although many in popular culture and the media do exactly that. You may also see this disorder abbreviated as **D.I.D.**

- **dissociative amnesia:** characterized by a large scale loss of memory for events or one's own identity. It can be very sudden in onset and in recovery, and often is associated with an injury or, perhaps, with a highly traumatic incident.

- **dissociative fugue:** this is sometimes called "traveling amnesia", because it is marked by amnesia and physical relocation. It is a rare condition, but you may have read of cases in which a person ends up hundreds of miles away from home, unaware of how they got there or who they are.

Where's the line? issues:

These disorders are rare and quite dramatic, so it is easier to see a clear line between "normality" and "abnormality" in these cases. But it may be interesting for you to discuss in class how much any or all of us "dissociate" from time to time. Some psychologists argue that all of us can be placed somewhere on a spectrum of dissociation, without calling any of us "disordered". Many of us too have "different personalities" in different situations, although we do not think of ourselves as suffering from D.I.D. Think of how you behave around your parents as compared to your peers, or how you are at soccer practice as compared to drama rehearsal, or what comes out in you during a conversation with a teacher as compared to a conversation with a boyfriend or girlfriend.

Dissociative identity disorder is one of the more controversial clinical labels today. It's very hard to wrap one's mind around just what it *is*, and there are some who say it doesn't really exist. This is not to say that there's "nothing wrong", but that perhaps it is a response to a therapist's expectations as much as anything else. You might want to consider this angle in your class discussions.

Etiology of Dissociative Disorders:

There are usually **organic causes** of dissociative amnesia and fugue; head injury is an obvious example. However, the **psychoanalytic or psychodynamic school of thought** offers interesting explanations as well. One could view all three of the disorders described above as powerful defense mechanisms, unconsciously built to protect oneself from a painful memory. Amnesia and fugue could be seen as kinds of repression. Dissociative identity disorder is highly correlated with early childhood abuse, and psychoanalysts contend that the condition is a complex attempt to escape the pain of that trauma.

The Schizophrenias

It's fairly common to hear this called the most serious of all mental illnesses. Symptoms of schizophrenia typically do not manifest themselves until the late teens or early twenties, and they are often quite severe and seriously impact one's ability to function in the world.

It is very common to confuse this with dissociative identity disorder, perhaps because the term 'schizophrenia' suggests "split personality" to people. The label refers instead to a split *from reality*. "Psychosis" is a synonymous but somewhat outmoded term for such a split.

The major symptoms (not all of which are present in all cases of schizophrenia) are:

- **hallucinations** (seeing, hearing or sensing something that doesn't actually exist)
- **delusions** (false beliefs, such as delusions of grandeur ("I'm Napoleon") or paranoid delusions ("Law enforcement officials have me under constant surveillance"))
- **inappropriate or flattened affect** (a sufferer with flat affect seems to experience no emotions at all)
- **jumbled thinking and behavior** (the victim's speech is very loosely connected, and words can be thrown together in odd, nonsensical ways – this is sometimes called "word salad")

You may encounter references to **"positive" and "negative" symptoms**. Don't think of these as value judgments, but rather in terms of *adding* or *subtracting*. Positive symptoms are those that a sufferer *has* that a healthy person does *not* (such as hallucinations or false beliefs), while negative symptoms refer to something the sufferer *lacks* that a healthy person *has* (as in the case of flattened affect).

The major types of schizophrenia are summarized below:

- **paranoid schizophrenia:** the central symptom here involves delusions, although the victim may also suffer from hallucinations etc. The delusions are usually of the paranoid kind, although they may be intermingled with delusions of grandeur

- **disorganized schizophrenia:** the central symptoms here are cognitive and emotional. Speech and thought are very confused, and emotions can be highly childlike or inappropriate

- **catatonic schizophrenia:** the central symptom here involves flattened affect, in which the victim demonstrates no emotion or responsivity and may even "freeze" in odd, contorted positions

- **undifferentiated schizophrenia:** this is sometimes thought of as a kind of "wastebasket" category, in that it describes schizophrenia that does not seem to fit into the other subtypes

Where's the line? issues:

Because this too is such a serious disorder the line of demarcation for "abnormality" is more clear than in other categories. Often, the victim has lived a normal childhood and adolescence and onset of the disease is sudden and frighteningly dramatic.

Etiology of Schizophrenia:

The **biomedical model** predominates in uncovering the possible roots of schizophrenia. Twin studies support the notion of a genetic predisposition for schizophrenia, as do studies of parents with schizophrenia and the rates of the disease in their biological children. This predisposition might be *triggered by environmental stressors* such as malnutrition. There is a correlation between the presence of schizophrenia and heightened *dopamine activity* in the brain, which may result from an excess of dopamine or an oversensitivity of dopamine receptors. Brain imaging techniques reveal that many individuals with schizophrenia have *enlarged ventricles* (fluid filled openings) in the brain. It's possible that these openings reflect a *loss of tissue* in the frontal lobes (the higher level "command center" of the human brain) and the temporal lobes (which may account for some of the language dysfunction of schizophrenia). There's video evidence supporting the idea that individuals who develop schizophrenia often demonstrated *unusual motor development and function* as little children. This too may involve frontal lobe problems. And there is a theory that a mother who has a *virus during pregnancy* is statistically more likely to bear a child who will develop schizophrenia. You can see there are lots of possibilities here, and as yet no definitive biological answer to the question "what causes schizophrenia?"

A **sociocultural perspective** on the disease focuses on poverty levels of sufferers and their home environments. There is a statistical correlation between the presence of schizophrenia and low socioeconomic status (however, this reminds us, like the biomedical examples above, of the dangers in inferring causation from correlation). Investigators have also looked at communication styles in the homes of those who develop schizophrenia, and some subscribe to a theory that suggests a relationship between poor or unreliable communication in the home and schizophrenia.

The **diathesis-stress model** is an attempt to tie some of these perspectives together. It suggests that biological predispositions interact with environmental triggers in the development of some disorders, such as schizophrenia. For example, an individual with no genetic "push" toward schizophrenia may not be harmfully impacted by unpredictable or erratic communication patterns in a household, while someone with a genetic predisposition could be.

Developmental Disorders

This category refers to disorders that are "usually first diagnosed in infancy, childhood or adolescence".

The major developmental disorders are summarized below:

- **autism:** this falls under the sub-category of "pervasive developmental disorders". It is characterized by a lack of appropriate social responsiveness and highly impaired communication. Those with autism may sit alone, seemingly disconnected from their surroundings for very long periods of time. They may rock back and forth or engage in other repetitive, seemingly aimless, sometimes self abusive behaviors. They often fail to use appropriate non-verbal communication such as eye contact or facial expression. It's very difficult to summarize the constellation of possible symptoms in this disorder, and it can look very different from case to case.

- **attention deficit/hyperactivity disorder:** like autism, this disorder is more common amongst boys, which is obviously a point of interest to researchers. It is characterized by impulsivity, sustained inattention and limited ability to focus on tasks. You might see it abbreviated as A.D.H.D.

- **conduct disorder:** some think of this as a childhood version of adult anti-social personality disorder, which we examine in the next section. Both are marked by frequent lying, stealing, manipulation and cruelty accompanied by a relative lack of remorse for such actions or empathy for those hurt by such behaviors

- **Tourette's Disorder:** commonly referred to as Tourette's *Syndrome*. Individuals with Tourette's display consistent vocal or motor 'tics', defined in the DSM as "sudden, rapid, recurrent, non-rhythmic, stereotyped motor movement or vocalization". Many suggest Tourette's is a relative of obsessive-compulsive disorder

- **different levels of mental retardation:** we touched on this topic in the last unit on "Testing and Individual Differences". Four levels are described in the DSM: mild, moderate, severe and profound, but it is unlikely that you would have to differentiate between them on the AP Exam or in the typical college introductory psychology class

Where's the line? issues:

In many schools today there is a debate about whether ADHD is over-diagnosed. Some ask for a clearer line to be drawn between "normal" childhood and adolescent behaviors and "hyperactivity". Once again, the "maladaptive" criterion is important in diagnosing developmental disorders; many children at some time or another engage in lying or stealing, but it is when such behavior is chronic and a consistent impediment to "normal" functioning for the child that a diagnosis of "conduct disorder" becomes a consideration.

Etiology of Developmental Disorders:

The roots of autism are still poorly understood. Attention deficit/hyperactivity disorder is often successfully treated with medication, which suggests a biomedical basis for that condition, perhaps in terms of reduced inhibitory neurotransmitter activity. If conduct disorder is indeed a relative of anti-social personality disorder, it too may be linked to lower than normal levels of physiological arousal, which is one theoretical explanation for sociopathic behavior.

Personality Disorders

It's difficult to get a good diagnostic grip on these disorders, and they are notoriously hard to treat successfully. They involve long term patterns of personality that disrupt one's life.

The essential personality disorders for AP Exam preparation are summarized below:

- **anti-social personality disorder:** this is <u>not</u> a reference to someone who is shy or socially withdrawn; rather, it refers to an individual who is rebellious, deceitful, manipulative, often hurtful, with no apparent sense of remorse or empathy. The term is essentially synonymous with 'sociopath' and 'psychopath'

- **narcissistic personality disorder:** marked by an exaggerated sense of one's own value and importance

- **histrionic personality disorder:** marked by an insatiable need and search for attention and a tendency toward highly emotional behavior

- **paranoid personality disorder:** persistent suspiciousness marked by a chronic sense of being observed and persecuted

- **borderline personality disorder:** the key word that dominates this diagnosis is 'instability'; it can be marked by sudden and intense rages, deep insecurity and fear of abandonment and general instability in relationships and emotional interaction

Where's the line? issues:

This is a good category for classroom discussion on the labeling issue. We all can think of people we know who are somewhat narcissistic, but do they meet the criteria for narcissistic personality disorder? We all know of cases in which a person was deeply hurt by the loss of a relationship and acted in somewhat irrational ways in response, but is that borderline personality disorder? Are these "disorders" or merely extremes within the "normal" range of human behavior?

Etiology of Personality Disorders:

There appear to be some **physiological differences** in those with anti-social personality disorder. These mainly involve reduced arousal levels. Such individuals do not seem to respond to arousing stimuli in the same way as those without the disorder. **Behaviorists** or **sociocultural theorists** might examine the home environments of those with anti-social personality disorder, to see if and how limitations on inappropriate actions were imposed during childhood. Behaviorists might also propose that those with personality disorders are somehow reinforced in their actions.

Somatoform Disorders

These are disorders with physical symptoms but no apparent physical cause. The causes seem to be *psychological*, but the symptoms are "real" and are not the result of malingering.

The somatoform disorders you should know for the AP test are summarized below:

- **conversion disorder:** so-called because the sufferer is essentially converting *psychological* stress into *physical* symptoms, as in a soldier who becomes paralyzed under the stress of battle and truly cannot move, even though no organic problem can be found

- **hypochondriasis:** this involves a preoccupation with the persistent fear that one has an illness, even in the face of medical evidence to the contrary

- **body dysmorphic disorder:** characterized by intense anxiety about a perceived physical deformity or defect

Where's the line? issues:

Conversion disorder is dramatic, clearcut and pretty near impossible to "fake", so the "normal vs. abnormal" line is clear. Hypochondriasis may present a problem however. Many people use the term "hypochondriac" in everyday conversation, but when is it clinically appropriate? Certainly if it is causing the individual significant personal distress that is one signal of a serious problem. The person's behavior may also be disturbing to co-workers or family members, which is another of the psychological criteria for 'abnormality'. It might be interesting for you to discuss possible cultural contributions to the presence of body dysmorphic disorder. In a world overrun by images of how one is "supposed" to look, is it more likely that individuals will be unable to see themselves accurately and affectionately?

Etiology of Somatoform Disorders:

A **psychoanalyst** would certainly focus on unconscious defense against trauma in explaining conversion disorder. Some **behaviorists** argue that such a condition might actually be a cry for attention, which if given would reinforce the presence of symptoms. This argument might also apply to those with hypochondriasis. A **cognitive** therapist might explore a hyponchondriac's exaggerated ways of thinking about and explaining bodily sensations that others might judge to be routine.

Eating Disorders

You are probably familiar with the basic symptoms of **anorexia nervosa** (marked by an intense fear of gaining weight or being fat which in turn leads to eating habits that result in substantially below normal body weight) and **bulimia nervosa** (characterized by an eating pattern of binging and purging), as they are very much a part of popular culture discussion.

Where's the line? issues:

Bulimia nervosa can be harder to diagnose because those who are bulimic are often not as obviously underweight as someone with anorexia. The DSM sets a threshold for an anorexic diagnosis at a body weight which is less than 85% of what would be expected for that individual. Our culture also makes this difficult – what, after all, is 'thin'? too thin? 'attractive'? unattractive? The media and society at large send all kinds of messages about such things which complicate the picture.

Etiology of Eating Disorders:

A **behaviorist** would focus on contingencies of reinforcement that may in the past have rewarded control. Certainly many would argue that "control" plays a role in the development of eating disorders, in the sense of being able to choose what, how and whether one eats. A proponent of **cognitive theory** might attribute eating disorders to the distorted self image that so many sufferers seem to have. Some link eating disorders to obsessive-compulsive disorder, and some medications for the latter condition help with eating disorders as well. Those most interested in **biomedical** explanations might also look at why eating disorders are so much more common in females than in males. Of course, that fact also requires **sociocultural** consideration, as does the fact that there are significant cultural differences in the rates of diagnosis of eating disorders.

Name Hall of Fame

David Rosenhan's important study of institutions and diagnostic labels is often referred to simply as "The Rosenhan Study", so it is imperative that you know his name. That's about it in this unit.

Essay Themes

This is a unit for you to emphasize in your studying. Several free response items in the past have focused on descriptions and treatments of psychological disorders. The major schools of psychological thought emerge again here, and you already know how important it is to be conversant with them. Even though the creators of the AP Psychology Exam are very careful about the distribution of items on the multiple choice section of the test (this unit is another that is allotted 7 to 9 % of those 100 questions), students have been known to report that "it seemed to be all about Abnormal Psych!" That may be because there is so much overlap between this unit and others, making it difficult to determine where one unit begins and another ends. This should further convince you to give Abnormal Psychology your full attention.

Test Preparation: Abnormal Psychology

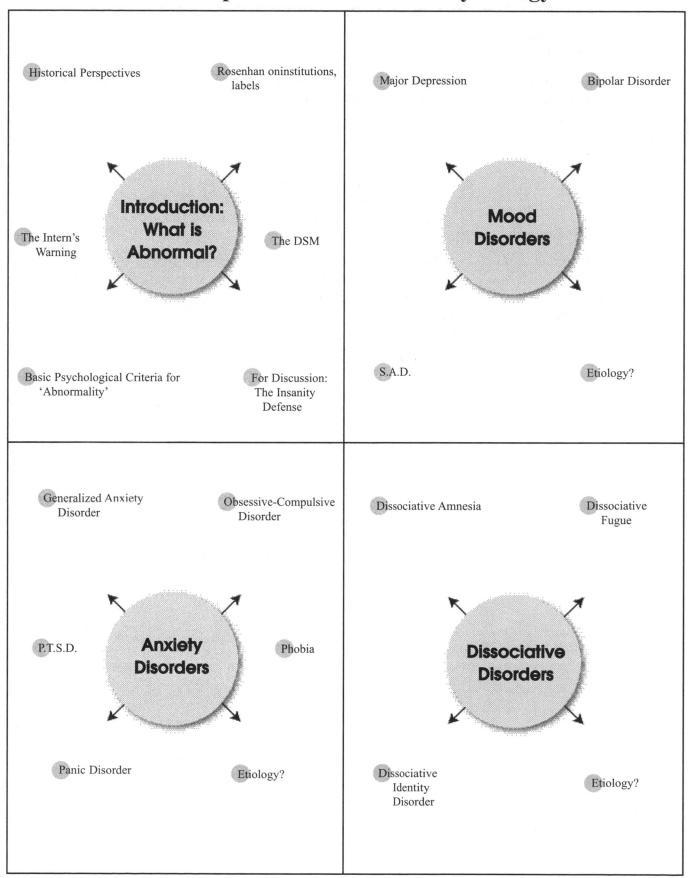

Introduction: What is Abnormal?

Historical Perspectives

Rosenhan oninstitutions, labels

The Intern's Warning

The DSM

Basic Psychological Criteria for 'Abnormality'

For Discussion: The Insanity Defense

Mood Disorders

Major Depression

Bipolar Disorder

S.A.D.

Etiology?

Anxiety Disorders

Generalized Anxiety Disorder

Obsessive-Compulsive Disorder

P.T.S.D.

Phobia

Panic Disorder

Etiology?

Dissociative Disorders

Dissociative Amnesia

Dissociative Fugue

Dissociative Identity Disorder

Etiology?

Test Preparation: Abnormal Psychology

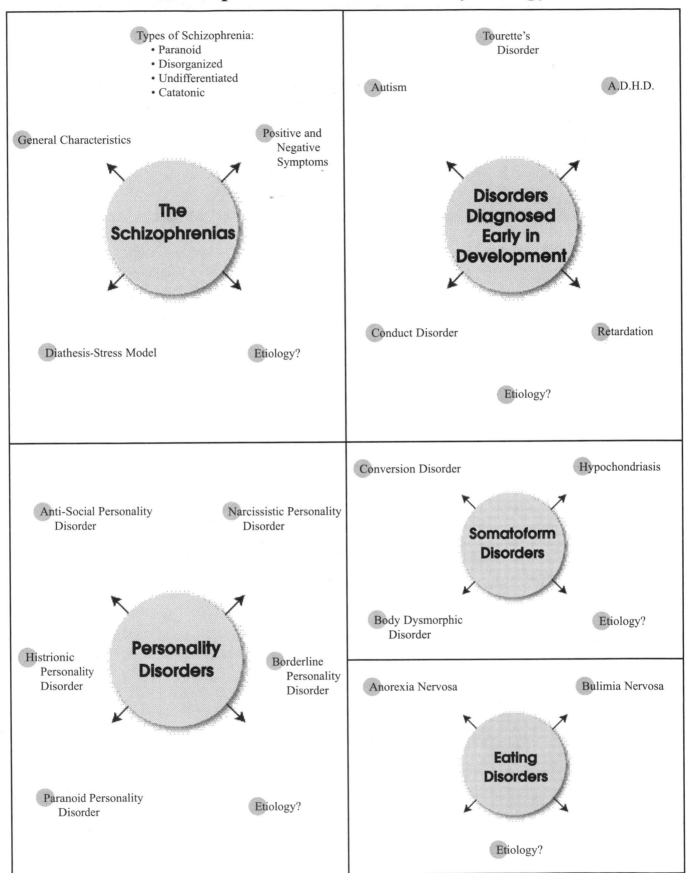

Types of Schizophrenia:
• Paranoid
• Disorganized
• Undifferentiated
• Catatonic

General Characteristics

Positive and Negative Symptoms

The Schizophrenias

Diathesis-Stress Model

Etiology?

Tourette's Disorder

Autism

A.D.H.D.

Disorders Diagnosed Early in Development

Conduct Disorder

Retardation

Etiology?

Anti-Social Personality Disorder

Narcissistic Personality Disorder

Histrionic Personality Disorder

Personality Disorders

Borderline Personality Disorder

Paranoid Personality Disorder

Etiology?

Conversion Disorder

Hypochondriasis

Somatoform Disorders

Body Dysmorphic Disorder

Etiology?

Anorexia Nervosa

Bulimia Nervosa

Eating Disorders

Etiology?

166

Practice Items

1. Twenty eight year old Jake's behavior is characterized by lack of self control, impulsiveness, consistent defiance of authority and a lack of empathy or remorse. These characteristics are most consistent with

   (A) factitious disorder
   (B) anti-social personality disorder
   (C) histrionic personality disorder
   (D) posttraumatic stress disorder
   (E) conduct disorder

2. Which of the following categories involve psychological stressors which translate into physical symptoms?

   (A) anxiety disorders
   (B) somatoform disorders
   (C) adjustment disorders
   (D) affective disorders
   (E) psychotic disorders

3. Tom and Jim are identical twins, while Matthew and Robert are fraternal twins. If Tom and Matthew are afflicted by schizophrenia

   (A) there is a better chance that Robert will also develop schizophrenia
   (B) there is a better chance that Jim will also develop schizophrenia
   (C) there is an equal chance that Robert and Jim will develop schizophrenia
   (D) Robert and Jim are statistically less likely to develop schizophrenia
   (E) Jim will develop schizophrenia and Robert may develop schizophrenia

4. The presence of dissociative identity disorder is

   (A) strongly correlated with physical or sexual abuse in childhood
   (B) strongly correlated with the presence of disorganized schizophrenia
   (C) strongly correlated with the presence of catatonic schizophrenia
   (D) typically temporary
   (E) linked to malfunctions in the dopamine circuit

5. Which of the following is NOT consistent with a general diagnosis of schizophrenia?

   (A) hallucinations
   (B) flattened affect
   (C) delusions
   (D) amnesia for recent events
   (E) disorganized thought processes

6. A cognitive theorist would most likely view anxiety as being the result of

   (A) unresolved unconscious conflict
   (B) flawed contingencies of reinforcement
   (C) self defeating, maladaptive thought processes
   (D) brain structure abnormalities
   (E) neurotransmitter abnormalities in the central nervous system

7. Enlarged ventricles in the brain, an excess of dopamine activity and frontal lobe dysfunction are all correlated with the presence of

   (A) eating disorders
   (B) bipolar disorder
   (C) schizophrenia
   (D) dissociative identity disorder
   (E) depersonalization disorder

8. You are a behavioral psychologist. A person you know has such a fear of horses that he refuses to go anywhere near a neighboring farm where several horses are stabled. If asked to explain this phobia, you would most likely argue that

   (A) horses are symbolic of the man's unconscious fear of his father
   (B) the man was born with a genetic predisposition for anxiety and fear
   (C) the man was likely deprived of loving interaction in early childhood
   (D) the man needs to be shown that his perception that horses are to be feared is distorted and unreasonable
   (E) the man is being reinforced for not going near the farm by a reduction in anxiety when he steers clear of it

9. Narcissistic personality disorder is characterized by

   (A) an inflated sense of one's uniqueness and importance
   (B) an unstable self image
   (C) catatonic behavior and a tendency toward social isolation
   (D) intense superstitiousness and other odd beliefs
   (E) social inhibition and feelings of inadequacy

10. A woman reports she feels disgustingly dirty unless she bathes and changes clothes at least four times a day, and that her house is not acceptable for visitors unless she scrubs the toilet twice daily. These characteristics are symptomatic of

   (A) dissociative fugue
   (B) obsessive-compulsive disorder
   (C) disorganized schizophrenia
   (D) schizotypal personality disorder
   (E) S.A.D.

11. Months after surviving a hurricane which destroyed his home, Louis feels persistent anxiety and irritability and experiences recurring nightmares about the disaster. These symptoms are consistent with

   (A) generalized anxiety disorder
   (B) conversion disorder
   (C) tardive dyskinesia
   (D) posttraumatic stress disorder
   (E) borderline personality disorder

12. Evidence suggests a correlation between the presence of major depression and

   (A) a damaged cerebellum
   (B) enlarged temporal lobes
   (C) elevated endorphin levels
   (D) lower than normal levels of dopamine and G.A.B.A. activity
   (E) lower than normal levels of serotonin and norepinephrine activity

13. Autism and A.D.H.D. are considered developmental disorders because

   (A) their symptoms worsen slowly over a period of years
   (B) even without medical intervention their symptoms tend to improve over time
   (C) the symptoms of each tend to emerge at the same point in adolescence
   (D) they are not neurological in origin
   (E) they are typically diagnosed in childhood

14. A disoriented 37 year old woman is discovered wandering in a park, and reports no recollection of her identity or how she got there. After an investigation the police learn she actually has a husband and child and lives over 200 miles away. This woman most likely suffers from

(A) dissociative fugue
(B) Rett's Disorder
(C) Tourette's Disorder
(D) schizoaffective disorder
(E) senile dementia

15. Benjamin experiences a pattern of severely depressed mood and lack of energy alternating with periods of greatly elevated emotions and activity levels. This is consistent with a diagnosis of

(A) impulse control disorder
(B) avoidant personality disorder
(C) bipolar disorder
(D) dysthymic disorder
(E) hypomania

Chapter XIII

Treatment of Psychological Disorders

Introduction

If you ever have the chance, take a course on the history of psychology. It is an often overlooked topic, but it's quite interesting. The history of the treatment of "psychological" disorders is fascinating, and tells us much about the times in which such therapies were used. We place the word psychological in quotation marks because some psychological conditions were thought at one time to be the work of demons or evil spirits who had possessed the body of the victim. Indeed, one historical treatment technique, called *trephining*, involved the drilling of a hole in the skull of the patient in an attempt to show such spirits the door.

The institutions which housed mental patients in the past were often frightening places. In some of them the public could pay to view institutionalized patients, much as one might visit a zoo. Reformers like **Philipe Pinel** in early 19th century France, his contemporary, Philadelphian **Benjamin Rush** and **Dorothea Dix** in 19th century America, along with many others, tried with some success to invite society to see that those suffering from mental illness required nurturance and treatment, not incarceration. In the late 20th century there was a widespread movement toward **de-institutionalization**, which was at least in part founded on the view that those with mental disorders could be helped and even completely cured. Today there is a wide array of professionals who offer such help.

A **psychiatrist** is a medical doctor with a specialty in mental health. Because he or she is an M.D., a psychiatrist can prescribe medications. A **clinical psychologist** may also be a 'doctor', but has a PhD rather than an M.D.; thus, if such a professional suggested medication as part of your treatment, he or she would have to refer you to a psychiatrist or other medical doctor to obtain a prescription. A **counselor or counseling psychologist** is another professional licensed to practice psychotherapy. It's likely that individual would have a master's degree or doctorate in clinical psychology or a related discipline.

As we turn now to the major therapeutic schools of thought, please keep in mind that many therapists of today are actually **eclectic** in their approach. They rely on many different techniques, borrowed from many different models, in their attempt to tailor treatment specifically to the individual patient at hand. In fact, research suggests that the key to a successful therapeutic experience depends most on the level of **warmth and trust in the relationship** between patient and therapist, not on the particular orientation of the psychologist. The therapist's ability to **offer an objective, caring and professional view** of the patient's life and issues seems to be of greatest importance.

Psychoanalytic/Psychodynamic Model

The label 'psychoanalyst' is *not* a catch-all term for any type of therapist, even though it is sometimes used as such in everyday language. A psychoanalyst is a particular kind of clinician, whose techniques are based on Sigmund Freud's and Carl Jung's theories of the unconscious mind. A psychoanalyst is usually a medical doctor. As part of a psychoanalyst's training, he or she would actually undergo analysis themselves. This focuses on **the achievement of insight through the uncovering of unconscious internal conflict**. Such analysis involves use of techniques like:

* **free association:** in classical psychoanalysis, the patient lies on a couch or sits on a chair while the analyst sits out of the sight line of the patient. This theoretically facilitates free association, in which the patient lets their mind roam freely from topic to topic, emotion to emotion. The idea is that the patient expresses whatever comes to mind and at some point reveals important things that might be at the heart of one's troubles. The release of such feelings can be **cathartic** for the patient

* **word association:** first developed by Carl Jung, this involves immediate, uncensored response to words given by the analyst. The idea is to say the first thing that comes to mind, without editing. Jung placed emphasis not only on what was said but how long it took to say it – delay in responding could imply **blocking** or **resistance**, which meant the patient was fighting what he or she really wanted to say

* **dream interpretation:** as you know, Freud referred to dreams as "the royal road to the unconscious" and many analysts today still rely heavily on interpretation of the latent content of dreams (the underlying, hidden themes in a dream), analyzing details which may be symbolic of issues in the patient's life

Over the long term of analysis, a psychoanalyst would likely expect and perhaps nurture to some extent a phenomenon known as **transference**. In this, the patient begins to feel feelings for the analyst that actually represent feelings they have toward a significant person in their life, such as a parent. There are obvious dangers in this, but if handled appropriately by the analyst it can offer insights into the patient's genuine emotions and conflicts. **Countertransference**, in which the analyst begins to project feelings from their own relationships onto the patient, is undesirable.

The more modern **psychodynamic** therapy is essentially a condensed version of the traditional psychoanalytic approach. One criticism of the latter is that it involved multiple weekly sessions which might continue for many years, making it prohibitively expensive for all but the wealthy. The psychodynamic approach attempts to address this issue by focusing a bit more on the here and now and how the present is impacted by unconscious, early childhood issues. The patient usually has once weekly sessions, and therapy is less long term than traditional analysis.

Psychoanalysis is also criticized because much of it is built on a kind of circular argument. For example: if an analyst contends that the patient is repressing a painful early childhood trauma, and the patient denies it, it's possible for the analyst to argue that the patient's resistance is proof of the repression. Since the unconscious mind is not observable, any conjectures as to what is going on in there must remain conjectures and cannot be "proven" or "disproven".

Behavioral Model

The behavioral treatment model is built on the fundamental premises of classical and operant conditioning along with social learning. Behavioral treatments per se are not *"talking cures"* like psychoanalysis or humanistic approaches. Rather, they directly address behaviors and the conditioning which supports them. You may wish to review the unit on Learning Theory to refresh your memory on the work of important behaviorists like B. F. Skinner and John B. Watson. Look as well at Ivan Pavlov's work in the classical conditioning of dogs, and Albert Bandura's concept of observational learning.

Token economies are built upon the principles of operant conditioning. In some schools and institutions, individuals are given reinforcers for desired behavior. These reinforcers may have no intrinsic value, but they can be traded in at some later point for something that truly is reinforcing for the individual, such as pizza, or free time, or vacation extensions. In one study a token economy was set up in which chimps performed tasks in exchange for poker chips which they could then use to "buy" bananas. The animals quickly learned to value the poker chips even though they have no inherent worth to a chimp.

Aversive therapy incorporates fundamentals of conditioning in attempting to stop problematic behaviors. A common example involves the use of *antabuse* for those who wish to stop drinking alcohol. The volunteer regularly takes antabuse, which has no effect unless it combines with alcohol. Such a combination induces nausea and vomiting. The idea is to associate the previously desirable act of drinking with unpleasant illness, resulting in an aversion to drinking.

Statistically, the most successful of all treatment approaches is that of **systematic desensitization** of phobias. The basic behavioral argument is that phobias are conditioned fears, so it is not surprising that those theorists believe simply in de-conditioning those responses. In order to extinguish an intense fear of rodents, for example, a behaviorist would first teach the patient some basic breathing and relaxation techniques. He or she would then ask the patient to list events associated with rodents which cause the patient fear. Such a list might include seeing a photograph of a rat, knowing that rats may be nearby, being in the same room as a rat and so on. The events would then be placed in order of intensity by the patient, with the most intense trigger at the top of the list.

The next step in this behavioral process involves exposure to the least provocative event on the list. The patient utilizes relaxation techniques to modulate their level of fear. When the patient learns to substitute relaxation for fear at this level of exposure, therapist and patient move onto the next most stressful event on the "anxiety hierarchy", and so on up the ladder of intensity. Systematic desensitization is sometimes called *counterconditioning* because of this idea of replacing one response with another, more desirable one.

In some rare cases, individuals have overcome phobias through full intensity exposure to the object of fear. It's possible, for example, that a person with a deep seated fear of leaving the home could be "cured" if forced out of the home by a fire or other emergency. If, after the expected period of extreme anxiety, the individual arrived at the realization that there was no danger in that environment, the phobic response might reach extinction. This kind of **flooding** is not a desirable therapeutic approach, for obvious ethical reasons, but **implosion or implosive therapy** is sometimes used by behaviorists. It is a kind of "mental flooding", in which the patient is guided to visualize a highly stressful exposure to the object of the phobia. In this way, the individual can learn to greet that image with relaxation rather than fear. Recently, behavioral therapists have begun to use **virtual reality technology** toward the same end.

One might also extinguish a phobia through the use of **modeling**. An individual suffering from a mouse phobia might watch the therapist or another "model" playing with or handling a mouse and learn to imitate that modeled behavior.

A long standing criticism of behavioral techniques is that they fail to address the root causes of the condition in question. They deal with the symptoms, critics say, but don't really get at the true issue. Some also critique behavioral approaches on the grounds that patients are conditioned and de-conditioned in the same way one might deal with pigeons or mice. These opponents argue that human emotion and thought processes are given short shrift in the behaviorists' world.

Cognitive Model

Perhaps because of the final criticism of behaviorism noted above, behaviorism is often wedded to the cognitive approach in therapy. The **cognitive-behavioral approach** combines the emphasis on overt behaviors from the behaviorist's perspective with the cognitivist's focus on the hurtful, irrational thought processes of the patient. A cognitive-behaviorist would therefore work to change the undesired behaviors of a patient while also attacking self defeating cognitions held by the individual.

You might remember from earlier units some references to the concept of **explanatory styles**, as formulated by **Martin Seligman**. He argued that some people have a pessimistic explanatory style, characterized by the tendency to blame bad events on themselves and to expect such events to be long lasting and to negatively impact one's entire life. This is but one example of a cognitive explanation for unhappiness. Two other cognitive views of therapy come from **Albert Ellis** and **Aaron Beck**. Ellis was the founder of **rational-emotive therapy (R.E.T.)**, in which the therapist boldly challenges the irrational or unjustifiable cognitions of the patient. The goal is to see the world and one's place in it more accurately, and to reduce self blame and self denigration. Beck proposed the concept of the **cognitive triad**, in which he theorized that many unhappy people have negative thoughts about themselves, events that occur around them and the future. Beck emphasized taking a realistic, objective look at these interpretations.

Of course, sometimes things really *are* bad, and your unhappiness is based in a quite reasonable response to difficult times. Some also find particular trouble with Ellis's R.E.T., because he was known to be quite confrontational with his patients.

Humanistic Model

The humanistic approach to therapy is usually viewed as the most optimistic and life affirming of the talking cures. Indeed, one criticism of the model is that it is naively positive about human motives and desires.

Humanists believe that the client is in charge of his or her own advancement. Humanists tend to prefer the term 'client' over 'patient' to emphasize this focus on the individual's need (and desire) to help him or herself. The humanistic therapist hopes to support the client in their quest for happiness by offering what **Carl Rogers** called **unconditional positive regard (U.P.R.)**. Rogers feared that most relationships in life were marked by **conditions of worth** (as in when someone seems to "love" you only because you're wealthy, or physically attractive), and that a healthy therapeutic situation would provide empathy and help with no strings attached and no judgments offered. Rogers **client centered therapy** (also called *person centered therapy*) is the hallmark humanistic treatment.

Humanist **Abraham Maslow** contended that most people want to become **self actualized**, to reach their fullest potential as human beings. Rogers too believed that people had a sense of their **ideal self,** which most individuals aspired to reach. Humanists like Rogers and Maslow would likely argue that the cause of most unhappiness is the knowledge that there is a chasm between one's **real self** (another Rogerian term) and one's ideal self. The goal of therapy is for the client to take on the task of closing that gap.

Gestalt therapy is a kind of humanistic approach, even though its founder, **Fritz Perls**, was trained as a psychoanalyst. You may recognize the term 'gestalt' from our study of Sensation and Perception; there, it referred to the human tendency to organize perceptions of the world into meaningful wholes. The goal of gestalt therapy is to help the client become more "whole" by pulling together the separate parts of one's self, just as all the king's men tried to re-assemble Humpty Dumpty's disparate pieces. The gestalt therapist encourages the client to face the unresolved turmoil in their life in the present moment. Thus, Perls was breaking from the psychoanalytic focus on the past, while also emphasizing the humanistic view that the burden of recovery lies with the client.

Group, Family and Community Approaches

There are many advantages to **meeting in a group with others who share similar problems**. It can be very reassuring early on simply to recognize that there are others who share similar problems. Those individuals can also offer thoughts and advice, based on their experiences, that may help the other members of the group. The simple act of affiliating with a group can be very comforting, and can offer opportunities to refine one's social skills and deepen all relationships in each member's life. Group therapy is also less expensive than one-on-one treatment.

"tough love groups"

Family therapy (or **family systems therapy**) brings the members of a family together to explore the dynamics within that complex group. This approach is based on the idea that each member of the family is part of a web of interdependence. Thus, the emphasis is on each individual as a part of the unit, and how the interactions between each component of the group impact each member.

Community psychology models focus, at a grass roots level, on prevention and early intervention. The goal is to help those with psychological problems at the local level, partly because many people can not afford or do not have access to larger institutions. In fact, the movement toward de-institutionalization, mentioned earlier in this unit, is part of the community psychology model. Ideally, individuals who are at risk for developing disorders, or who have already begun to exhibit symptoms, are cared for more quickly, comfortably and conveniently at the local level.

Biomedical Model

The obvious emphasis here is on physical interventions which directly address the symptoms of various disorders.

A dramatically controversial and now largely outmoded technique is that of psychosurgery. In the middle of the 20th century especially, surgical procedures were sometimes done on violent patients. The **prefrontal lobotomy**, for example, involved the disconnection of the frontal lobes (the "executive" portion of the cortex) from the thalamus in the mid-brain. This often succeeded in eliminating aggression in the patients, but also tended to leave them emotionally and cognitively impaired for the rest of their lives.

Electroconvulsive therapy (ECT) is another controversial treatment which is still sometimes utilized today, although in a more evolved form than earlier in the 20th century. It is very occasionally used as a treatment for severe depression which has been resistant to other forms of therapy. The patient receives muscle relaxants and is briefly put to sleep . Next, an electric current is administered. The goal is to induce a seizure, and something about the seizure often alleviates, at least temporarily, the symptoms of the depression. It is still not particularly well understood just how that process "works". It is a popular misconception that "shock treatments" are used as punishment in institutions. While E.C.T. remains controversial, it is not used to threaten or punish patients. It is, however, still sometimes marked by side effects such as memory impairment.

A very new procedure called **repetitive transcranial magnetic stimulation (rTMS)** is being proposed as an alternative to E.C.T. In it, the brain is stimulated using electromagnets. Like E.C.T., there are questions about just what it does and how it works, but many individuals who have not benefited from other therapeutic approaches have found relief from their depression after rTMS treatments.

Another technique that addresses the biological roots of a disorder is the use of **light therapy** for sufferers of seasonal affective disorder. That is characterized by depression which comes with the change of seasons. The reduced levels of light during winter seem to be at the root of this mood disorder, so patients are often systematically exposed to light in order to alleviate symptoms.

As you may recall from the last chapter, **lithium carbonate** is one of several treatments used to help those with bipolar disorder, and the one that you are most likely to encounter on the Advanced Placement Exam.

Three other categories of psychotropic drugs are **anti-depressant**, **anti-anxiety** and **anti-psychotic** medications:

Early anti-depressants such the **the tricyclics** and **MAO inhibitors** operated by increasing norepinephrine and serotonin activity in the brain. Even more popular now are a group of drugs known as **selective serotonin reuptake inhibitors (S.S.R.I.'s)**. As their name suggests, these medications slow the reuptake of serotonin, leaving more of it in the synapse and thus facilitating more serotonin activity. Prozac is a selective serotonin reuptake inhibitor which is used not only as an anti-depressant but also for obsessive-compulsive disorder, eating disorders, and more.

The major group of **anti-anxiety medications** (or tranquilizers) which is most likely to appear on the AP Exam are the benzodiazepenes. Two well known examples from this group are **Valium** and **Xanax**. In essence, these drugs stimulate inhibition. They increase levels of G.A.B.A. activity; you may recall that G.A.B.A. is the most plentiful inhibitory neurotransmitter in the brain.

Anti-psychotic drugs operate on the neurotransmitter dopamine. Schizophrenia (once known as a "psychotic" disorder) is marked by unusually high levels of dopamine, and medications for it block or inhibit dopamine activity.

Many of the above mentioned drugs can have side effects, ranging from dry mouth to irritability to drowsiness to sexual dysfunction. Anti-psychotic drugs were once notorious for occasional severe side effects such as *tardive dyskinesia*. It is marked by facial tics and contortions, lip smacking and other involuntary movements, and can be irreversible if not caught early. As therapists have learned more about appropriate dosage levels, such side effects are less common than before.

It is impossible to say in a sentence or two which therapeutic approach is best. As mentioned earlier, the success of talking cures seems more related to the relationship between sufferer and therapist than to the academic orientation of the professional. It's also quite important to recognize that the success of any particular treatment depends on the disorder. Systematic desensitization is a very effective treatment for phobias, but how would one apply it to schizophrenia? Naturally, no one would prescribe an anti-psychotic medication to an individual suffering from generalized anxiety disorder. A talking therapy which focuses on early childhood trauma might be very appropriate for an individual with dissociative identity disorder but not someone with seasonal affective disorder. It seems wise to tailor the therapy to the specific needs of the patient.

Name Hall of Fame

Sigmund Freud and **B.F. Skinner**.... sound familiar?

There are other people to know in this unit. On the AP Examination, the name **Albert Ellis** is usually mentioned in the same breath with his rational-emotive therapy, from the cognitive school of thought. **Aaron Beck** may deserve just as much recognition in that area, although in the past he has shown up less often on the exam. Neo-Freudians like **Carl Jung**, **Alfred Adler** and **Karen Horney** may appear, as you already know. You met **David Rosenhan** in the last unit on Abnormal Psychology and his research on institutionalization and labeling fits in this chapter as well, and **Abraham Maslow's** name has figured prominently in units on Motivation and Personality Theory, along with this one.

Carl Rogers is so closely linked to his client or person centered therapy that it is often referred to as a "Rogerian" approach, so know his name as well.

Essay Themes

As we mentioned in the last unit, clinical psychology has been a common topic for free response items on past Advanced Placement Examinations. Fortunately, your grasp on the treatment unit should have been enhanced by your earlier study of Personality Theory. As you saw there, knowing about the **major schools of psychological thought** is of paramount importance for success on the big test.

Test Preparation: Treatment of Psychological Disorders

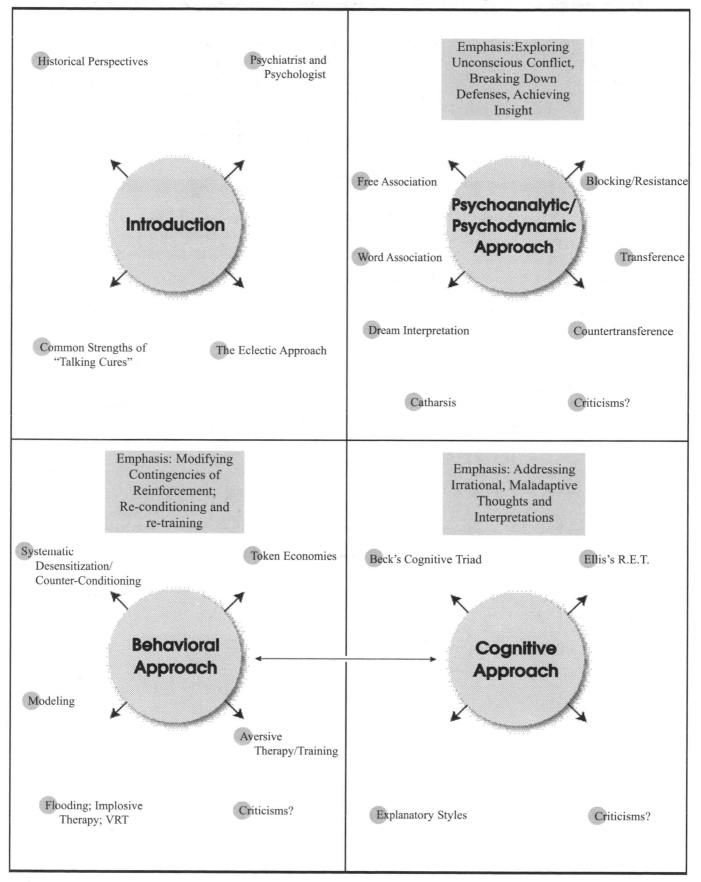

Historical Perspectives

Psychiatrist and Psychologist

Introduction

Common Strengths of "Talking Cures"

The Eclectic Approach

Emphasis:Exploring Unconscious Conflict, Breaking Down Defenses, Achieving Insight

Free Association

Blocking/Resistance

Psychoanalytic/ Psychodynamic Approach

Word Association

Transference

Dream Interpretation

Countertransference

Catharsis

Criticisms?

Emphasis: Modifying Contingencies of Reinforcement; Re-conditioning and re-training

Systematic Desensitization/ Counter-Conditioning

Token Economies

Behavioral Approach

Modeling

Aversive Therapy/Training

Flooding; Implosive Therapy; VRT

Criticisms?

Emphasis: Addressing Irrational, Maladaptive Thoughts and Interpretations

Beck's Cognitive Triad

Ellis's R.E.T.

Cognitive Approach

Explanatory Styles

Criticisms?

179

Test Preparation: Treatment of Psychological Disorders

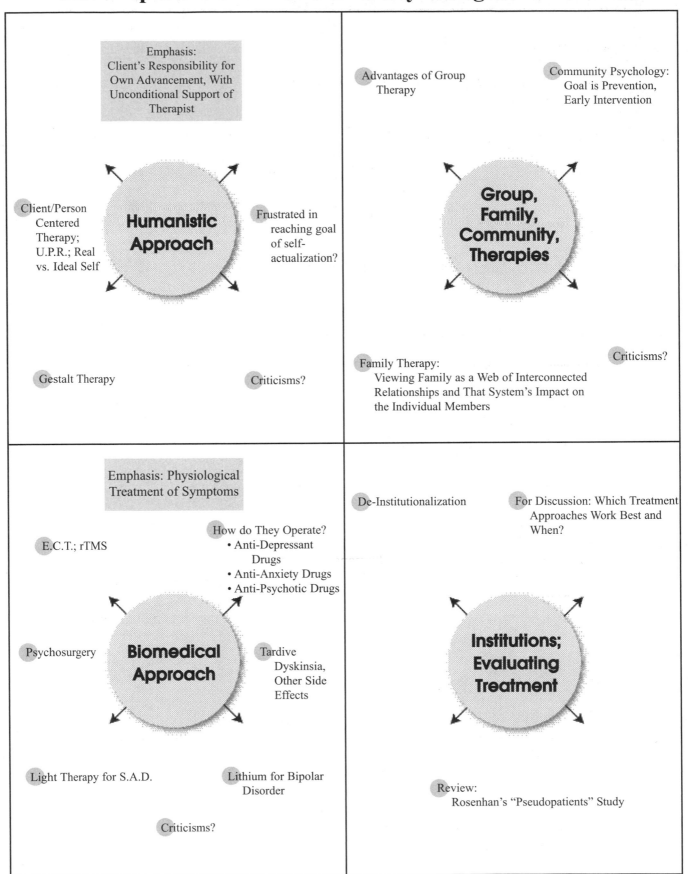

Emphasis: Client's Responsibility for Own Advancement, With Unconditional Support of Therapist

Humanistic Approach

Client/Person Centered Therapy; U.P.R.; Real vs. Ideal Self

Frustrated in reaching goal of self-actualization?

Gestalt Therapy

Criticisms?

Advantages of Group Therapy

Community Psychology: Goal is Prevention, Early Intervention

Group, Family, Community, Therapies

Family Therapy: Viewing Family as a Web of Interconnected Relationships and That System's Impact on the Individual Members

Criticisms?

Emphasis: Physiological Treatment of Symptoms

E.C.T.; rTMS

How do They Operate?
• Anti-Depressant Drugs
• Anti-Anxiety Drugs
• Anti-Psychotic Drugs

Biomedical Approach

Psychosurgery

Tardive Dyskinsia, Other Side Effects

Light Therapy for S.A.D.

Lithium for Bipolar Disorder

Criticisms?

De-Institutionalization

For Discussion: Which Treatment Approaches Work Best and When?

Institutions; Evaluating Treatment

Review: Rosenhan's "Pseudopatients" Study

180

Practice Items

1. A humanistic therapist would most likely criticize a behavioral therapist on the following grounds:

    (A) behavioral approaches tend to get stuck in interpretations of the root causes of the patient's behaviors
    (B) behavioral approaches ignore the importance of uncovering the powerful unconscious conflict rooted in early childhood
    (C) behavioral approaches lack empirical support for their claims of success
    (D) behavioral approaches are not empathetic and supportive enough of the whole person
    (E) behavioral approaches put too much of the burden on the client for their own healing

2. Lithium carbonate is a common treatment for

    (A) seasonal affective disorder
    (B) major depression
    (C) social phobia
    (D) bipolar disorder
    (E) anti-social personality disorder

3. The major goal of the community psychology movement is

    (A) establishment of token economies operated on a community level
    (B) prevention or early intervention
    (C) to build and administer more humane mental institutions in more communities
    (D) to identify those communities with higher than normal rates of mental illness and establish institutions there
    (E) to make behavioral and cognitive therapies more readily available in small towns

4. A behaviorist would likely criticize the psychoanalytic/psychodynamic approach on the grounds that psychoanalysts

    (A) focus too much attention on the self defeating thoughts of the patient
    (B) overemphasize the impact of current family dynamics on the individual's dysfunction
    (C) expend too much effort on alleged, unobservable causes of problems that may be illusory
    (D) progress so quickly that the patient does not reap long term benefits
    (E) look to foster self-actualization at the expense of addressing the actual symptoms of disorders

5. According to Carl Rogers, the role of the therapist in client centered therapy is to

    (A) help modify the self destructive thinking of the client
    (B) help the client see where they've been at fault
    (C) offer warmth, empathy and support
    (D) condition the client to behave more adaptively
    (E) enable the client to transfer negative emotions onto the therapist

6. The purpose of free association techniques is to

    (A) facilitate self-actualization
    (B) help bring unconscious conflict to the surface
    (C) focus the patient on the here and now
    (D) add structure to the patient's thought processes
    (E) help the patient to relax with the therapeutic process

7. A family systems therapist is most likely to

    (A) focus attention at first on the thoughts and behaviors of the most maladjusted family members
    (B) focus attention at first on the thoughts and behaviors of the most well adjusted family members
    (C) view each family member not in isolation but as a part of the whole family unit
    (D) explore the individual perspectives of each family member to encourage a sense of personal autonomy in relation to the family unit
    (E) encourage each individual member of the family to examine the contingencies of reinforcement which have governed their behaviors in the family unit

8. Tardive dyskinesia is

    (A) a major potential side effect of some anti-psychotic medications
    (B) a recently developed anti-anxiety medication
    (C) a recently developed anti-depressant medication
    (D) likely to result from electroconvulsive therapy
    (E) the most common form of psychodynamic therapy

9. Which of the following suggests catharsis has occurred?

    (A) Nate unexpectedly remembers how much he liked the girl who sat next to him in seventh grade
    (B) William resists telling his therapist about the resentment he feels toward his brother
    (C) Whitney's idea of success is owning a lot of jewelry
    (D) Alexis displays anger toward her analyst that appears to reflect anger toward her mother
    (E) Pat feels significantly better after weeping over a family tragedy

10. Which of the following techniques would likely be most effective in treating an intense fear of elevators?

    (A) aversive conditioning
    (B) dream analysis
    (C) systematic desensitization
    (D) priming
    (E) rTMS

11. Albert Ellis's rational emotive therapy was designed to

    (A) teach breathing and other relaxation techniques to his patients
    (B) challenge the self defeating cognitions of his patients
    (C) explore the models the patient had been exposed to in early childhood
    (D) utilize introspection to uncover examples of childhood trauma
    (E) facilitate the release of patients' emotions

12. Valium is

    (A) an anti-anxiety medication
    (B) an anti-psychotic medication
    (C) an anti-depressant medication
    (D) a neuroleptic
    (E) a tricyclic

13. The most effective treatment for seasonal affective disorder is

    (A) electroconvulsive therapy
    (B) modeling
    (C) aversive therapy
    (D) light therapy
    (E) gestalt therapy

14. Prozac helps some who suffer from depression by

     (A) blocking transmission of substance p
     (B) stimulating transmission of endorphins
     (C) encouraging the reuptake of dopamine
     (D) sensitizing norepinephrine receptors
     (E) blocking the reuptake of serotonin

15. Aaron Beck's cognitive triad refers to a patient's thoughts about

     (A) themselves, events in their life and the future
     (B) themselves, significant others and peripheral others
     (C) significant others, peripheral others and self image
     (D) the past, the present and the future
     (E) the world, the self and others

Chapter XIV

Social Psychology

Group Interaction

Social psychology examines the impact of groups on individuals. It is essentially the study of the interconnectedness of humans. Perhaps it is an illusion to think of ourselves as "independent" beings at all; each of us is so interdependent with the environment and the people around us. Some Buddhist meditation masters call this "interbeing" and point out how difficult it is to separate "ourselves" from everything else. Social psychology specifically explores the human interplay between self and others.

If you have ever done something in a group that you would not have done when alone, then you already have some knowledge about social psychology. **De-individuation** is a term coined to account for some individual behaviors in group settings. It usually refers to negative behavior, although it could describe any sense of the loss of identity and personal responsibility in a crowd. De-individuation helps to explain why an otherwise kind hearted, law abiding person commits a theft during a riot. It accounts for why individuals do things at a huge concert or a packed sporting event that they would not imagine doing otherwise. It's as if the group makes the individual feel more anonymous.

Sometimes individuals behave in ways that are unproductive simply because they fear *others* might do so. This is a **social trap**. When trying to merge onto a road in a crowded city, it would probably be best for all if every individual driver were patient and cooperative. A "first you go and then I'll go" ethic might actually help everyone involved – however each individual involved not only has to play along but has to believe that everyone else will play along too. Cooperation could serve the self interest of all, but everyone must cooperate and trust that others will do the same. The so-called **tragedy of the commons** is a kind of social trap. Imagine a group of shepherds who share a common grazing area which is just the right size to accommodate their flocks. One shepherd, with a perfectly reasonable desire for self improvement, decides that if he acquires one or two more animals, he can do his work better and turn a better profit besides. This self interested but understandable act will have a ripple effect on all the other shepherds, who now must share the common ground with too many sheep. If more than one shepherd has such an inclination, the problem is exacerbated. Eventually, even those who first moved to expand can also be hurt. Even when one's long term self interest is best supported by cooperation, people often end up competing, to the detriment of all.

It is possible to unite groups in a common cause through the introduction of **superordinate goals**. If a group, even a contentious one, is given a task that can be accomplished only with the cooperation of all members, that group tends to bond. Members rally around the cause to attack that overarching problem, and the effort ties them together as one.

It is not the case, however, that individuals always *want* to be "tied together as one". Research into personal space demonstrates that. While there is significant cultural and situational variation, as a general rule individuals tend to possess a sense of **personal space** which is not to be invaded without permission. Researcher Edward Hall once postulated that Americans set the boundaries of their personal territory at two or three feet; in other cultures, the bubble is bigger or smaller, but there *is* a bubble nonetheless. When that bubble is broken, people may avoid eye contact, cross arms or legs, shift the body or actually move away to reestablish a comfortable relationship. There are numerous exceptions to this of course; intimacy is often expressed through physical closeness, the rules may be different at a crowded party as compared to a library, and Hall also discussed areas of *public space* which may manifest at a beach or on an uncrowded bus. The phenomenon of territoriality is not a likely topic for the AP Examination, but it may be interesting for you to investigate it further.

Two very important concepts related to more formal group activities are group think and group polarization. Either or both may well show up on an AP Exam. In **group think**, members of a group find themselves "going along" with the flow of the group or the apparent wishes of that group's leader. Criticisms are no longer raised, alternative solutions no longer offered. Sometimes this results from each individual member's desire for a harmonious group environment, sometimes because members are deferring to a strong , perhaps even feared, leader. Today, some wise group leaders actually designate specific members of the group to be naysayers; it is that person's primary job to pose questions, offer critiques, and generally insure that group think does not occur.

In **group polarization**, group decisions end up as extreme versions of the individual members' predispositions. Get a bunch of violent people together to discuss possible military strategies and it is likely that the final group proposal will be a more aggressive one than any of the individual participants would have offered. It was once thought that groups tended to make more dangerous decisions in general than the individual members would have (the so-called *"risky shift"*), but research suggests it is more accurate to say that the group simply exaggerates the predispositions of the individuals.

In **social loafing** individuals in a group exert less effort than they would if on their own. This can be conscious but is more usually unconscious. In a tug of war game, teammates might each report they were pulling with all their might, and they might even believe that was so, but research suggests that the efforts of the entire group make it easier for each *individual* member to slack a bit.

Finally, we look at how a group of people <u>observing</u> an individual can influence that person's performance. If you are participating in a spelling bee competition or a math team event, does having an audience watching hurt you or help you? How about playing in a softball game or running in a track meet – does a big crowd help you to do better? Research in social psychology suggests that the audience influences you in ways that depend upon the task you are performing. If it is a task that you know well, and is one in which you have had success, the audience tends to aid your performance. This is known as **social facilitation**. If, on the other hand, an audience gathers round when you are trying to do something you've never done before, it's likely their presence will hinder your performance. This is called **social inhibition**. If you have won spelling competitions in each of the last five years, you'll get an additional boost from the presence of others this time around. If you sometimes misspell your own name, an audience will probably cause you to stumble even more in your spelling efforts.

Obedience to Authority

Some people use the terms 'obedience', 'compliance' and 'conformity' interchangeably, but there are definite distinctions between them. To conform is to adjust your thoughts or actions to agree with a reference group or a norm. **Obedience** refers to doing a thing because someone, often an authority figure, told you to do so, whether you like it or not. It's a bit harsher than compliance – there's an order and a person follows that order. If someone wins your *compliance*, they have essentially persuaded you to choose to do what they want you to do; to <u>comply</u> with a request implies some level of agreement on your part. More on that in a moment. First, we turn to obedience.

Stanley Milgram's study in the early 1960's on obedience to authority remains one of the most famous and controversial studies in all of psychology. Milgram wrote an entire book on the subject, and it is difficult to do justice to his work and all of its implications in this space. Simply stated, Milgram created a situation in which an authority figure (in this case, a man in a lab coat, at Yale University) ordered a volunteer to "teach" another volunteer, and to punish that "learner" if and when he made a mistake (in Milgram's original work, the learners and teachers were all men). The volunteers were led to believe that they were participating in a study on the effects of punishment on learning and memory, but Milgram was actually interested in the behavior of the "teachers" – would they physically punish another volunteer if commanded to do so?

Electric shocks were used as the punisher. The teacher could administer over two dozen levels of increasingly severe shock to the learner, up to a maximum of 450 volts. The teacher was given a low level "sample shock" before the session began, to give him a sense of what the shocks were like. The teacher was also personally introduced to the learner before things got underway. The teaching and learning was conducted via microphone – there was no visual contact after the teacher was allowed to see the learner hooked up to the shock apparatus. The teacher and learner could each hear the other quite easily; the communication alternated between questions, answers and grunts or cries of pain from the frequently incorrect learner.

Before running his study, Milgram asked many respected colleagues to forecast the outcome. They predicted that only one teacher in a thousand would administer the maximum amount of shocks, up to 450 volts, and that most would stop at around 120 volts (which would've required 3 or 4 wrong answers from the learner and the subsequent punishments delivered by the teacher).

In Milgram's original study, with 40 male teachers ranging in age from 20 to 50, approximately 2/3 went "all the way", and all teachers administered at least some shocks. This despite the fact that the learner, who had openly complained of a past heart condition upon meeting the teacher, groaned, screamed, refused to answer, screamed some more, and then stopped responding altogether in the course of the session.

In fact, no shocks were really given. The "learner" was actually in on the whole operation with Milgram. His responses and cries of pain were scripted, such that each teacher heard the same reactions to the same questions at the same points in the process. Of course the volunteer teacher didn't know any of that.

There is much to discuss in regard to this study, but we haven't the space here to touch on the variations later built into the study (introducing visual contact between teacher and learner, having the authority figure give the orders but then leave the room during the actual "teaching", and many more). The ethical guidelines for psychological research we discussed in the chapter on Research Methodology are in many ways based on the Milgram study (of course, if these volunteers had been told, for example, that "they had the right to discontinue participation at any time", Milgram would not have had much of a study). For the purposes of your AP Exam preparation and laying a foundation for future study of psychology, know that Milgram attributed the behavior of the teachers to the power of the situation. In watching film of Milgram's sessions, it is difficult not to be judgmental about the personalities of the people involved. How could they do this stuff to a screaming man with a heart condition?? Milgram would likely ask us how certain we are of what *we* would do in such a situation. In fact, when the situation was somewhat less overwhelming, results <u>were</u> a bit different. If, for example, a volunteer teacher was allowed to see another teacher refuse to continue, obedience in the first teacher went way down. When the authority figure left the room or delivered instructions by phone, obedience went down. In the original setup, the authority figure never threatened the teacher (although they did prompt teachers with phrases like "you must continue" or "the experiment requires that you continue"), but it appears the physical presence of that authority did make it harder to disobey. Investigate Milgram's work on your own – it is a very rich area for discussion and reflection.

Just in case you encounter them on the AP Exam, and because it may serve you well in the real world, we'll look at two methods of persuasion sometimes used to win compliance. They go by interesting names: **the foot-in-the-door technique** and **the door-in-the-face technique**.

If you hope to make a big commission by selling the most expensive guitar possible to a prospective buyer, you might employ a foot-in-the-door approach by first showing guitars of lesser value, while encouraging the shopper to commit to the idea of buying from you. You might invite the shopper to test out one or more of your guitars, again in an attempt to win a small commitment from him or her. Only then would you move onto the more expensive models, now that the shopper has committed, even in small ways, to the idea of buying. The technique is based on methods sometimes employed in the past by door-to-door salespeople, who operated on the assumption that if they could just "get their foot in the door", their chance of sales success was high.

The door-in-the-face technique involves starting big and then "settling". To sell the most expensive guitar possible, you might begin by showing a custom made model with a price affordable only to the wealthiest of buyers. After rejecting that purchase, coming down to a lower price is much easier for the potential buyer. A $900 guitar looks quite inexpensive compared to a $10,000 instrument. The seller thus invites the buyer to slam the door in his face, at first, in order to win compliance on a less costly, but still profitable sale. When law suits are filed requesting exorbitant settlements, or when professional athletes publicly ask for astronomical salaries, the rationale behind the numbers might well be built on the door-in-the-face approach.

Conformity

As you saw in the last section, **conformity** refers to a kind of "going along" with others or with some societal expectation. **Solomon Asch** conducted studies in the 1950's on conformity to group pressure. He seated a number of individuals together and asked them to verbally respond to some questions. All but one of the participants were confederates of Asch's, and, on some of the questions, he had coached them to give obviously incorrect answers. The idea was to see if the target volunteer went along with those answers, even against his better judgment. Asch discovered that people were quite likely to conform to the group pressure, even on items that a control group (whose members had been asked the same questions without the public group pressure) almost never answered incorrectly. It was not the case that those in his experimental setup didn't "know" the correct answers, but that having as few as three others give different responses made it very hard to resist the group consensus. Asch found that rates of conformity even increased as the size of the group increased, up to a ceiling of six or seven members; after that point, adding more confederates did not impact the results. The factor that was even more important than the size of the group was *the unanimity of the group*. As you might imagine, if even one confederate did not go along with the group, that made it much easier for the target volunteer to avoid conforming as well.

Another study you must know about is **Philip Zimbardo's "mock prison"** of the early 1970's. Zimbardo asked for student volunteers to play roles in a "prison" established at Stanford University. He was interested in the dynamics of incarceration and prison psychology. Volunteers were randomly assigned as guards and prisoners in what was designed to be a two week role play of prison life. Zimbardo had to discontinue the study after less than one week, because the volunteers had gotten too immersed in their roles. Many of the guards conformed so much to what was "expected" of the role that they began to punish, humiliate and generally make life miserable for the "prisoners", who largely tended to play the roles of powerless inmates. This study is another which contributed to today's ethical guidelines in psychological research, as many felt and still feel it was unnecessarily dangerous. You can probably think of one or two of your school mates that you would not want to have as a guard at your mock prison.

Altruism/Prosocial Behavior

When do people help others, and what factors contribute to that sort of pro-social behavior? These are questions that have probably been asked for a very long time, and they were asked again in the 1960's when a woman named Kitty Genovese was stabbed to death in New York City. Over the course of approximately 30 minutes one evening, Genovese was stabbed repeatedly while being chased by a man in the immediate area of her own apartment building. She eventually died from her wounds. Social psychologists are very interested in this tragedy because no one helped Ms. Genovese, although police later discovered that over three dozen individuals clearly heard the commotion. One neighbor called the assault into police, but only after Ms. Genovese was dead and apparently only after first calling a friend out of town to ask for advice.

Why did so many people fail to help? Psychologists offer some explanations which, collectively, comprise what is called **the bystander effect**. The fact that there *were* so many people is the basis of one explanation known as **diffusion of responsibility**. Individuals in such a situation seem to think "someone else will do it". And then, the longer things go with nobody intervening, the more likely it is that each individual will come to doubt whether anything actually needs to be done. This is called **pluralistic ignorance**. There is also an element of fear in this scenario; individuals may fear embarrassment if they intervene in a situation when help really wasn't needed, and the longer no one helps, the more it can appear that help is not needed. Of course, in the Genovese case, fear of physical harm was also a factor in the bystanders' inaction.

John Darley and Bibb Latane conducted research in response to the Genovese case which supports all of this. They found that individuals who were led to believe that a person nearby was having a seizure were more likely to help, more quickly, if they felt they were the only person aware of the situation.

Attribution Theory

In the 1950's, Fritz Heider proposed **attribution theory** to account for how each of us assigns responsibility for decisions and outcomes. He coined two terms for this: **dispositional (or personal) attributions** and **situational attributions**. If a close friend of yours wins an important tennis match, you may be more likely to attribute the friend's success to her hard work and exceptional ability (a dispositional attribution). If your friend loses a key match, you may be more likely to attribute the loss to external factors, such as bad weather or a poor umpire (a situational attribution). Heider argued that humans are often prone to the **fundamental attribution error** (or **F.A.E.**), in which they tend to disproportionately make dispositional attributions over situational ones, especially if the behavior they're evaluating is distressing or ambiguous.

We often commit the F.A.E. while driving in traffic – that person who is traveling so slowly in front of us must simply be an incompetent driver. There are many possible situational factors influencing that person's driving, but we typically give those less weight. However, we give such variables lots of weight when *we* are the ones driving slowly. In such a case, we tend to apply the **self serving bias**; if our behavior is irritating to others, it surely was a matter of an overwhelming or unavoidable circumstance, not a weakness of our own! Many of us commit the fundamental attribution error when learning about Milgrams' obedience study described earlier; we're inclined to think there's something wrong with the character of volunteers who obeyed the authority figure and we give less attention to the impact of situational forces on their decisions.

In **self handicapping**, a person offers a kind of preliminary "excuse" which they can then fall back on if they indeed do poorly on a task. If a man fears that he will fail miserably in the concert tomorrow, he may stay up very, very late tonight, and make certain everyone *knows* that he did; this provides a ready-made excuse (or attribution) if his performance is disappointing.

There is subtle but strong psychological incentive to want to believe that ours is a **just world**. This allows us to explain the misfortunes others suffer as being the result of some behavior of theirs – and *we* will be careful not to behave that way ourselves. This creates a sense of control in one's life. Some people may even read the obituary of someone the same age as themselves and look for evidence in the story of behavior that led to the death (heavy cigarette smoking for example). This may allow the reader to feel the passing was not random, that it had a "cause", that the world is an orderly place, and that he can avoid the dangers that placed that person in jeopardy.

Some psychologists believe that many of our actions are driven by the **illusion of control** – why do people so commonly push a button calling for the elevator when that button is already pushed? Some argue that it gives one a sense that it is they who are calling for the elevator, that no one else is in control of their destination or mode of travel!

Attitudes

What comes first – attitudes or behaviors? Do we humans tend to have views and judgments that govern our behaviors, or do we first act and then account for those actions by constructing attitudes which are consistent with the behaviors?

In the unit on Motivation, we touched on **cognitive dissonance theory**. It addresses this interplay between behaviors and attitudes. Essentially, we seem to strive to keep our behaviors, cognitions and attitudes consistent with one another. When they are not in agreement, the result is cognitive dissonance, a term Leon Festinger coined to describe the internal tension we experience when what we think doesn't jibe with what we do. If you claim to have a passionate interest in conservation, you will want to act in ways that are in line with that attitude. If one day you find yourself throwing plastic bags carelessly around a pristine camp site, you are likely to feel some anxiety. To relieve this dissonance, you must either change your behaviors or modify your stated attitude.

In the earlier unit on Thinking and Language Acquisition we looked at **confirmation bias**, which is relevant to this section as well. Once we have an attitude or opinion, we tend to look to support it, while sometimes overlooking evidence that might refute it. Thus, long held beliefs and attitudes can be quite resistant to change.

Another concept that is relevant to many units in introductory psychology is the **self fulfilling prophecy**. We mentioned it specifically in the earlier section on Intelligence Testing and the chapter on Psychological Disorders. In it, our own expectations actually cause them to come true. At times our attitudes about someone or something can be transparent enough that they actually influence outcomes. In a study in the late 1960's, elementary school teachers in the Boston area were led to believe that some of their new students were especially ready to blossom academically. In fact, the students were chosen at random. But, by the end of the school year those students <u>had</u> significantly improved from the year before and in comparison to their schoolmates, who did not benefit from the apparently unconscious treatment the teachers' gave to the targeted kids. Those teachers *believed* that the students were going to do well, and thus they did.

Bias/Prejudice

You may have been exposed in history classes to a study conducted by a third grade teacher in Iowa in the late 1960's which is sometimes called **the blue eyes/brown eyes study**. The teacher told her class that people with blue eyes were superior to those with brown eyes. Blue-eyed students in her class were allowed to place a stigmatizing collar on the brown-eyed kids, and in general the teacher began to treat the brown-eyed children as inferior. So too did the blue-eyed children, and very quickly at that. Many people still question the wisdom of this study, although the teacher has conducted follow-up sessions with the class which seem to indicate little long term negative fall out. The study certainly did seem to demonstrate how quickly and easily one can turn one group of people against another. History tells us it is all too easy to **scapegoat** those you deem inferior, blaming them for all wrongs.

This may be attributable to **in-group bias**. Humans seem to have a strong tendency to favor the groups to which they belong. "We" are the in-group, and "they" are the out-group. "We" share common values and attitudes; "they" are different from us. **Ethnocentrism** is a related term referring to the tendency to think that your nation or culture is superior to others. This can also result in a tendency to see other cultures as simply versions of one's own; it's hard to appreciate another society or culture if you are trapped in an ethnocentric view of the world.

Interestingly however, while members of out-groups are seen to be different from those in the in-group (and, obviously, that relationship is all relative – you see the groups to which you belong as in-groups, while others may think of you as an out-group), often the members of that out-group are *not* seen as being particularly different from *each other*. This is called **out-group homogeneity bias**. Those who are in a group to which you do not belong and with which you are unfamiliar are judged to be more similar (or homogenous) than they really are. Thus, a Hispanic man who witnesses a crime perpetrated by an Asian man may genuinely have difficulty distinguishing between that man and other Asians, not because "he's a racist" but because he has not had enough experience and interaction with Asian people.

Stereotyping is linked to out-group homogeneity bias. Because a woman does not know the members of a group to which she does not belong, she may simply rely on generalizations about those members. You might remember from our study of Sensation and Perception that we often rely on **schemas** in arriving at our perceptions of the world, and we seem to have cultural, racial and gender schemas as well.

Attraction and Relationships

Even though you may resist this idea, research in Social Psychology indicates that the keys to attraction are **similarity** and physical **proximity**. It may at times be true that "opposites attract", but it is not a useful generalization. And, even though many of us have romantic ideas about seemingly preordained meetings with those we are supposed to be with, it appears that we are simply more likely to link up with people who are nearby. We tend to like people and things that are familiar to us; **the mere exposure effect** is based on the idea that we have more positive feelings about things to which we are frequently exposed.

We will end this chapter with a very brief look at an upbeat topic: love. Robert Sternberg has attempted to define certain types of love, a bold move in a world where so many people prefer to think of it as a mysterious, indefinable energy. In Sternberg's **triangular theory of love**, he argues that *consummate love* is made up of passion (the intense desire to be with the other person), intimacy (emotional closeness, openness and sharing) and commitment (the desire to maintain the relationship). Specific forms of 'love' are made up of different combinations of those three elements. For example *romantic love* has passion and intimacy but lacks commitment, *companionate love* is made up of intimacy and commitment but lacks passion, *empty love* has commitment but lacks intimacy and passion, and *infatuation* has passion but no commitment or intimacy. It's unlikely you will have to identify these types on the Advanced Placement Examination, but the theory certainly offers fodder for discussion.

Name Hall of Fame

You first saw **Stanley Milgram's** name way back in the first unit on Research Methodology. His is a name you ought to know for the AP Exam. The same can be said of **Solomon Asch**, famous for his studies on conformity to group pressure, and **Philip Zimbardo**, who conducted the controversial "mock prison" study at Stanford University. You need to know attribution theory well, but probably not the name **Fritz Heider**, even though his is the name most associated with it. No other names from this unit would make the hall of fame.

Essay Themes

Surprisingly, this unit has not been a frequent focus of free response items on past AP Exams, perhaps because it is almost always placed at the end of textbooks and college courses, and thus some kindly types on the test development committee felt many students and teachers couldn't reasonably get to it.

There are indeed many kindly types on the committee, but it is not a safe bet to assume that there'll be no Social Psychology free response items! The area is certainly rich with possibilities – it's not too hard to imagine an item which asks about **obedience and conformity**, perhaps with direct reference to the work of Milgram and Asch. Attribution theory, **the study of attitudes** and **the concept of prejudice** could all easily be tied into elements of other units, which makes them especially attractive to the authors of the test. One essay in the past assessed student grasp of experimental design using a study that was an almost exact replica of Darley and Latane's work on the bystander effect. So, you can see that this is a very important unit indeed.

Test Preparation: Social Psychology

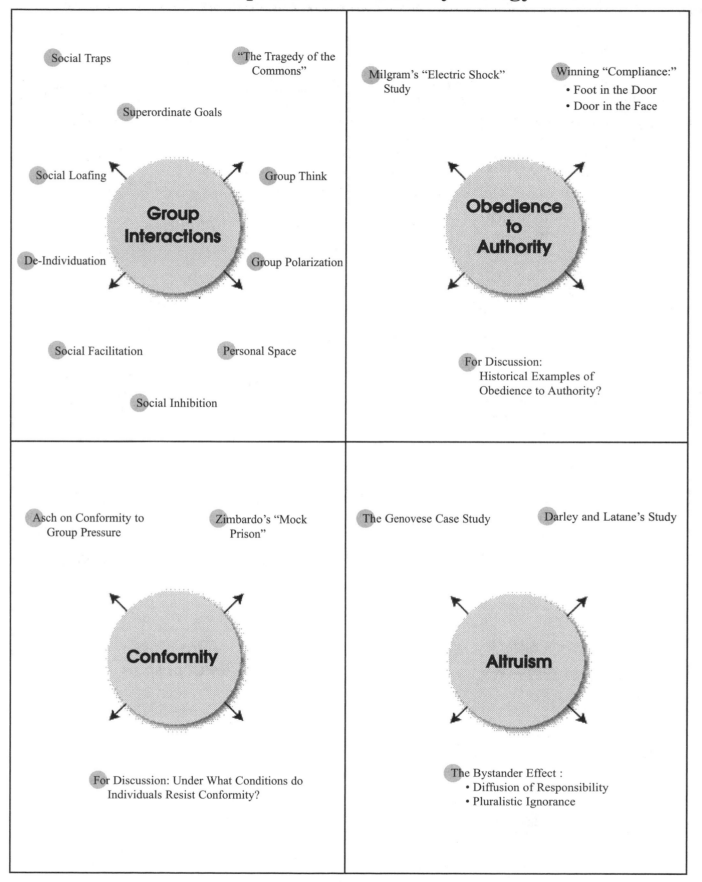

Group Interactions

- Social Traps
- "The Tragedy of the Commons"
- Superordinate Goals
- Social Loafing
- Group Think
- De-Individuation
- Group Polarization
- Social Facilitation
- Personal Space
- Social Inhibition

Obedience to Authority

- Milgram's "Electric Shock" Study
- Winning "Compliance:"
  - Foot in the Door
  - Door in the Face

For Discussion:
Historical Examples of Obedience to Authority?

Conformity

- Asch on Conformity to Group Pressure
- Zimbardo's "Mock Prison"

For Discussion: Under What Conditions do Individuals Resist Conformity?

Altruism

- The Genovese Case Study
- Darley and Latane's Study
- The Bystander Effect :
  - Diffusion of Responsibility
  - Pluralistic Ignorance

195

Test Preparation: Social Psychology

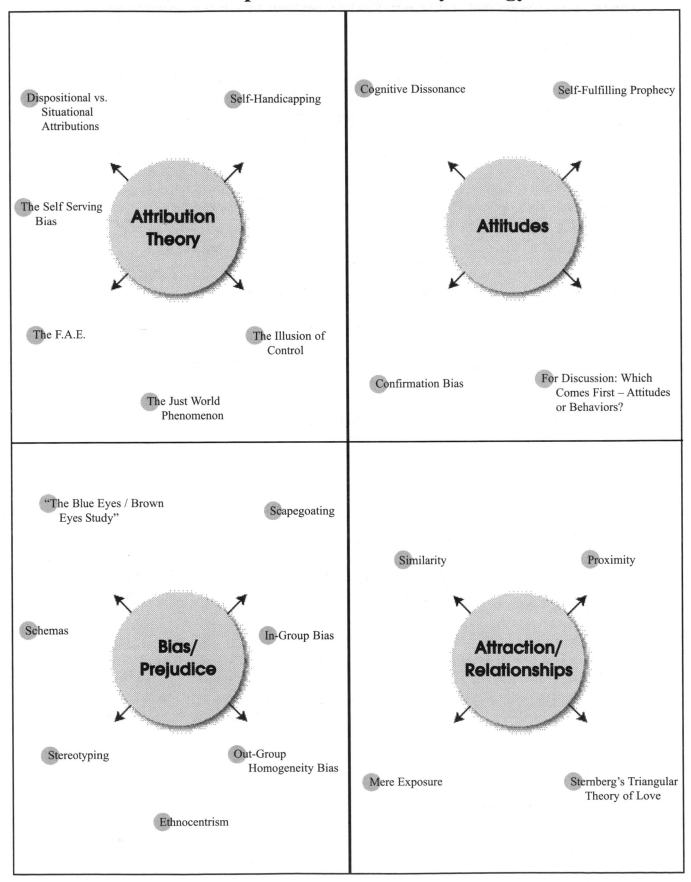

Dispositional vs. Situational Attributions

Self-Handicapping

The Self Serving Bias

Attribution Theory

The F.A.E.

The Illusion of Control

The Just World Phenomenon

Cognitive Dissonance

Self-Fulfilling Prophecy

Attitudes

Confirmation Bias

For Discussion: Which Comes First – Attitudes or Behaviors?

"The Blue Eyes / Brown Eyes Study"

Scapegoating

Schemas

Bias/ Prejudice

In-Group Bias

Stereotyping

Out-Group Homogeneity Bias

Ethnocentrism

Similarity

Proximity

Attraction/ Relationships

Mere Exposure

Sternberg's Triangular Theory of Love

196

Practice Items

1. The head of a government agency proposes an idea to a group of advisors. The group quickly reaches consensus, as no contradictory or critical opinions are offered, despite the fact that there are substantial weaknesses in the boss's proposal. This is an example of

    (A) the risky shift
    (B) social facilitation
    (C) social inhibition
    (D) group polarization
    (E) group think

2. In Solomon Asch's studies on conformity to group pressure

    (A) subjects were most likely to conform to the behaviors of people they'd previously known
    (B) subjects conformed more often when there was unanimity among Asch's confederates
    (C) women were most likely to conform to the behavior of other women
    (D) women were most likely to conform to the behavior of men
    (E) male subjects conformed 100 % of the time when Asch's confederates were also males

3. The central conclusion from Philip Zimbardo's "mock prison" study was that

    (A) student volunteers will obey older authority figures
    (B) college students are prone to aggression
    (C) many individuals exhibit strong tendencies toward autocratic behavior and therefore should not be placed in positions of authority
    (D) highly suggestible volunteers should not be chosen as research participants
    (E) individuals tend to conform to role expectations

4. A classmate loudly announces that he is certain he will do poorly on that morning's national exam because he had to stay up the entire previous night with a distraught friend. This public pronouncement could be viewed by a psychologist as an example of

    (A) assimilation
    (B) self efficacy
    (C) self modulation
    (D) self handicapping
    (E) cognitive dissonance

5. The presence of an audience seems to help the performance of a respected concert violinist, who gives her finest performance in front of the largest crowd she's ever faced. This is an illustration of

   (A) group polarization
   (B) social inhibition
   (C) social facilitation
   (D) accommodation
   (E) pluralism

6. In which of the following variations would you expect the lowest levels of obedience in Stanley Milgrams's "electric shock" study on obedience to authority?

   (A) when the "learner" is a male
   (B) when the "learner" is kept out of visual contact with the "teacher"
   (C) when the "teacher" can instruct another participant to administer the punishment
   (D) when the authority figure does not threaten but only verbally prompts the "teacher"
   (E) when the authority figure leaves the room after giving the instructions

7. According to the theory of diffusion of responsibility, the single biggest factor predicting whether a bystander will help someone in need is

   (A) the number of other bystanders
   (B) the duration of the incident
   (C) whether the person in need verbally requests assistance
   (D) the amount of potential threat involved
   (E) whether they themselves have been helped by others in the past

8. Which of the following is the best illustration of de-individuation?

   (A) in a survey, the most common response to the question "what would you do if you could do anything you wanted, with no possibility of anyone knowing?" is "rob a bank"
   (B) a man has a significant loss of self esteem after failing repeatedly at a job he thought he'd love
   (C) a woman behaves cruelly toward a girl from a foreign culture
   (D) a student decides to let others in his group do the math problems because he considers math to be a weakness of his
   (E) a police officer focuses his attention on one suspect and ignores other possibilities

9. Muzafer Sherif applied principles of social psychology to reduce tension and encourage healthy relations between male members of two rival groups at a summer camp by

   (A) introducing the members to each other
   (B) inviting the two groups of campers to share meals together
   (C) arranging competitive games between the two camps
   (D) asking the parents of each set of campers to model the desired behavior
   (E) creating a superordinate goal which required cooperation from both groups

10. The tendency to "blame the victim" in a rape case might best be attributed to

    (A) the blind spot
    (B) in-group bias
    (C) instrumental aggression
    (D) the just world phenomenon
    (E) ethnocentrism

11. Students watch video of a study in conformity and laugh raucously at the conforming participants while calling them names and referring to them as 'weak' and 'stupid'. Their failure to consider the power of the situation in the study is an example of

    (A) stimulus variability
    (B) organismic variability
    (C) the fundamental attribution error
    (D) cognitive dissonance
    (E) pluralistic ignorance

12. According to Robert Sternberg, a relationship that has a sense of intimacy and commitment but lacks passion is called

    (A) non-love
    (B) empty love
    (C) companionate love
    (D) consummate love
    (E) fatuous love

13. Evidence suggests that individuals tend to be attracted to others who are

    (A) nearly opposite in terms of interests
    (B) similar to themselves in outlook and values
    (C) physically more attractive than them
    (D) unlikely to criticize them
    (E) more intelligent than them

14. According to attribution theory, a student who receives the highest score in the class on an exam is most likely to attribute that score to

   (A) the teacher's skill
   (B) the simplicity of the test itself
   (C) a flawed scoring system
   (D) his own ability and effort
   (E) the inherent relevance of the material tested

15. A researcher wants to see if she can entice people to volunteer two hours a week working with recently released felons. She first asks potential volunteers if they believe in giving a helping hand to prisoners who've served their time on good behavior. Several weeks later, she returns to those who answered 'yes' to that survey question and asks if they are willing to work with the released felons. A large percentage agree to do so. The researcher has utilized

   (A) the foot-in-the-door approach
   (B) the door-in-the-face approach
   (C) the concept of reciprocity
   (D) the norm of social responsibility
   (E) complicity techniques

Chapter XV

Preparation to Take the Examination

On the Advanced Placement Psychology exam you'll get **70 minutes** to answer **100 multiple choice questions**. The free response, or "essay" section of the exam is administered only after the multiple choice portion is completed – you can't go ahead to it if you finish the multiple choice early. You'll have **50 minutes** to respond to **two essay questions**.

The directions provided for you before the multiple choice section don't tell you much of anything – besides, you've probably taken more than your share of such tests before. However, the directions for the free response section are worth looking at beforehand:

Directions: You have 50 minutes to answer BOTH of the following questions. It is not enough to answer a question by merely listing facts. You should present a cogent argument based on your critical analysis of the question posed, using appropriate psychological terminology.

Pay special attention to the words **"cogent argument"** and **"appropriate psychological terminology"**. The exam readers (a collection of highly qualified high school advanced placement psych teachers and college psych professors) find it difficult to score responses that circle around the question with a collection of "facts" but never really offer a thesis supported by evidence. Readers can also be annoyed by responses that rely mostly on "pop psychology" or "man-in-the-street" knowledge and intuition. You want to show them you took a rigorous, college-level psychology course, and that you have a firm grasp of actual psych terminology and concepts. As you write your answers you also ought to think about making the reader's job as easy as possible. Focused, clear writing will please them and thus benefit you!

At this point you may want to look back at the first chapter in this book to review the "top ten tips" for success on each section of the examination. Here's an abbreviated version of those suggestions:

Tips for the multiple choice section:

- **Slow down.** Be aware of the clock, yes, but know that 70 minutes is a pretty reasonable amount of time for 100 items, if you're well prepared
- Remember that the **multiple choice items are arranged in order of difficulty**. It's a decent general rule not to talk yourself out of answers that come easily to you early in the exam. Again, if you're well prepared, the first 20 or so items will likely *be* fairly easy for you.

- If you have time to review a bit at the end of the session, try to discipline yourself to **revisit only those items you'd marked** as being potentially problematic. Revaluating and changing answers isn't a bad thing per se, but you obviously want to avoid talking yourself out of responses that don't need changing.

- Remember that this section is **worth 66% of your total exam score**. Even though you may get tired as the section progresses, hang in there, because these items carry a lot of weight.

- It is certainly to your advantage to **answer any question on which you can eliminate even ONE answer choice as being definitely wrong**. The 1/4 point deduction for each wrong answer is supposed to discourage purely random guessing, but if you've worked through this book you should be able to use process of elimination and thus make a reasonable answer choice even on the most difficult items on the exam.

Don't look for patterns in your responses. The exam will likely have a pretty balanced distribution of "A's", "B's", "C's", "D's" and "E's" in the end, but you should never answer a question based on reasoning like "that's too many "B's" in a row". You could conceivably have four "B's" in a row – don't worry about it.

One strategy that can be quite effective is to block the answer choices and answer the question to yourself first before even looking at the distractors. This can spare you unnecessary time debating with yourself about an item you really do know.

Tips for the free response section:

- The sample exams that follow will give you a chance to **practice pacing**, which is very important on the essays.

- **Budget your time and stick to that plan**; 50 minutes will pass quickly!

- Your exam proctor should give you a warning at the 25 minute mark that you're halfway home (you may want to specifically ask for that). If you haven't begun the second of your essays by then, go to it!

- **Consider doing the question you know best first**. It'll be very frustrating if you take an inordinate amount of time struggling with essay #1 only to find you have limited time to answer the second question which you know very well.

- Remember that **the two essays each carry the same scoring weight**. Even if one looks bigger or appears to have more points to earn in it, don't be deceived!

- **Know what the question is specifically asking** and systematically address all of it. That seems obvious, but a large percentage of test takers simply don't do it.

- Your job is to tell the readers what you know. It can be helpful to pretend that they don't know anything; **they're smart but don't know psychology, and you're explaining it to them**, using genuine psychological terminology.

- For those of you who are handwriting-impaired, have mercy on your readers. They sit for several hours a day for over a week reading responses to the same free response item, which is challenging under any circumstances. But completely illegible penmanship can be exasperating for a reader, because he or she can't really decipher what you know. The readers want to give you the credit you deserve – they really do. Make it easy for them!

GO ON TO THE NEXT PAGE

Sample Examination I

Section I

1. A baby looks behind a door for a ball that has just rolled behind it. In developmental terms, this would serve as evidence that the child had mastered

   (A) reversibility
   (B) object permanence
   (C) circular movement
   (D) conservation
   (E) attachment

2. According to Jean Piaget, formal operational thinking is characterized by

   (A) language acquisition
   (B) the earliest forms of logical reasoning
   (C) the ability to reason abstractly and hypothetically
   (D) the inability to cognitively take the perspective of another
   (E) mastery of conservation of mass and liquid

3. A researcher is conducting an experiment on the effects of subliminal perception. At random, she assigns 50 volunteers to group #1 who will knowingly listen to a tape with an "appetite suppressant" subliminal message (masked by pleasant ocean wave sounds) and 50 volunteers to group #2 who are told nothing and who listen to an "ocean sounds" tape that has no subliminal message on it. She further assigns 50 volunteers to group #3 who are told that they are hearing a subliminal "appetite suppressant" tape even though they hear a tape with no message at all, and 50 more volunteers to group #4 which receives an oral lecture on appetite control. Which of the following is the "placebo" group in this study?

   (A) group # 1
   (B) group # 2
   (C) group # 3
   (D) group # 4
   (E) there is no placebo group in this study

4. Which of the following is most predictive of attraction between two humans?

   (A) similarity and physical proximity
   (B) complementarity and shared cultural experience
   (C) age similarity and IQ similarity
   (D) socioeconomic background
   (E) education level

205

5. Free association and dream analysis are therapeutic techniques most associated with

    (A) gestalt therapy
    (B) psychoanalysis
    (C) rational emotive therapy
    (D) client centered therapy
    (E) counterconditioning

6. Telephone and social security numbers both illustrate this concept in memory:

    (A) rehearsal
    (B) the link method
    (C) the method of loci
    (D) confabulation
    (E) chunking

7. The inability to solve a problem because some element of it is viewed only in terms of its most typical uses is called

    (A) functional fixedness
    (B) meta-analysis
    (C) metacognition
    (D) regularization
    (E) polarization

8. In Albert Bandura's "Bobo Doll" experiment on social learning, the control group

    (A) immediately beat Bobo upon being placed in a room with the doll
    (B) were shown a video in which Bobo was attacked by adult models
    (C) did not view the video showing adults beating up Bobo
    (D) hesitated at first but eventually beat Bobo when placed in a room with the doll
    (E) behaved identically to the experimental groups in the experiment

9. According to Martin Seligman, the belief that one cannot control unpleasant or punishing outcomes is called

    (A) learned helplessness
    (B) lateral inhibition
    (C) latent inhibition
    (D) latent learning
    (E) a mental map

10. A student is informed that she has finished in the 49th percentile on a national achievement test. What does this indicate?

    (A) she got 49% of the items on the test correct
    (B) she got 51% of the items on the test correct
    (C) there is a 49% likelihood that the test actually measures what it purports to measure
    (D) she performed at the same level as or better than 49% of those who took the same test
    (E) she performed at the same level as or better than 51% of those who took the same test

11. Which of the following has proven to be the most effective treatment for phobias?

    (A) person centered therapy
    (B) psychotropic medications
    (C) systematic desensitization
    (D) the cognitive triad
    (E) transcranial magnetic stimulation

12. The type of schizophrenia marked most by physical immobility or repetitive, purposeless mannerisms is called

    (A) undifferentiated schizophrenia
    (B) paranoid schizophrenia
    (C) catatonic schizophrenia
    (D) hebephrenic schizophrenia
    (E) disorganized schizophrenia

13. Charles Spearman's concept of "G" refers to

    (A) the first stage in the grieving process
    (B) general intelligence
    (C) gender
    (D) group think
    (E) generativity in late adulthood

14. A 34 year old man demonstrates poor self control, impulsiveness, chronic deceitfulness and a seeming lack of empathy. These characteristics are most consistent with a diagnosis of

    (A) fetishism
    (B) P.T.S.D.
    (C) S.A.D.
    (D) anti-social personality disorder
    (E) schizoaffective disorder

15. A teacher reads an essay and gives it a grade of "B-". Three days later, the author of the essay submits the same paper again, amongst a pile of essays from another section of the course. This time, the teacher gives the essay a grade of "D". This result is an illustration of weak

   (A) criterion validity
   (B) face validity
   (C) norming
   (D) inter-rater reliability
   (E) intra-rater reliability

16. In order to study whether boys in elementary school are more aggressive in their interactions than girls, you decide to watch them at play during recess without their knowledge. You are conducting

   (A) an unethical study
   (B) correlational research
   (C) a longitudinal study
   (D) a cross-sectional study
   (E) a naturalistic observation

17. Janet receives the following quiz scores, calculated on a 10 point scale: 7, 9, 7, 10, 7, 7, 9

Which of the following is the most accurate representation of the central tendency of this distribution?

   (A) the standard deviation is >1, the mean is 8 and the mode is 7
   (B) the standard deviation is <1, the mean is 8 and the mode is 7
   (C) the mean is 8, the median is 7 and the mode is 7
   (D) the mean is 8, the median is 7 and the mode is 10
   (E) the mean is 8, the median is 10 and the mode is 7

18. In an experiment designed to examine whether crowding affects levels of hostility, crowding is

   (A) an extraneous variable
   (B) a confound
   (C) the result of the null hypothesis
   (D) the dependent variable
   (E) the independent variable

19. In John B. Watson's classical conditioning of a fear response in a small boy called "Little Albert", the unconditioned stimulus was

(A) fear of a white rat
(B) fear of all white, furry things
(C) Albert's attempt to escape
(D) a white rat
(E) a loud noise

20. Which of the following best describes the capacity of long term memory (LTM)?

(A) it can generally hold 5 to 9 unrelated pieces of information
(B) it can generally hold only what the sensory memory can hold
(C) there appear to be no limits to its capacity
(D) it can generally hold about the same amount of information as short term memory (STM)
(E) there appear to be limits only in terms of retaining procedural memories

21. Symptoms of schizophrenia

(A) usually manifest themselves during late adolescence or early adulthood
(B) usually manifest themselves as a response to a clear environmental trigger
(C) include the presence of two or more distinct identities housed within the one individual
(D) always include either visual or auditory hallucinations
(E) are often misinterpreted as characteristic of somatoform disorder

22. Theories of motivation which assume the presence of a biological imperative to maintain an ideally balanced internal state are considered

(A) Darwinist
(B) reductionist
(C) mechanistic
(D) phenomenological
(E) homeostatic

23. According to Sigmund Freud, it is during this stage of psychosexual development, roughly between the ages of 3 to 6 years old, when a male child unconsciously experiences the Oedipal Conflict:

(A) the genital stage
(B) the latency stage
(C) the phallic stage
(D) the anal stage
(E) the oral stage

24. Cells in the visual cortex which respond to specific lines and angles in the visual field are called

    (A) global cells
    (B) complex cells
    (C) simple cells
    (D) feature detector cells
    (E) bipolar cells

25. Hearing impairment caused by damage to hair cells or the auditory nerve is called

    (A) agnosia
    (B) aphasia
    (C) anosmia
    (D) perceptive deafness
    (E) conductive deafness

26. The closer an object is to the viewer, the faster it appears to move. This depth cue is called

    (A) texture gradient
    (B) the phi phenomenon
    (C) interposition
    (D) the autokinetic effect
    (E) motion parallax

27. Daniel jumps out of the shower twice, wrongly believing he has heard the telephone ring. In signal detection theory, each would be termed

    (A) a correct rejection
    (B) a subliminal
    (C) a false alarm
    (D) a false negative
    (E) a miss

28. In the last quarter of the 19th century, the study of the relationship between the physical stimuli in the world and the psychological interpretations of those stimuli was called

    (A) gestalt psychology
    (B) introspection
    (C) structuralism
    (D) psychophysics
    (E) cognitivism

29. Operant responses are easiest to extinguish when they are originally learned through which of the following reinforcement schedules?

    (A) continuous
    (B) negative
    (C) intermittent
    (D) variable ratio
    (E) variable interval

30. Which of the following is NOT true of hypnosis?

    (A) the hypnotic subject must choose to submit to the hypnotist and cooperate with the hypnotist's suggestions
    (B) brain wave measurements of hypnotized subjects are most similar to those of ordinary waking consciousness
    (C) hypnotized subjects will never do anything dangerous or harmful to themselves or to others
    (D) hypnosis has often been effectively used as an anesthetic in dental surgery
    (E) hypnosis has often been effectively used to treat addictive behaviors

31. In a sleep laboratory, a volunteer is repeatedly awakened just before entering R.E.M sleep. After such deprivation, when the volunteer is allowed to sleep normally

    (A) she has difficulty maintaining sleep
    (B) she has substantially longer sleep sessions with relatively little R.E.M. sleep
    (C) she has more frequent and longer lasting R.E.M. periods
    (D) E.E.G. readouts of stage three and four sleep are dramatically altered in comparison to control group readings
    (E) there is no measurable difference in R.E.M. sleep between the volunteer and control subjects

32. A researcher classically conditions a dog to salivate at the sound of a buzzer by repeatedly pairing that sound with the arrival of food. Next, the researcher repeatedly pairs an image of a black square with the sound of the buzzer; soon, the presence of the black square elicits a salivary response in the dog. This is an example of

    (A) extinction
    (B) higher order conditioning
    (C) discrimination
    (D) spontaneous recovery
    (E) generalization

33. Evidence indicates that, through interaction with the world, the human brain wires and rewires its synaptic connections throughout life. This is called

    (A) biological salience
    (B) biological readiness
    (C) brain plasticity
    (D) depolarization
    (E) polarization

34. We might say that a man is rewarded for opening an umbrella in that it ends the unpleasantness of rain falling on him. This is an example of

    (A) simultaneous conditioning
    (B) negative reinforcement
    (C) positive reinforcement
    (D) primary reinforcement
    (E) omission training

35. A guitar instructor is frustrated by one of her students who joined the teacher after having played the instrument on her own for the past year. The instructor discovers that the student has developed habits that now make it difficult to learn to finger more complex chord shapes. This is an example of

    (A) overjustification
    (B) overlearning
    (C) the law of diminishing returns
    (D) contingency
    (E) negative transfer

36. According to incentive theorists, the thrust of human motivation is based on

    (A) survival of ones' genes
    (B) external goal attainment
    (C) inborn biological imperatives
    (D) higher level judgment and planning
    (E) self esteem

37. Disturbances in mood, sleep and appetite are most likely correlated with reduced levels of

    (A) serotonin activity
    (B) G.A.B.A. activity
    (C) activity in the medulla
    (D) function in the corpus callosum
    (E) cerebral lateralization

38. The visual cliff is

    (A) both a monocular and a binocular depth cue
    (B) misperceived because of contrast effects
    (C) an example of a reversible figure
    (D) used by developmental psychologists to explore preference for familiar images
    (E) an apparatus used to examine depth perception in infants

39. A politician who has firmly held convictions about a particular economic policy no longer welcomes information or evidence that might contradict her beliefs. This is best explained by

    (A) the illusion of control
    (B) the availability heuristic
    (C) confirmation bias
    (D) her algorithmic approaches to problem solving
    (E) prototype matching theory

40. A team of researchers has been unable to solve a design problem. The leader of the team suggests they stop work, in the hope that team members may have new insights when they return to the problem after a rest period away from it. This reasoning is based on the concept of

    (A) divergent thinking
    (B) convergent thinking
    (C) incubation
    (D) feature analysis
    (E) meta-analysis

41. Wolfgang Kohler's research on insight learning in chimpanzees suggested that the chimps

    (A) had unusual difficulty understanding the problems given to them
    (B) could at best only mimic what Kohler himself first demonstrated to them
    (C) seemed unable to generalize their solutions to other similar problems
    (D) could not solve problems which required more than two or three steps in the solution
    (E) seemed to reflect and then reach rather sudden solutions to the problems presented to them

42. Kristen is in love with the idea of becoming a social worker, but also has a deep desire to attend the local university to study law. This is an example of

    (A) an approach-approach conflict
    (B) an approach-avoidance conflict
    (C) an avoidance-avoidance conflict
    (D) a multiple approach-avoidance conflict
    (E) a multiple approach-approach conflict

43. A child says "I ain't going nowhere" and his aunt corrects him, saying "No, it's 'I'm not going anywhere'". The child responds, "Well, you know what I meant". He is defending his use of

    (A) psycholinguistics
    (B) prescriptive grammar
    (C) descriptive grammar
    (D) morphemes
    (E) linguistic relativity

44. "The feathers will get wet. There's no telling how fast the legs are moving. It would be nice to know where they plan to go". These sentences would be significantly easier to recall if you knew they were part of a story about ducks swimming in a pond. This is an illustration of

    (A) the primacy effect
    (B) the recency effect
    (C) semantic distinctiveness
    (D) the effect of context on memory
    (E) proactive interference

45. A high school student expects to receive a college acceptance letter on Saturday. The mail carrier always delivers the mail at precisely 10 AM on Saturdays; the student does not check for her letter before 10 AM, but does check immediately at that time. Essentially, the student is

    (A) undergoing extinction trials
    (B) experiencing classical conditioning
    (C) on a fixed ratio schedule of reinforcement
    (D) on a fixed interval schedule of reinforcement
    (E) on a variable interval schedule of reinforcement

46. A man is warned to expect poor behavior from his nephew during a weekend camping trip. As soon as the youngster arrives, the man behaves as if he expects trouble from the boy, and the boy does indeed behave rudely and irresponsibly for the entire trip. A psychologist might account for this by citing the concept of

    (A) the self fulfilling prophecy
    (B) conformity
    (C) compliance
    (D) situational attribution
    (E) discrepancy theory

47. The gland of the endocrine system most responsible for the metabolization of glucose is

    (A) the adrenal medulla
    (B) the adrenal cortex
    (C) the pituitary gland
    (D) the thyroid
    (E) the pancreas

48. During pregnancy, which of the following is least likely to function as a teratogen?

    (A) exposure to high levels of lead
    (B) x-ray exposure
    (C) alcohol
    (D) vigorous exercise
    (E) stress

49. The idea of catharsis as a kind of safety valve which releases unconscious aggression is most clearly associated with

    (A) arousal theory
    (B) drive reduction theory
    (C) sociobiology
    (D) psychoanalysis
    (E) the theory of natural selection

50. Carol Gilligan's criticism of Lawrence Kohlberg's theory of moral development is based on the argument that

    (A) Kolhberg misinterpreted cultural differences in responses
    (B) Kohlberg's stages are too narrowly defined
    (C) Kohlberg's theory underestimates the cognitive ability of younger children
    (D) Kohlberg's theory does not account well for differences between male and female responses
    (E) Kohlberg's "Heinz Dilemma" was poorly understood by most participants in the study

51. Which of the following is the best example of semantic memory?

    (A) remembering exactly what you were doing when you heard about the terrorist attacks on September 11, 2001
    (B) knowing what acetylcholine is
    (C) typing well even into old age
    (D) remembering your seventh birthday party
    (E) retaining the basic elements of your golf swing after years of not playing

52. The J.N.D. is a

    (A) projective test
    (B) measure of the minimum amount of detectable change between two stimuli
    (C) method of measuring levels of neural activity
    (D) method of viewing brain structure
    (E) manual used by therapists to help diagnose mental disorders

53. The cognitive developmental process of dealing with new information by attempting to fit it into previously held schemas is called

    (A) modeling
    (B) discrimination
    (C) synthesis
    (D) accommodation
    (E) assimilation

54. According to David Elkind, the phenomena of the personal fable and the imaginary audience are associated with

    (A) old age
    (B) middle age
    (C) young adulthood
    (D) adolescence
    (E) the preschool years

55. According to set point theory, when a heavy person diets but implements no other lifestyle changes, his or her metabolism is likely to

    (A) attenuate
    (B) atrophy
    (C) accelerate
    (D) decelerate
    (E) maintain homeostasis

56. Which of the following would serve as the best evidence in support of critical period theory?

    (A) a student runs out of time on a standardized test even though he knew the material very well
    (B) a three year old child is not corrected when he says "I eated candy this morning"
    (C) a child understands the meaning of certain sentences even though she cannot yet speak herself
    (D) a seven year old child is penalized for thinking divergently in class
    (E) a 12 year old child with no previous exposure to spoken language now has great difficulty learning any language even with professional training

57. The motor cortex in humans is housed in the

    (A) basal ganglia
    (B) frontal lobe
    (C) temporal lobe
    (D) parietal lobe
    (E) somatosensory cortex

58. Which of the following is characteristic of the human "fight or flight" response?

    (A) increased respiration, increased blood pressure, decreased blood flow to the digestive system
    (B) constriction of pupils, increased heart rate, increased salivation
    (C) decreased salivation, decreased respiration, dilation of pupils
    (D) increased heart rate, decreased epinephrine activity, decreased salivation
    (E) decreased heart rate, increased respiration, decreased blood flow to the digestive system

59. Which of the following would serve as the best argument against Abraham Maslow's hierarchy of needs?

    (A) most humans aspire to reach their fullest potential
    (B) animals and humans have different motivations
    (C) motivation is a multi-layered, interactive phenomenon
    (D) some individuals seek companionship even in the absence of satisfactory amounts of food and water
    (E) human emotional response is too variable individual-to-individual to offer meaningful generalizations about it

60. A theorist who believes that dreaming is largely a matter of repeated neural activation in the cortex which the "dreamer" then tries to pull together into a meaningful story line is a proponent of

    (A) activation-synthesis theory
    (B) psychoanalytic theory
    (C) opponent process theory
    (D) adaptive non-responding theory
    (E) cognitive dissonance theory

61. According to neo-Freudian Carl Jung, the fact that similar themes appear in folk and fairy tales of many different cultures over centuries is evidence for the existence of

    (A) anima and animus
    (B) archetypes in the collective unconscious
    (C) an inborn basic anxiety
    (D) the typical human progression through psychosexual stages of development
    (E) cultural transmission of central human problems and methods for addressing them

62. Which of the following are each associated with trait theory?

    (A) the collective unconscious and the inferiority complex
    (B) operant conditioning and modeling
    (C) cardinal traits and U.P.R.
    (D) the 16 PF and the Big Five
    (E) "G" and specialized skills

63. An ethologist would be most concerned with examining

    (A) sign stimuli and instinctive fixed action patterns
    (B) cultural influences on individual behavior
    (C) human emotional potential
    (D) human intellectual potential
    (E) human neural circuitry

64. Milton's quote "The mind is it's own place and in itself can make a heaven of hell, a hell of heaven" best summarizes

    (A) cognitive personality theory
    (B) client centered therapeutic approaches
    (C) the essence of the superego
    (D) attribution theory
    (E) psychodynamics

65. Which of the following is the best example of the defense mechanism known as displacement?

(A) David claims his co-workers don't work hard enough, although they all see him as the laziest person in their workplace
(B) Ty throws himself into volunteer work after being laid off from his job
(C) Craig misses work for several days but does not take responsibility by calling his superiors
(D) Giselle has no recollection of a tornado that destroyed her childhood home
(E) Anna's former boyfriend calls her to report he is engaged to another woman; Anna congratulates him, but after hanging up the phone throws a plant against the wall

66. According to Carl Rogers, what is the result for individuals who are in relationships characterized by unconditional positive regard?

(A) they become spoiled and narcissistic
(B) they reject genuine affection when it is offered later in life
(C) they are more open to love but simultaneously more distrustful of it
(D) they become more defensive, withdrawn and cynical about the real motives of others
(E) they are happier, more well adjusted and closer to their ideal sense of self

67. Which of the following is NOT characteristic of a manic episode?

(A) inflated self esteem or grandiosity
(B) persistently elevated mood
(C) heightened attention
(D) a "push of speech", or the seeming pressure to keep talking
(E) engagement in activities that have a potential for painful consequences

68. Thomas Szasz once said "Give a child a hammer and suddenly everything needs to be pounded". This illustrates

(A) the potential dangers in the use of diagnostic labels in clinical psychology
(B) the concepts of observational learning and modeling
(C) the argument that humans are inherently aggressive
(D) the need for diagnostic criteria for abnormality
(E) the power of discontinuity theories

69. A developmental psychologist would be most likely to utilize which of the following to examine an infant's preferences?

   (A) habituation techniques
   (B) feature detection
   (C) feature analysis
   (D) double blind methodology
   (E) stimulus generalization

70. For nearly two years you have been working at a job which makes you very tense and unhappy, but find yourself telling your friends that it's really a very nice work environment that you enjoy. Researchers like Leon Festinger would argue that your words are an attempt to relieve a state of

   (A) homeostasis
   (B) equilibrium
   (C) overjustification
   (D) self actualization
   (E) cognitive dissonance

71. Sam is highly emotional and dramatic, and has a seemingly insatiable desire to be the center of attention. This is most consistent with a diagnosis of

   (A) narcissistic personality disorder
   (B) borderline personality disorder
   (C) histrionic personality disorder
   (D) sociopathy
   (E) psychopathy

72. Which of the following would be considered the least productive and most potentially harmful occurrence during psychoanalysis?

   (A) word association
   (B) assimilation
   (C) transference
   (D) countertransference
   (E) catharsis

73. In Philip Zimbardo's "mock prison" study

    (A) student volunteers conformed, sometimes to dangerous extremes, to the role expectations associated with 'guards' and 'prisoners'
    (B) riots broke out among all those acting as inmates, in protest against their treatment by those playing the roles of guards
    (C) the social hierarchy of the prison population quickly began to mirror the social hierarchies which tend to develop in actual prisons
    (D) the 'guards' in the prison affiliated with the 'prisoners', in joint opposition against the 'warden'
    (E) it was difficult to obtain a representative sample of volunteers because so few individuals were willing to play the role of 'prisoner'

74. Which of the following is NOT a component of Howard Gardner's theory of multiple intelligences?

    (A) naturalistic intelligence
    (B) fluid intelligence
    (C) interpersonal intelligence
    (D) logical-mathematical intelligence
    (E) bodily-kinesthetic intelligence

75. Token economies are based on the principles of

    (A) operant conditioning
    (B) classical conditioning
    (C) modeling
    (D) social learning
    (E) humanism

76. Which of the following is NOT generally seen as an advantage of group therapy approaches?

    (A) group therapy can minimize the sense that one authority figure must "cure" the patient
    (B) group therapy helps individuals to see that others do indeed share their problems
    (C) group therapy discussions can focus entirely on each member's personal stories
    (D) group therapy can offer more options to individuals as they hear how others with similar problems deal with them
    (E) group therapy is less expensive than one on one therapy

77. Two individuals decline to cooperate with each other even when cooperation would actually have served the self interests of both. This describes

    (A) the concept of self monitoring
    (B) the predominance of superordinate goals
    (C) social comparison theory
    (D) confirmation bias
    (E) a social trap

78. Jessie and Jon are driving on the highway at rush hour when a car suddenly cuts in front of them in order to reach a poorly marked exit. Jon loudly criticizes the driver of the other vehicle for his poor judgment and driving skills, while Jessie points out that the circumstances may have required the other driver to do what he did. Jon's response is best explained by

    (A) rational emotive theory
    (B) the fundamental attribution error
    (C) social diffusion
    (D) the norm of social responsibility
    (E) impression formation theory

79. In a study on group problem solving it is discovered that individual members of groups tend to exert less effort than they would have if working alone. This is called

    (A) the tragedy of the commons
    (B) contiguity
    (C) contingency
    (D) social loafing
    (E) dynamics theory

80. The dissociative state known as 'fugue' is sometimes referred to as

    (A) traveling amnesia
    (B) a factitious disorder
    (C) psychosis
    (D) neurosis
    (E) somatization

81. The "flow" of a neural message is

    (A) cell body to axon to terminal buttons to axon hillock
    (B) cell body to axon hillock to dendrites to terminal buttons
    (C) axon hillock to cell body to terminal buttons to axon
    (D) dendrites to cell body to terminal buttons to axon
    (E) dendrites to cell body to axon to terminal buttons

82. Which of the following psychotropic drugs operates by blocking the reuptake of serotonin?

    (A) Clozapine
    (B) Prozac
    (C) Valium
    (D) Librium
    (E) Xanax

83. These provide neurons with nutrients while also insulating them and essentially holding them in place:

    (A) glial cells
    (B) afferent neurons
    (C) efferent neurons
    (D) neurotransmitters
    (E) neuromodulators

84. Which of the following is the most likely value for "r" resulting from a study of the correlation between air temperature and the incidence of urban violence?

    (A) −1.0
    (B) +1.0
    (C) −.74
    (D) +.53
    (E) +.14

85. A man who unconsciously resents a rival in the workplace frequently showers that rival with praise. According to a proponent of Freudian psychoanalytic theory, this is an example of

    (A) a rationalization
    (B) reaction formation
    (C) identification
    (D) regression
    (E) suppression

86. A researcher administers a battery of ten personality tests to a client. When she statistically analyzes the results, she discovers that the results from tests 3, 5 and 7 are highly correlated with each other, and concludes that those three assessments all measure the same key component of personality. The researcher has utilized

    (A) factor analysis
    (B) face validity
    (C) concurrent validity
    (D) test/retest reliability
    (E) standardization

87. Which of the following quotes is most closely associated with humanistic personality theory?

    (A) "People largely disturb themselves by thinking in a self defeating, illogical, and unrealistic manner"
    (B) "The goal of the human soul is conquest, perfection, security, superiority"
    (C) "It's as if Freud supplied to us the sick half of psychology and we must now fill it out with the healthy half"
    (D) "That we have found the tendency to conform in our society so strong ... is a matter of concern"
    (E) "The essence of obedience is that a person comes to view himself as the instrument for carrying out another person's wishes, and he therefore no longer regards himself as responsible for his actions"

88. S.A.T. scores range from 200 to 800. Angela, who earned a 600 on the S.A.T. verbal section brags "Sam got a 300 on the same section! I did twice as well as him!" What is the flaw in her reasoning?

    (A) Angela could only meaningfully do such a calculation using ratio data
    (B) S.A.T. scores are ordinal data
    (C) S.A.T. scores are nominal data
    (D) the S.A.T. is not a reliable assessment
    (E) Angela and Sam may well have significantly different educational backgrounds

89. A 55 year old man suffers a stroke which leaves him with anterograde amnesia. This means he is

    (A) able to recall what he experiences but only with the use of mnemonics
    (B) able to recall semantic memories only
    (C) unable to recall his own identity, old friends and family members
    (D) unable to retain memory of events which have occurred since the stroke
    (E) unable to recall details of the stroke itself, although the rest of his memory remains intact

90. The blocking of G.A.B.A receptors would most likely result in

    (A) seizures
    (B) reduced perception of pain
    (C) hypersomnia
    (D) apnea
    (E) hallucinations

91. The change in the electrical charge of a neuron when it "fires" its neural message is called

    (A) reuptake
    (B) the action potential
    (C) absolute refraction
    (D) relative refraction
    (E) potentiation

92. During Erik Erikson's fourth stage of psychosocial development, a seven year old girl is repeatedly frustrated by her attempts to learn in math class. For the child this might result in a lifelong sense of

    (A) trust issues
    (B) stagnation
    (C) isolation from peers
    (D) inferiority
    (E) role confusion

93. In group polarization

    (A) the individual members of a group leave the group setting with an inflated sense of their own importance to the group
    (B) the individual members of a group leave the group setting with an unrealistically negative view of their contributions to the group
    (C) members of a group tend to divide themselves into opposing "sides" even when such a division did not exist before the group came together
    (D) group size becomes the major determinant as to whether the group effectively completes its assigned tasks
    (E) a group's judgments and decisions tend to be more extreme than those of any individual member of the group

94. In the study of human perception and size constancy, an object as it actually exists in the world is called the

    (A) distal stimulus
    (B) proximal stimulus
    (C) U.C.S.
    (D) refractory image
    (E) illusory image

95. Which of the following is the best visual representation of a positively skewed distribution?

(A)

(B)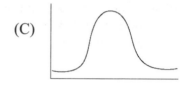

(C)

((D))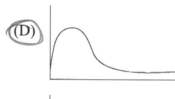

(E)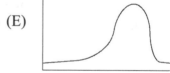

96. Which part of the human brain is most analagous to a bell over the entryway of a store, which signals those working in the store that a customer has arrived and requires attention?

(A) the septum
(B) the striatum
(C) the cerebrum
(D) the amygdala
(E) the reticular activating system

97. Prevention and early intervention are the major goals of this therapeutic approach:

(A) group therapy
(B) community psychology
(C) humanism
(D) token economies
(E) behavior modification

98. An assessment of 'intelligence' that has an insufficient operational definition of the concept would therefore most likely lack

    (A) norms
    (B) a representative sample
    (C) confounds
    (D) intra-rater reliability
    (E) construct validity

99. Ms. Williams teaches at a high school where students are randomly assigned to classes without reference to past performance or supposed ability level. After her first unit of the course, she gives a history exam to one class of 25 seniors during first period in room 204. She administers the same test to a second class of 25 seniors during the last period of the day in room 105. The mean performance of the first class is nine points higher than that of the second class, and Ms. Williams concludes that it is her "smart class". Which of the following are confounding variables in this scenario?

    (A) the exam itself and Ms. Williams
    (B) the time of administration of the tests and the two rooms
    (C) Ms. Williams and the two classes
    (D) the two classes and the two rooms
    (E) the high school and the two classes

100. A man who runs a horse stable gives a tour to a friend, introducing each individual horse by name, although the friend cannot discriminate one animal from another. This is best accounted for by

    (A) scapegoating
    (B) the self serving bias
    (C) social inhibition
    (D) pluralistic ignorance
    (E) outgroup homogeneity bias

Sample Examination I

Section I

Directions: You have 50 minutes to answer BOTH of the following questions. It is not enough to answer a question by merely listing facts. You should present a cogent argument based on your critical analysis of the questions posed, using appropriate psychological terminology.

1. Surrounding people, stimuli and circumstances can have a significant impact on human behavior and mental processes. Describe each of the following and explain how each can be specifically dependent on aspects of the immediate situation:

    • human perception
    • context dependent memory
    • Schachter-Singer / two-factor theory of emotional response
    • the bystander effect
    • conformity
    • de-individuation
    • social facilitation

2. Describe each of the following and tell how each might have played a role in your preparation for and taking of this examination:

    • the pre-frontal cortex
    • Wernicke's area
    • the hippocampus
    • short-term memory capacity
    • mnemonic devices
    • the law of effect in operant conditioning
    • the sympathetic nervous system

GO ON TO THE NEXT PAGE

Sample Examination II

Section I

1. In the following group of values, what is the mode?: 8, 9, 10, 10, 12, 15, 15, 15

   (A) 10
   (B) 11
   (C) 11.75
   (D) 12
   (E) 15

2. This brain structure seems most responsible for the formation of new memories:

   (A) the hippocampus
   (B) Broca's Area
   (C) Wernicke's Area
   (D) the amygdala
   (E) the caudate nucleus

3. Which of the following best describes the capacity of short term memory in humans?

   (A) it seems to have unlimited capacity
   (B) it can hold 7 + or − 2 unrelated pieces of information
   (C) it can hold material for several minutes even with no specific rehearsal
   (D) it can hold material for a maximum of a second or two if no processing is carried out
   (E) no valid studies of short term memory have been conducted to accurately ascertain its capacity

4. A six year old child reports that the two sets of coins in the following arrays have the same amount:

O O O O O O O
O O O O O O O

The same child is then shown this array and reports that the bottom row "has more":

O O O O O O O
O O O O O O O

The child's responses indicate she has not yet mastered:

(A) continuity
(B) contiguity
(C) conservation
(D) assimilation
(E) accommodation

5. In the first part of the 20th century, several German psychologists argued that humans consistently attempt to organize sensory stimuli into coherent wholes. This contention became the theme of

(A) later research into institutionalization of mental patients
(B) gestalt psychology
(C) the community mental health movement
(D) the behavioral school of thought
(E) IQ testing

6. Which of the following sleep disorders is marked by repeated stoppages of breathing during the night's sleep?

(A) bruxism
(B) enuresis
(C) narcolepsy
(D) apnea
(E) somniloquy

7. With which theorist would experts most associate the following quote?: "The great problems of life – sexuality, of course, among others – are always related to the primordial images of the collective unconscious"

   (A) B.F. Skinner
   (B) Abraham Maslow
   (C) Carl Jung
   (D) Sigmund Freud
   (E) Mary Ainsworth

8. According to Erik Erikson, the psychosocial task of adolescence is to resolve the conflict of

   (A) initiative vs. guilt
   (B) identity vs. role confusion
   (C) intimacy vs. isolation
   (D) industry vs. inferiority
   (E) generativity vs. stagnation

9. Which of the following does a healthy newborn human possess from birth?

   (A) the moro reflex
   (B) stranger anxiety
   (C) separation anxiety
   (D) attachment to the primary human food source
   (E) a sense of object permanence

10. The false belief that one is constantly under surveillance by the FBI and CIA is an example of

    (A) dissociative identity disorder
    (B) a delusion
    (C) overgeneralization
    (D) a hallucination
    (E) egocentrism

11. Daniel suffers from sleep disturbance, irritability, difficulty concentrating, markedly reduced interest in significant activities, and recurrent, intrusive recollections and dreams about a previously threatening event. Experts would likely diagnose this as

    (A) major depressive disorder, recurrent
    (B) major depressive disorder, single episode
    (C) Tourette's disorder
    (D) generalized anxiety disorder
    (E) post-traumatic stress disorder

12. The affective disorder marked by shifts between deep depression and euphoric, wildly optimistic mania is called

    (A) bipolar disorder
    (B) dysthymia
    (C) seasonal affective disorder
    (D) obsessive compulsive disorder
    (E) conversion disorder

13. Research in social psychology suggests that people are most likely to be attracted to those who are

    (A) unattainable
    (B) dissimilar to them
    (C) similar to them
    (D) opposite from them
    (E) safe and secure choices

14. Diffusion of responsibility is a central characteristic of

    (A) prototype matching theory
    (B) the bystander effect
    (C) the law of effect
    (D) sociobiology
    (E) attribution theory

15. Autism is characterized by

    (A) hyperactivity
    (B) rapidly cycling mood swings
    (C) impaired social interaction and communication
    (D) deceitfulness and an apparent lack of remorse or empathy
    (E) visual and auditory hallucinations

16. With what school of psychological thought would you most associate the concept of unconditional positive regard?

   (A) Trait Theory
   (B) Psychoanalytic Theory
   (C) Cognitive Theory
   (D) Behavioral Theory
   (E) Humanistic Theory

17. This limbic system structure seems most responsible for regulating appetite, thirst and core body temperature:

   (A) the basal ganglia
   (B) the pons
   (C) the hypothalamus
   (D) the medulla
   (E) the cerebellum

18. According to Sigmund Freud, dreams can be interpreted for their underlying symbolism, which he referred to as

   (A) latent content
   (B) manifest content
   (C) catharsis
   (D) transference
   (E) discrimination

19. Deep sleep is characterized by

   (A) the loss of control of the major muscle groups
   (B) the presence of delta wave activity on an EEG
   (C) the presence of alpha wave activity on an EEG
   (D) the presence of sleep spindles on an EEG
   (E) the presence of low amplitude, very rapid electrical brain wave activity

20. Which of the following sets of techniques is most closely associated with behavioral treatment?

   (A) implosive therapy, virtual reality therapy, token economies
   (B) the empty chair, the hot seat, the exaggeration game
   (C) aversive therapy, flooding, transference
   (D) transference, countertransference, dream analysis
   (E) free association, word association, flooding

21. Harry Harlow discovered that infant monkeys would seek safety from a soft, cloth surrogate mother rather than a hard, wire surrogate mother, even when the wire mother was the only one to provide food to the infant. Harlow's finding supports the notion that infants require

    (A) socialization
    (B) contact comfort
    (C) psychosocial development
    (D) constancy
    (E) continuity

22. The major problem threatening the validity of a "naturalistic observation" is that

    (A) the subjects may react to or be influenced by the observation if they realize they are being observed
    (B) the subjects' behavior cannot be controlled
    (C) the observer is unable to predict the behaviors of the subjects
    (D) the observer cannot statistically analyze the findings in a meaningful way
    (E) the observer will have difficulty establishing the necessary control group

23. Which of the following is the most likely criticism a psychoanalyst would make of behavioral therapeutic approaches?

    (A) the behaviorist pays too much attention to the emotional needs of the patient
    (B) the behaviorist focuses too heavily on the unhealthy relationships in a patient's life
    (C) the behaviorist gives too little attention to the underlying causes of disorders
    (D) there is no measurable evidence to assess the success or failure of behavioral techniques
    (E) there is no theoretical framework upon which behavioral techniques are built

24. The contention that basic human emotions are universally expressed and understood is supported by Paul Ekman's research into

    (A) body language
    (B) linguistic relativity
    (C) chimpanzees and their emotional responses
    (D) facial expressions of emotions
    (E) the limbic system

25. An airport security officer believes a passenger is carrying a weapon, but on close inspection discovers she is not. In signal detection theory, the officer's original judgment would be termed a

    (A) false alarm
    (B) false negative
    (C) miss
    (D) correct rejection
    (E) hit

26. Electroconvulsive therapy (ECT) is used as a treatment in rare cases of severe

    (A) personality disorder
    (B) anti-social behavior
    (C) catatonic schizophrenia
    (D) depression
    (E) dysthymia

27. According to research conducted by Solomon Asch, when are individuals least likely to conform to group pressure?

    (A) when the group size reaches as high as six or seven individuals
    (B) when the behavior by the group is clearly inappropriate or incorrect
    (C) when there is no unanimity in the group
    (D) when the conformity experiment is conducted by a female
    (E) when the individual did not previously know any of the members of the group

28. Which of the following is the order in Abraham Maslow's "hierarchy of needs", ranging from lowest to highest level of need?

    (A) psychological needs, safety needs, need to belong, need for self efficacy, need to survive
    (B) physiological needs, safety needs, need to belong, esteem needs, self actualization
    (C) physiological needs, esteem needs, need to belong, need for self efficacy, self actualization
    (D) physiological needs, need to belong, esteem needs, need to pursue happiness, self actualization
    (E) need for survival, esteem needs, need for control, need to pursue happiness, need for belonging

29. A statistician looks at the amount of agreement between three different judges who score the performances of Olympic ice skaters. The statistician is most probably investigating

    (A) test bias
    (B) ethnocentrism
    (C) inter-rater reliability
    (D) intra-rater reliability
    (E) the normal curve

30. Eight year old Aaron gives an in-class report entitled "How I Spent My Summer Vacation". Preparation for it relied most upon

    (A) echoic memory
    (B) eidetic memory
    (C) iconic memory
    (D) episodic memory
    (E) semantic memory

31. As his Calculus teacher passes out the final examination, Bernard feels his heart begin to pound, his palms sweat and his mouth go dry. These physiological responses are activated by his

    (A) central nervous system
    (B) skeletal nervous system
    (C) somatic nervous system
    (D) sympathetic nervous system
    (E) parasympathetic nervous system

32. An aptitude test would be used to

    (A) assess the extent to which an individual has mastered a body of information
    (B) assess how well an instructor taught a body of information
    (C) establish a baseline for comparison to other assessments
    (D) predict the correlation between two variables
    (E) determine how well suited the test taker is for a particular job or role

33. Which of the following is an advantage of longitudinal studies over cross sectional studies?

(A) subject mortality is more likely in longitudinal studies
(B) the independent variable is more easily manipulated in longitudinal studies
(C) the dependent variable is more easily measured in longitudinal studies
(D) it is easier to control sample size in longitudinal studies
(E) the sample is consistent in longitudinal studies

34. In human language acquisition, babbling is typically followed by

(A) cooing and telegraphic speech respectively
(B) cooing and holophrastic speech respectively
(C) semantics and meta-linguistics respectively
(D) telegraphic speech and holophrastic speech respectively
(E) holophrastic speech and telegraphic speech respectively

35. The central emphasis in family therapy is to

(A) modify the contingencies of reinforcement inherent in the family dynamic
(B) look at the family as a collection of very distinct and independent individuals
(C) place the burden for healing on each of the family members themselves
(D) view the family as a web of interdependent relationships
(E) explore the unconscious sources of conflict within the family unit

36. When Jillian was diagnosed with cancer, she believed that she must have "done something wrong" to deserve such an illness. Her belief is best explained by

(A) the just world phenomenon
(B) suppression
(C) repression
(D) reaction formation
(E) a situational attribution

37. You are betting on the flip of a normal, two sided coin. It has come up 'tails' on seven consecutive flips – you bet the next flip will be 'heads', figuring it is due to come up. This decision is based on

(A) correlational data
(B) the gambler's fallacy
(C) replication
(D) the positive skew of the coin flips
(E) counterbalancing

38. The section of the human brain which is apparently most responsible for higher level reasoning, social judgment and planning is

    (A) the frontal lobe
    (B) the parietal lobe
    (C) the occipital lobe
    (D) the somatic nervous system
    (E) the autonomic nervous system

39. A pigeon is reinforced with food for pecking at a red disk. However, the pigeon does not peck at other red objects. This is called

    (A) second order conditioning
    (B) higher order conditioning
    (C) discrimination
    (D) temporal conditioning
    (E) latent learning

40. Activation of the parasympathetic branch of the autonomic nervous system would result in

    (A) dilation of the pupils
    (B) an increase in heart and respiration rates
    (C) a decrease in salivation and digestive activity
    (D) inhibition of bladder constriction
    (E) a decrease in heart rate

41. Julia buys herself a new car, and now notices far more of the same model and color of car than she ever did before her purchase. This is an illustration of

    (A) top down processing
    (B) bottom up processing
    (C) a stimulus variable
    (D) the phi phenomenon
    (E) context dependence

42. Research into free running rhythms suggests that

    (A) there is little significant individual variation in sleep patterns
    (B) the body adapts quickly to sleep deprivation
    (C) the brain is most active during non-R.E.M. sleep
    (D) individuals who are deprived of R.E.M. sleep will get more R.E.M. once they are allowed to return to normal sleep without interruption
    (E) when individuals are allowed to sleep whenever they wish, with no reference to day/night or time cues, their bodies tend to operate on a 25 hour clock

43. The receptors for audition are called

(A) pheromones
(B) taste cells
(C) the semicircular canals
(D) hair cells
(E) rods and cones

44. In an experiment examining the impact of uniform color on referee's perceptions of aggression in football games, the uniform color is

(A) an extraneous variable
(B) a confounding variable
(C) an independent variable
(D) a dependent variable
(E) an intervening variable

45. Which of the following is an example of a negative correlation?

(A) a statistical analysis indicates there is no clear relationship between IQ and levels of prejudice
(B) a dog learns that chewing on the furniture consistently leads to an unpleasant consequence, so it stops chewing the furniture
(C) a study suggests a strong upward connection between hours spent watching television and weight in pounds of American adolescents
(D) a school district reports that their low scores on a national achievement test are directly related to low salaries for teachers in the district
(E) a researcher discovers that as education levels increase, levels of obedience to authority decrease

46. Two mountaineers are carrying packs of identical weight. Each time they stop to rest, one secretly puts a light object from his pack into his companion's pack. He hopes to lighten his own load and reasons that his companion will not notice such small changes in a pack that is already heavy. Such reasoning is an application of

(A) Weber's Law
(B) saturation principles
(C) The Law of Pragnanz
(D) The Whorfian Hypothesis
(E) Steven's Power Law

47. After living in a new apartment for over a year, you have become so accustomed to the nightly passing of a train near your window that you no longer notice it until one night it does not pass by. This is an illustration of

    (A) dichotic listening
    (B) opponent process theory
    (C) sublimation
    (D) habituation
    (E) polarization

48. According to Albert Bandura, under which of the following conditions would a child be most likely to imitate a modeled behavior?

    (A) when the model is unknown to the child
    (B) when the model is the same age as the child
    (C) when the modeled behavior is reinforced and the child has a sense of self efficacy about that behavior
    (D) when the model is the same sex and approximate size of the child
    (E) when the modeled behavior is not harmful to self or others

49. The smallest units of language that carry meaning are called

    (A) prototypes
    (B) prelinguistic utterances
    (C) phonemes
    (D) morphemes
    (E) pragmatics

50. A child who solves a novel arithmetic problem explains how he arrived at his solution. This is an example of

    (A) metacognition
    (B) an internal locus of control
    (C) an external locus of control
    (D) self handicapping
    (E) self actualization

51. A preoperational child nods her head repeatedly while speaking on the phone, seemingly unaware that the listener cannot see what she is doing. Jean Piaget would likely view this as evidence of

    (A) egocentrism
    (B) reversibility
    (C) artificialism
    (D) animism
    (E) habituation

52. According to George Kelly, individuals build and revise their own "personal constructs" which help them to understand and explain the world to themselves. Such a conception fits best under

    (A) cognitive theory
    (B) gestalt theory
    (C) phenomenology
    (D) introspection
    (E) functionalism

53. Which of the following is an example of a variable ratio schedule of reinforcement?

    (A) receiving five dollars every Friday for completing household tasks
    (B) receiving five dollars for every "A" you earn on your high school report card
    (C) winning the lottery after playing many times
    (D) receiving a dollar for every mile you walk in a charity "Walk-a-Thon"
    (E) getting increased use of the family car upon reaching the age of 18

54. Research suggests that the most well adjusted and socially competent adults tend to come from homes governed by which of the following parenting styles?

    (A) permissive
    (B) indulgent
    (C) democratic
    (D) authoritarian
    (E) authoritative

55. In which of the following variations of Stanley Milgram's "electric shock" obedience study was there the highest rate of obedience to the authority figure?

    (A) when the authority figure threatened the volunteers with physical harm if they did not obey
    (B) when the volunteers were paid
    (C) when the volunteers were female
    (D) when the volunteers were allowed to instruct a second party to actually execute the orders of the authority figure
    (E) when the orders given by the authority figure were not deemed to be dangerous by the volunteers

56. According to arousal theory,

    (A) females score consistently higher on measures of baseline physiological arousal than males
    (B) males score consistently higher on measures of baseline physiological arousal than females
    (C) there is little statistical correlation between levels of physiological activation and task performance
    (D) organisms will perform complex tasks best if they have a moderate level of activation
    (E) the great majority of humans tend to seek high levels of sensation and arousal

57. In Hans Selye's general adaptation syndrome, an individual progresses in order through these stages in response to stress:

    (A) response, relief, reactance
    (B) reaction, response, relief
    (C) resistance, alarm, stress onset
    (D) alarm, resistance, exhaustion
    (E) appraisal, response, relief

58. In statistics, the standard deviation is a measurement of

    (A) the spread of scores in relation to the mean
    (B) the difference between the lowest and highest scores in a distribution
    (C) the typical difference between the independent variable and the dependent variable
    (D) the typical difference between any experimental group and the control group
    (E) central tendency

59. Set point theory suggests that humans have

    (A) one range of weight and body fat percentage that is species specific
    (B) a biological regulatory mechanism which determines how much fat the body will carry
    (C) only two established body types, mesomorph and endomorph
    (D) a set weight or body fat level that is culturally determined
    (E) established desirable weight levels that continue to change over time

60. Wilson loves his fiance deeply, but also feels significant anxiety about making a lifelong commitment at this stage of his life. Psychologist Kurt Lewin would label this

    (A) a multiple avoidance conflict
    (B) a multiple approach conflict
    (C) an avoidance-avoidance conflict
    (D) an approach-avoidance conflict
    (E) an approach-approach conflict

61. Gordon Allport used the term 'cardinal trait' to refer to

    (A) one of the five or so most important personality characteristics in an individual
    (B) personality traits that are consistently found in most individuals across cultures and over time
    (C) a single characteristic in an individual that is consistent across situations and over time
    (D) the most primitive, survival-based human characteristics
    (E) the characteristics in humans that arise only when under severe and enduring stress

62. Humanistic personality theory is most frequently criticized on the grounds that it is

    (A) too restrictive of human freedom
    (B) unrealistically optimistic about human nature and motives
    (C) too pessimistic about the individual's willingness to control his or her own destiny
    (D) heavily biased in favor of the influence of early childhood experiences
    (E) heavily biased in favor of the male perspective at the expense of female experience

63. Cross culturally, even babies born blind begin to demonstrate a "social smile" at about the same ages. This serves as evidence of _____ in human development.

    (A) socialization
    (B) maturation
    (C) acculturation
    (D) enculturation
    (E) adaptation

64. A sculptor who has powerful but unconscious sexual urges does only nude sculptures, vehemently arguing that it is the only "true" art form. A psychoanalyst would say that which of the following defense mechanisms is at work in this scenario?

    (A) regression
    (B) suppression
    (C) internalization
    (D) sublimation
    (E) identification

65. A history examination purportedly assessing knowledge of the pre-Civil War American South has several items on it about post-war Reconstruction. The exam lacks

    (A) constancy
    (B) reliability
    (C) content validity
    (D) criterion validity
    (E) efficacy

66. Anti-psychotic medications typically operate by

    (A) blocking dopamine activity
    (B) suppressing hormonal secretions
    (C) encouraging the release of endorphins
    (D) activating the peripheral nervous system
    (E) modulating limbic system function

67. In order to "standardize" an assessment, a group is administered the test

    (A) to determine if it is reliable
    (B) to determine if it is valid
    (C) to establish the extent to which the sample is representative
    (D) and those results are used as the norm against which future test takers are compared
    (E) and it is evaluated for its accuracy in testing what it claims to be testing

68. Raymond Cattell argued that there are two basic kinds of intelligence; of those, which is most closely associated with reasoning, novel problem solving and understanding of the relationship between ideas?

    (A) fluid intelligence
    (B) "G"
    (C) crystallized intelligence
    (D) multiplicity
    (E) primary intelligence

69. Psychologist David Rosenhan and several others had themselves admitted to mental institutions by falsely claiming to hear voices. Once admitted, each pseudopatient acted perfectly normally and never again reported hearing voices. Which of the following best summarizes the results of this study?

    (A) both the staff and the patients already residing in the institutions discovered the pseudopatients were misrepresenting their symptoms within one week
    (B) the study had to be discontinued after one week because each of those taking part had become dangerously overmedicated
    (C) no members of the staff caught onto the charade, interpreting the day-to-day behaviors of the pseudopatients only in the context of the diagnosis each had been given
    (D) the pseudopatients were kept against their will in the institutions for periods ranging from twelve to fifteen months
    (E) the original diagnoses of each of the pseudopatients were changed at least three times within an average of two months

70. A therapist asks her patient not to "awful-ize" the loss of his girlfriend. The therapist appears to be a proponent of which of the following treatment approaches?

    (A) client centered therapy
    (B) gestalt therapy
    (C) Jungian psychoanalysis
    (D) organic therapy
    (E) rational emotive therapy

71. Which of the following quotes is most representative of a major current trend in the study of intelligence and its assessment, associated with researchers such as Howard Gardner and Robert Sternberg?

    (A) "Even at low levels of intelligence... we find a command of language that is totally unattainable by an ape" (Noam Chomsky)
    (B) "People with a high need for achievement are not gamblers; they are challenged to win by personal effort, not by luck" (David McClelland)
    (C) "Everyone is ignorant, only on different subjects" (Will Rogers)
    (D) "How many people, one wonders, are sane but not recognized as such in our psychiatric institutions?" (David Rosenhan)
    (E) "Often the momentary situation which, at least in part, determines the behavior of a person is disregarded and the behavior is taken as a manifestation of personal characteristics" (Fritz Heider)

72. A young boy is suddenly stricken with blindness for which there seems to be no organic cause after witnessing a near fatal accident involving his sister. He is probably suffering from

    (A) panic disorder
    (B) generalized anxiety disorder
    (C) a fugue episode
    (D) hypochondriasis
    (E) a conversion disorder

73. The debate over whether development occurs gradually and almost imperceptibly, or in a stage-like way marked by clearly observed divisions is an argument over

    (A) cognitive vs. social forces
    (B) continuity vs. discontinuity
    (C) nature vs. nurture
    (D) adaptation and habituation
    (E) situational or dispositional attributions

74. All auditory, visual, somasthetic and gustatory signals are routed through this large structure in the center of the brain:

(A) the thalamus
(B) the putamen
(C) the cerebellum
(D) the association cortex
(E) the pons

75. The fact that weak incoming stimuli do not result in the transmission of weak neural messages is evidence for

(A) the existence of a relative refractory period
(B) the existence of an absolute refractory period
(C) the all-or-none law
(D) reuptake
(E) the process of neural networking

76. Edward Tolman discovered that rats that had been exposed to a maze would not actually demonstrate their learning of it unless reinforced for doing so. He called this

(A) trial and error learning
(B) latent learning
(C) insight learning
(D) temporal conditioning
(E) positive transfer

77. Objects nearer to you seem to move more quickly than objects far away, which can help you in determining depth or distance. This phenomenon is called

(A) motion parallax
(B) accommodation
(C) interposition
(D) shadowing
(E) the autokinetic effect

78. As students return from college to visit a high school teacher, the teacher finds she has difficulty remembering some of their names. She explains this by saying that she's learned so many new names during the current school year that she now has trouble recalling all of her former students. This is an example of

    (A) constructive memory
    (B) reconstructive memory
    (C) situational schemas
    (D) proactive interference
    (E) retroactive interference

79. Which of the following is the best example of social inhibition?

    (A) a woman who is very good at using a rifle performs even better as a crowd gathers around her at a carnival target shooting game
    (B) a child refuses to imitate aggression modeled by an adult
    (C) a child enthusiastically imitates aggression modeled by an adult
    (D) a man refuses to contribute to a charity when approached by a volunteer in an airport
    (E) a man who is a poor bowler bowls even worse than usual when several friends watch him perform

80. In a classical conditioning study, a cat is shown a red light which is followed by an air puff to the eye, leading to reflexive blinking in the animal. After several such pairings, the cat blinks as soon as the red light is presented. Which of the following illustrates blocking in this scenario?

    (A) the cat continues to blink at the presentation of the red light, even though red lights had not had such an effect before the study
    (B) the cat begins to blink at green and blue lights as well
    (C) the cat blinks at red lights, but not at other, similar stimuli
    (D) the next day, the cat is very slow to acquire conditioning when the procedure is repeated with a tone in place of the red light
    (E) attempts to extinguish the blinking response fail

81. Recalling and naming the glands of the endocrine system is an example of

    (A) semantic memory
    (B) procedural memory
    (C) working memory
    (D) maintenance memory
    (E) constructive memory

82. According to this theory, the auditory cortex identifies the pitch of 40 hz sounds because neurons along the basilar membrane processing that auditory input fire 40 times per second:

    (A) dissonance theory
    (B) prototype theory
    (C) feature analysis theory
    (D) frequency theory
    (E) volley theory

83. The kinesthetic system

    (A) is housed in the parietal lobe
    (B) is housed in the inner ear
    (C) tells you where your body parts are in space and in relation to each other
    (D) provides information on whole body balance and head position
    (E) provides information about sensations of temperature and pressure

84. Which of the following is the best example of state dependent memory?

    (A) an eyewitness supplies two different versions of events to two different questioners
    (B) an eyewitness supplies two different versions of events because of the different ways questions are put to him
    (C) a man who learned new material while in a depressed mood actually does better in recalling that material when in a similarly depressed condition
    (D) a girl who learned a vocabulary list in room 207 feels she will do better on a test of those words if she can take the test in room 207
    (E) the victim of a crime does not recall details of the crime well because of the highly emotional nature of the events

85. A therapist treats a patient who has an intense fear of heights by asking the patient to repeatedly envision standing on the ledge of a thirtieth floor window, while the patient remains safe in the therapist's office. This is an example of

    (A) gestalt therapy
    (B) flooding
    (C) aversive conditioning
    (D) systematic desensitization
    (E) implosive therapy

86. The original Wechsler Intelligence tests

    (A) were designed only for children
    (B) were designed only for adults
    (C) required greater language skills than previous intelligence assessments
    (D) were more performance-based than the previous language-based assessments
    (E) were the first to sample a wide range of individuals

87. A grandmother promises her grandson he can swim in the pool after dinner if he eats his vegetables. This is an application of

    (A) contiguity
    (B) the Premack Principle
    (C) simultaneous conditioning
    (D) retroactive interference
    (E) chaining

88. Robert Rescorla argued that classical conditioning will only occur if there is contingency, which means

    (A) the UCS reliably predicts the presentation of the CS
    (B) the CS reliably predicts the presentation of the UCS
    (C) the CS is previously unknown to the learner
    (D) the learner has had previous exposure to the CS and the UCS
    (E) the CS and the UCS are also presented in reverse order

89. Which of the following is NOT a defensible conclusion based on current research into the biological basis of schizophrenia?

    (A) the presence of the disease is correlated with frontal lobe dysfunction
    (B) the ventricles in the brain of sufferers tend to be enlarged
    (C) an excess of dopamine activity is correlated with the disorder
    (D) the presence of the disease is often linked to abnormalities in motor development in childhood
    (E) a child's risk of developing the disorder does not change when both his biological parents have the disease

90. Positron Emission Tomography (P.E.T.)

    (A) mimics the activation of the sympathetic nervous system to allow for study of human emotional response
    (B) tracks and measures the flow of slightly radioactive glucose to determine the location and level of neural activity
    (C) records brain wave activity
    (D) is used in conjunction with polygraphs in work with lie detection
    (E) is used to treat major depression

91. When sodium channels on a cell membrane open, the electrical charge within the cell briefly becomes more positive than the charge outside of the cell. This is called

    (A) self propagation
    (B) the absolute refractory period
    (C) the relative refractory period
    (D) polarization
    (E) depolarization

92. A child waits all afternoon for his father to arrive home to punish the boy for his misbehavior earlier in the day. The sound of his father's car on the gravel in the driveway signals his arrival, and the boy is then spanked for his earlier transgression. For some time afterward, the boy feels a sense of anxiety whenever he hears the sound of a car on gravel. In this scenario, what are the conditioned stimulus, unconditioned stimulus, unconditioned response and conditioned response respectively?

    (A) anxiety, pain from the spanking, the sound of the gravel, fear of his father
    (B) the spanking, his father, pain from the spanking, anxiety
    (C) the spanking, his father, anxiety, pain from the spanking
    (D) the sound of the gravel, anxiety, the spanking, pain from the spanking
    (E) the sound of the gravel, the spanking, pain from the spanking, anxiety

93. Which of the following theories of emotional response proposes that the thalamus processes awareness of physiological changes and the psychological interpretation of those changes simultaneously?

    (A) opponent process theory
    (B) James-Lange Theory
    (C) Cannon-Bard Theory
    (D) Two Factor Theory
    (E) Schachter-Singer Theory

94. Selena, who feels deep seated discomfort about her physical appearance, tells her partner "I know you think I'm fat", and the partner vigorously disputes her claim. A psychoanalyst might interpret Alyson's statement as being an example of

    (A) projection
    (B) identification
    (C) rationalization
    (D) reaction formation
    (E) displacement

95. While Jean Piaget argued that children largely develop through biological maturation, Lev Vygotsky argued for internalization, which is

    (A) a process by which children develop by absorbing information from the social context they inhabit
    (B) largely dependent on the physical health of the child in the first year of life
    (C) driven by instinctive, reflexive responses
    (D) strictly based upon biological imperatives
    (E) most influenced by birth order variables

96. Which of the following best illustrates the fundamental attribution error in attempting to account for why a lone driver would not stop to help you while your car was broken down by the side of the road?

    (A) "He must have believed it was too dangerous to stop"
    (B) "He's obviously not a considerate person!"
    (C) "You just can't figure out why people do what they do"
    (D) "No one else would've stopped either"
    (E) "I must have looked too sloppy and disheveled"

97. A study reveals that Asian volunteers have difficulty identifying different Hispanic individuals if the volunteers have had little or no previous exposure to Hispanic people. This is supported by the concept of

    (A) pluralistic ignorance
    (B) scapegoating
    (C) bottom up processing
    (D) in-group bias
    (E) outgroup homogeneity bias

98. Glial cells

   (A) support the function of the message sending neurons in the brain
   (B) are most numerous in the earliest stages of neural development
   (C) carry messages from the skin receptors to the central nervous system
   (D) carry messages from the central nervous system to the muscles and glands
   (E) lack a nucleus

99. Chris has a period of relative calm shattered by a rush of intense anxiety and worry, irritability, restlessness and difficulty concentrating, which seem to have no apparent cause. These symptoms are most consistent with a diagnosis of

   (A) borderline personality disorder
   (B) agoraphobia
   (C) generalized anxiety disorder
   (D) panic disorder
   (E) somatization disorder

100. Blocking neural receptor sites for acetylcholine would most likely result in

   (A) hypersomnia
   (B) memory disturbance
   (C) insomnia
   (D) narcolepsy
   (E) delusional thinking

Sample Examination II

Section II

Directions: You have 50 minutes to answer BOTH of the following questions. It is not enough to answer a question by merely listing facts. You should present a cogent argument based on your critical analysis of the questions posed, using appropriate psychological terminology.

1. "Nothing is easier than self deceit. For what each man wishes, that he also believes to be true" (Demonsthenes, 384-322 B.C.E.)

   Construct an argument in support of this statement, making detailed reference to each of the following in your response:

   - self fulfilling prophecy
   - confirmation bias
   - David Rosenhan's study on institutionalization
   - cognitive dissonance
   - the placebo effect
   - constructive memory

2. Describe each of the following and discuss why each might be a misnomer, (" a name wrongly or unsuitably applied to a particular person or object") or a misleading term if read literally:

   - color blindness
   - absolute threshold
   - negative reinforcement
   - positive symptoms of schizophrenia
   - anti-social personality disorder
   - positively and negatively skewed distributions

Sample Examination III

Section I

1. Repeating the methods used in a previous experiment to determine whether using those same methods again will lead to the same results is called

   (A) rehearsal
   (B) counterbalancing
   (C) automaticity
   (D) regression
   (E) replication

2. The Diagnostic and Statistical Manual (DSM)

   (A) offers guidelines on basic treatment of mental disorders
   (B) provides statistical evidence to support the use of certain treatment approaches over others
   (C) is a classification symptom for mental disorders
   (D) is the most statistically reliable self report assessment of personality
   (E) explains the scoring system used in evaluating responses to Rorschach ink blots

3. The brief period after the "firing" of a neuron during which the neuron cannot be reactivated is called

   (A) sublimation
   (B) kinesis
   (C) depolarization
   (D) the refractory period
   (E) the resting state

4. Which of the following is the most accurate statement about the capacity and duration of short term memory?

   (A) it theoretically has an unlimited capacity over an unlimited period of time
   (B) it is so variable from one individual to another that it is essentially meaningless to generalize about its capacity or duration
   (C) typically, an individual can hold seven + / - two items in it, for 20 to 30 seconds
   (D) its capacity and duration invariably decrease after adolescence
   (E) its capacity and duration invariably increase after adolescence

257

5. While playing with your eight month old cousin, you hide behind the couch out of her sight. A moment later, she crawls around the couch and "finds" you. She has demonstrated a grasp of

   (A) object permanence
   (B) conservation
   (C) animism
   (D) artificialism
   (E) reciprocity

6. If an individual were to reach his or her fullest potential, becoming a fully creative, productive, spontaneous and empathetic person, Abraham Maslow would say they were

   (A) fully functioning
   (B) homeostatic
   (C) self actualized
   (D) in an approach-approach mode
   (E) acculturated

7. With what theorist would you associate the following quote?: "The ego's relation to the id might be compared with that of a rider to his horse".

   (A) Edward Thorndike
   (B) Sigmund Freud
   (C) B.F. Skinner
   (D) Albert Bandura
   (E) Carl Rogers

8. A child's story is given the following scores by seven different raters using a ten point scale to evaluate the creativity of the child's work: 4,3,4,5,7,4,5. What is the median score?

   (A) 3.0
   (B) 4.0
   (C) 4.6
   (D) 5.0
   (E) 7.0

9. The earliest forms of intelligence tests compared the chronological age of the test taker to his

   (A) physical appearance or phenotype
   (B) performance on non-linguistic tasks
   (C) mental age
   (D) level of emotional development
   (E) siblings

10. Those who suffer from this rare dissociative disorder have two or more distinct personalities housed in their one body:

    (A) schizophrenia
    (B) bipolar disorder
    (C) somatization
    (D) dissociative fugue
    (E) dissociative identity disorder

11. The conflicting statements "I love to smoke cigarettes" and "I know cigarette smoking is bad for my health" illustrate a condition of internal tension known as

    (A) cognitive dissonance
    (B) a contrast effect
    (C) convergent thinking
    (D) countertransference
    (E) self handicapping

12. The temporary reappearance, after extinction, of a previously conditioned response is called

    (A) acquisition
    (B) spontaneous recovery
    (C) retrieval
    (D) retroactive interference
    (E) remission

13. According to Jean Piaget, a child in the concrete operational stage of cognitive development learns that the amount of matter does not increase or decrease merely because of a change in its form or appearance. At this point, the child has mastered

    (A) conservation
    (B) functional fixedness
    (C) abstract thought
    (D) externalization
    (E) proximal development

14. Which of the following is a limitation of correlational research?

    (A) strong positive correlations are rare

    (B) strong negative correlations are rare

    (C) if two variables are found to have zero correlation we assume they have no relationship at all

    (D) it is more difficult to conduct than experimental research

    (E) correlational data only reflect that a relationship exists between two variables but does not indicate whether either causes the other to occur

15. A doctor gently strokes the cheek of a healthy newborn child. What will the neonate reflexively do in response?

    (A) a neonate would be unresponsive to such stimulation in the first hours of life

    (B) pull her arms and legs into the midline of her body

    (C) turn her head in the direction of the touch, rooting for a food source

    (D) imitate the modeled behavior

    (E) demonstrate visually directed reaching

16. Paul Ekman and his colleagues concluded from studies in the 1970's on facial expressions of emotions that

    (A) individuals vary widely in their ability to recognize genuine emotions via facial expression alone

    (B) there were specific and significant differences between residents of Brazil and Chile in recognition of facial expressions

    (C) trained professionals tend to outperform amateurs in lie detection through facial expression

    (D) facial expressions often contradict messages transmitted through body language

    (E) the meaning and understanding of basic facial expressions is universal across cultures

17. Lawrence Kohlberg's theory of the development of moral reasoning is characterized by

    (A) a progression from judgment based on reward and punishment, to reasoning rooted in social expectations and finally to a reliance on abstract moral principles

    (B) a consistent focus on age variations in moral reasoning, especially in adolescence and adulthood

    (C) the belief that humans are born with a sense of morality housed in the collective unconscious

    (D) an emphasis on just vs. unjust consequences for immoral or amoral behavior

    (E) the generalization that there are significant cultural differences in moral judgment and behavior

18. Which of the following interact to help in regulating appetite and thirst?

    (A) the hippocampus and the cerebellum
    (B) the thalamus and the prefrontal cortex
    (C) the hypothalamus and the hippocampus
    (D) the hypothalamus and the pituitary gland
    (E) the pons and the prefrontal cortex

19. Daniel is investigating why his car won't start. He systematically looks at every part of the engine, one after another, believing that while it may take him a long time to find the problem, he is guaranteed to eventually find a solution. Daniel has used

    (A) a decision matrix
    (B) the representativeness heuristic
    (C) an algorithmic approach
    (D) brainstorming
    (E) concept perseverance

20. Increased recall for items placed early in a list one is trying to remember is called

    (A) the primacy effect
    (B) the recency effect
    (C) the distinctiveness effect
    (D) semantic memory
    (E) crystallized memory

21. If the consequence of a behavior brings pleasure or satisfaction, it is likely the behavior will be repeated under similar circumstances. This is a description of

    (A) classical conditioning
    (B) the law of effect
    (C) omission training
    (D) aversive training
    (E) the law of pragnanz

22. Jenna tutors other students because it makes her feel helpful, while her friend Vanessa tutors students strictly for pay. Their rationales respectively demonstrate the difference between

    (A) primary and secondary drives
    (B) primary and secondary reinforcers
    (C) instinctive and appetitive drives
    (D) innate and socialized motivation
    (E) intrinsic and extrinsic motivation

23. An individual with schizophrenia dominated by extreme motor immobility and sometimes by assumption of odd postures would likely be classified as

   (A) undifferentiated type
   (B) disorganized type
   (C) catatonic type
   (D) residual type
   (E) paranoid type

24. Humanists like Carl Rogers contend that a central cause of depression or anxiety is

   (A) the realization of a gap between one's real self and one's ideal self
   (B) fixation in a psychosexual stage of development
   (C) unresolved unconscious conflict
   (D) inconsistent, irrational communication styles in the family
   (E) a genetic predisposition

25. A man who is a heavy smoker self-administers an electric shock every time he desires a puff of a cigarette. This is an example of which behavior modification strategy?

   (A) systematic desensitization
   (B) modeling
   (C) aversive conditioning
   (D) V.R.T.
   (E) shaping

26. Benzodiazapenes like Valium are considered to be

   (A) anti-depressant medications
   (B) anti-psychotic medications
   (C) anti-anxiety medications
   (D) hallucinogens
   (E) narcotics

27. On the first day of practice a new coach notices a player and says to an assistant "he looks like trouble to me". The coach is then particularly harsh and public in his criticisms of the player, who becomes more and more troublesome as time goes by. A psychologist might attribute the player's problematic behavior to

   (A) social loafing
   (B) a self fulfilling prophecy
   (C) the self serving bias
   (D) situational attributions
   (E) the just world phenomenon

28. Which of the following is the most accurate progression, from greatest to smallest amount of somatosensory surface area given over in the cortex to the listed body parts?

    (A) fingers, back, feet
    (B) elbows, back, feet
    (C) back, buttocks, lips
    (D) lips, palm of hand, upper arm
    (E) lips, upper arm, fingers

29. Brianna has a persistent, long standing and intensely exaggerated sense of her self importance and uniqueness. This is most consistent with a diagnosis of

    (A) dysthymia
    (B) cyclothymia
    (C) conduct disorder
    (D) histrionic personality disorder
    (E) narcissistic personality disorder

30. The assertion that there is no connection between the independent variable and the dependent variable in an experiment is called

    (A) the control
    (B) statistical significance
    (C) experimenter bias
    (D) the null hypothesis
    (E) a skewed result

31. The limbic system structure that seems most responsible for identifying the emotional relevance of input is the

    (A) nucleus accumbens
    (B) amygdala
    (C) basal ganglia
    (D) septum
    (E) R.A.S.

32. The difference between an interval scale of measurement and a ratio scale of measurement is that

    (A) a ratio scale does not indicate the difference between scores
    (B) a ratio scale merely names or lists itcms
    (C) a ratio scale has an absolute zero point
    (D) an interval scale has an absolute zero point
    (E) an interval scale does not provide a range of scores

33. The sense of head position and whole body balance is called

    (A) the kinesthetic sense
    (B) the somasthetic sense
    (C) synesthesis
    (D) the vestibular sense
    (E) redintegration

* The next two items each refer to the same scenario:

   Two young soldiers are training to become radar operators, learning to detect the presence of aircraft in computer simulations.

34. The teacher positions a simulated aircraft on the respective screens of the trainees, but both fail to detect its presence. In signal detection theory, this is called

    (A) a hit
    (B) a miss
    (C) a false alarm
    (D) a false positive
    (E) an attribution error

35. Which of the following is an example of a correct rejection in this scenario?

    (A) one of the trainees rightly disagrees with his training partner when the partner erroneously claims there is an aircraft present
    (B) both trainees wrongly report that an aircraft is present
    (C) both trainees rightly report that an aircraft is present
    (D) both trainees fail to detect an aircraft that was present
    (E) the two trainees disagree as to the intensity of a particular radar signal

36. The fovea

    (A) houses all the receptors for vision
    (B) is located in the center of the retina and is responsible for visual acuity
    (C) falls in the center of the human "blind spot"
    (D) allows light to enter the eye
    (E) is the colored membrane in front of the eye

37. The inability to detect smells is known as

    (A) enuresis
    (B) anosmia
    (C) prospagnosia
    (D) aphasia
    (E) apraxia

38. According to opponent process theory, a boy who stares for a full minute at a red valentine sent to him by a classmate who then looks at a neutral background will experience

    (A) a green afterimage
    (B) a red afterimage
    (C) a blue afterimage
    (D) an upside-down afterimage
    (E) a black and white afterimage

39. Which of the following characterizes the statistical relationship between age and average amount of nightly sleep?

    (A) there is no consistent pattern in this relationship
    (B) the younger the child the less they sleep
    (C) the average amount of sleep any individual gets fluctuates regularly as we age
    (D) the two are negatively correlated
    (E) the two are positively correlated

40. The auditory cortex is located in

    (A) the limbic system
    (B) the frontal lobes
    (C) the prefrontal cortex
    (D) the temporal lobes
    (E) the parietal lobes

41. A young child learns to become conscious of being in the dream state and can control to some extent the progression of dream events. This is an application of

    (A) R.E.M. rebound
    (B) hypersomnia
    (C) lucid dreaming
    (D) latent content
    (E) manifest content

42. Which of the following is the best example of negative reinforcement?

    (A) being spanked for failing to clean your room
    (B) eating a handful of candy which reduces your sadness and boredom
    (C) being threatened with physical punishment without its being carried out
    (D) being made to sit quietly on a chair for exactly two minutes
    (E) drinking a huge amount of water before competing in a long road race

43. For a mere five seconds, a woman is shown a drawing which contains pictures of thirty unrelated items. She is then able to recall each of the items and place them in their exact location in the original drawing. It is reasonable to assume this woman possesses

    (A) eidetic memory
    (B) flashbulb memory
    (C) associative memory
    (D) frontal lobe hypertrophy
    (E) an enlarged amygdala

44. Loss of hearing which results from damage to the ossicles or blockages in the auditory canal is called

    (A) tectorial inhibition
    (B) lateral inhibition
    (C) perceptive deafness
    (D) nerve deafness
    (E) conductive deafness

45. In his description of a bank robber's getaway car, an eyewitness unintentionally adds details that were not actually present. This is an example of

    (A) priming
    (B) constructive memory
    (C) the serial position effect
    (D) implicit memory
    (E) declarative memory

46. The large band of fibers connecting the left and right hemispheres of the cortex, allowing those two sides of the brain to communicate with each other, is called the

    (A) cerebellum
    (B) cerebrum
    (C) corpus callosum
    (D) septum
    (E) reticular formation

47. Developmentally, which of the following is a transitional object?

    (A) a wedding ring
    (B) a birth certificate
    (C) a child's first reading book
    (D) a cup of juice
    (E) a stuffed animal

48. When a young girl grasps the idea that she will remain a girl throughout her life she has attained a sense of

    (A) androgyny
    (B) acculturation
    (C) gender identity
    (D) gender role
    (E) gender constancy

49. To an ethologist, a complex pattern of organized, unlearned behavior that is species-specific is called

    (A) a drive
    (B) a need
    (C) an affective response
    (D) an instinct
    (E) a motive

50. Set point theory suggests that humans possess

    (A) an internal mechanism which regulates how much fat the body will carry
    (B) a culturally established range of expectations for male and female role behaviors
    (C) an individually established range of expectations for male and female role behaviors
    (D) a biological tendency to seek safety and control
    (E) an innate drive toward affiliation

51. Which of the following is best characterized as a retrieval problem in memory?

    (A) flashbulb memory
    (B) tip-of-the-tongue phenomenon
    (C) leveling
    (D) sharpening
    (E) working memory

52. The developmental process in which an individual modifies preexisting schemas to account for new information or learning is called

    (A) synthesis
    (B) accommodation
    (C) assimilation
    (D) summation
    (E) elaboration

53. According to Yerkes-Dodson Law, for optimum performance on a difficult task

    (A) the performer must have prior experience with the task
    (B) a high level of arousal is required
    (C) a moderate level of arousal is desirable
    (D) distractions must be eliminated
    (E) emotionality must be essentially absent

54. A mother publicly demonstrates exaggerated concern and love for her children, although she unconsciously feels trapped and frustrated by motherhood. To a Freudian psychoanalyst this is an example of

    (A) suppression
    (B) repression
    (C) regression
    (D) reaction formation
    (E) projection

55. Humanistic personality theorists would likely object to psychoanalytic and behavioral approaches on the grounds that both are

    (A) not applicable to mentally healthy individuals
    (B) essentially unmeasurable
    (C) too idealistic about human nature
    (D) too pessimistic and deterministic
    (E) needlessly complex

56. Volunteers are shown a photograph and asked to write a story about it. The stories are then scored and analyzed. This is most likely a

    (A) Q-Sort
    (B) Strong Preference Test
    (C) Thematic Apperception Test (T.A.T.)
    (D) Rorschach Test
    (E) Myers-Briggs Inventory

57. Somatoform disorders are characterized by

(A) physical symptoms which have no apparent physiological basis
(B) heightened levels of arousal in the central nervous system
(C) reduced levels of arousal in the central nervous system
(D) persistent fear of becoming mentally ill
(E) chronic abnormalities in gross motor function

58. Research into fluid intelligence suggests

(A) a 20 year old man will generally outperform a 70 year old man in measures of it
(B) a 70 year old man will generally outperform a 20 year old man in measures of it
(C) that females generally outperform males in measures of it
(D) that it is culture-specific
(E) that it develops after adolescence

59. In a statistical study, the correlation coefficient for the IQ scores of identical twins raised separately is found to be +.60. This

(A) suggests that there is no basis for hypothesizing a genetic predisposition for intelligence
(B) serves as fairly strong evidence for the argument that there is a genetic component to intelligence
(C) means there is no clear connection between upbringing and performance on assessments of intelligence
(D) demonstrates that correlational research is not useful in looking at a variable such as IQ
(E) highlights flaws in the operational definitions of intelligence

60. Which of the following is the best example of problems with inter-rater reliability?

(A) two different inventories are found to not actually measure what they claim to measure
(B) a musician performs badly in rehearsals but excels during actual performance
(C) a college professor has one of her teaching assistants grade all her students' exams
(D) two driving schools use starkly different approaches in teaching their driving students
(E) three talent show judges have widely divergent views of who the best contestant is

61. Chris exhibits intense lack of trust and fear of abandonment along with a very low frustration threshold. This is accompanied by extreme instability of mood and behavior. Chris's symptoms most closely fit which of the following personality disorders?

    (A) schizoaffective
    (B) schizotypal
    (C) borderline
    (D) passive aggressive
    (E) anti-social

62. Carefully controlled exposure to high levels of light is an often successful treatment approach used for

    (A) hypochondriasis
    (B) conversion disorder
    (C) Tourette's disorder
    (D) seasonal affective disorder
    (E) dissociative fugue

63. A hospital housing the mentally ill wishes to confirm the preliminary diagnosis of a patient. Which of the following assessments would staff members most likely use?

    (A) the W.I.S.C.
    (B) the W.A.I.S.
    (C) the California Psychological Inventory
    (D) the Bulit-R
    (E) the Minnesota Multiphasic Personality Inventory (M.M.P.I.)

64. Nobel Prize winner Roger Sperry found that when he instantaneously displayed images to patients who had recently undergone split brain surgery that

    (A) they were able to verbally report what had been shown to their right eye but not what had been shown to their left eye
    (B) they were able to verbally report what had been shown to the left eye but not what had been shown to their right eye
    (C) they were unable to verbally report having seen anything at all displayed to either eye, but could draw what they had seen
    (D) they were unable to report in any way anything they had seen in either eye
    (E) even though they had just had the surgery they had learned to adapt immediately and could thus verbally report anything that had been displayed to either eye

65. This portion of the brain, located on the back border of the frontal lobe, regulates voluntary movement in the various parts of the body:

   (A) Wernicke's Area
   (B) the central sulcus
   (C) the motor cortex
   (D) the Sylvian fissure
   (E) the caudate nucleus

66. A police officer ignores evidence that might exonerate a suspect because the officer is already convinced of the suspect's guilt. This is an example of

   (A) factor analysis
   (B) confirmation bias
   (C) hindsight bias
   (D) cognitive consistency
   (E) prototype matching

67. A fund raiser hopes to get nearby residents to contribute money to a charitable endeavor. First, she has volunteers visit those residents, asking them to display a small sticker in their windows which states support for that cause. One month later, the volunteers return to ask for a contribution to the cause, and they easily reach their goal. The fund raiser relied on which of the following persuasion techniques?

   (A) reciprocity
   (B) mutuality
   (C) the foot-in-the-door technique
   (D) the door-in-the-face technique
   (E) the self enhancement technique

68. Which of the following is the best example of the defense mechanism known as sublimation?

   (A) Michael is concerned about the size of his ears and feels certain that everyone is constantly looking at them
   (B) Dee Dee does poorly on a biology exam and says "I don't want to be a biologist anyway"
   (C) Anne has powerful, unconscious aggressive urges and decides to become a surgeon
   (D) Dustin is attracted to pornographic material but he also leads a community censorship program against pornography
   (E) Shaunna and Ed are told that their child has a terminal illness but remain convinced the child will recover

69. One researcher investigating cheating in American colleges and universities distributes a survey on the topic to juniors at a local community college; a second researcher interested in the same topic interviews two students recently expelled from a major university in a cheating scandal. Which of the following disadvantages is essentially present in both approaches?

    (A) both are very limited in generalizability
    (B) both contain data tainted by the very presence of the researcher
    (C) both fail to control for confounding variables
    (D) both fail to control for the placebo effect
    (E) both are prone to subject mortality

70. The introduction of a superordinate goal would likely

    (A) contribute to increased cooperation and liking between two groups
    (B) reduce levels of intrinsic motivation
    (C) serve as a secondary reinforcer
    (D) cause friction in a group of more than three members
    (E) extinguish a conditioned response

71. Edward Tolman discovered that rats which had been exposed to a maze first and then asked to run the maze to completion only demonstrated that they had actually learned the maze when reinforced for doing so. He called this

    (A) trial and error learning
    (B) latent learning
    (C) insight learning
    (D) observational learning
    (E) predisposed learning

72. This neurotransmitter seems involved in transmission of messages regarding muscular control and of pleasure:

    (A) substance p
    (B) dopamine
    (C) acetylcholine
    (D) beta-endorphin
    (E) noradrenaline

73. In designing and administering a survey regarding attitudes about domestic violence, which of the following is the best example of demand characteristic?

    (A) the researchers come to believe that respondents are giving them the answers they seem to want to hear
    (B) the researchers discover they have framed the items in ambiguous ways
    (C) the respondents are not a representative sample of the population
    (D) the sample size is not large enough
    (E) informed consent was not secured

74. R.E.M. sleep is often referred to as "paradoxical sleep" because in it brain activity is quite high while there is

    (A) a reduction in blood pressure
    (B) a slowed heart rate
    (C) a slowed rate of breathing
    (D) a sharp decrease in muscular control and tone
    (E) an increase in delta wave activity

75. At the start of her course, a chemistry professor administers an assessment designed to measure aptitude in the study of chemistry. At the end of the course she finds a strongly negative correlation between scores on the aptitude test and final grades for the chemistry course. This result indicates the aptitude test lacks

    (A) split half reliability
    (B) intra-rater reliability
    (C) test/retest reliability
    (D) test/retest validity
    (E) predictive validity

76. A psychoanalyst believes that her patient has begun to experience and express feelings toward her that actually mirror the feelings the patient feels for her own mother. Sigmund Freud called this

    (A) catharsis
    (B) gestalt
    (C) resistance
    (D) countertransference
    (E) transference

77. The ciliary muscles help adjust the shape of the lens of the eye to facilitate the focus of near and far objects. This is called

    (A) assimilation
    (B) convergence
    (C) accommodation
    (D) refraction
    (E) summation

78. Blocking the reuptake of a neurotransmitter would result in

    (A) increased transmission of that neurotransmitter's signals
    (B) the cessation of activity in the central nervous system
    (C) the cessation of activity in the peripheral nervous system
    (D) seizures
    (E) coma

79. Neo-Freudian Carl Jung might argue that a man who publicly takes pride in never having cried may be unconsciously rejecting

    (A) his father
    (B) himself
    (C) the shadow portion of his psyche
    (D) anima in the collective unconscious
    (E) the id

80. Which of the following best summarizes the essence of cognitive theory?

    (A) "Men are disturbed not by things but by the views they take of them" (Epictetus)
    (B) "Nothing is so carefully secured as this, that whilst we live we shall learn" (Ralph Waldo Emerson)
    (C) "You can discover what your enemy fears most by observing the means he uses to frighten you" (Eric Hoffer)
    (D) "Be not afraid of life" (William James)
    (E) "Human temperaments are combinations of psychological profiles, behaviors, thoughts and emotions along with their presumed biological foundation" (Jerome Kagan)

81. Which of the following is the most defensible conclusion one can reach from Stanley Milgram's "electric shock" obedience study?

    (A) obedience was usually a function of the particular personality types of those administering the shocks
    (B) volunteers with a history of rebelliousness and resistance to authority were much less likely to obey than others
    (C) obedience seems to be linked most to the nature of the orders given; people are highly unlikely to follow orders which inflict harm on others
    (D) obedience appears to be a function of the power of the situation and is less attributable to the personalities of those who receive the orders
    (E) individuals are much more likely to obey male authority figures than female authority figures

82. The tendency for decisions made by a group to be more extreme than those that would've been made by any single member of the group is called

    (A) group polarization
    (B) group compliance
    (C) group think
    (D) the sleeper effect
    (E) the autokinetic effect

83. A teenager who is normally shy and reserved and has not been drinking dances wildly while shirtless in the midst of a large crowd at a concert. His atypical behavior is best explained by

    (A) social inhibition
    (B) attribution theory
    (C) the sleeper effect
    (D) false consensus
    (E) de-individuation

84. Telegraphic speech

    (A) is semantically correct and qualifies as prescriptive grammar
    (B) qualifies as neither prescriptive nor descriptive grammar
    (C) qualifies as descriptive grammar
    (D) involves expressions of one word which still convey meaning
    (E) occurs developmentally during adolescence

85. A woman who is furious about issues at her workplace returns home and spanks her child for no apparent reason, then explains the behavior by saying "discipline is good for a child". What two defense mechanisms are at work here?

    (A) identification and suppression
    (B) suppression and identification
    (C) displacement and rationalization
    (D) displacement and projection
    (E) internalization and identification

86. Tourette's disorder, autism and conduct disorder all fall under the category of

    (A) impulse control disorders
    (B) disorders first diagnosed in infancy, childhood or adolescence
    (C) factitious disorders
    (D) dissociative disorders
    (E) anxiety disorders

87. The use of virtual reality therapy has proven to be effective in extinguishing

    (A) schizophrenia
    (B) dissociative identity disorder
    (C) dissociative fugue
    (D) conversion disorder
    (E) phobias

88. Damage to Broca's area would most likely result in

    (A) Parkinson's Disease
    (B) obsessive compulsive disorder
    (C) P.T.S.D.
    (D) expressive aphasia
    (E) asynchronous physical development

89. A criticism of trait theory is that

    (A) there is no reasonable way to measure the presence of personality traits
    (B) there may be relatively little consistency in personality traits across situations
    (C) it is too optimistic about essential human nature
    (D) it is too pessimistic about essential human nature
    (E) it overemphasizes the role of human decision making in the growth of personality

90. A woman is saddened by a romantic breakup. She decides to date several different men in an attempt to forget her old partner, but she sometimes finds herself accidentally calling her new dates by her old boyfriend's name. This is an example of

   (A) inhibition theory
   (B) encoding specificity
   (C) structural encoding
   (D) proactive interference
   (E) retroactive interference

* The next two items are in reference to the following scenario:

A cat has become classically conditioned to run into a room in response to the sound of a can opener, after that sound has been repeatedly paired with the presentation of food. Next, the researcher conducts several trials in which she presents a red light, followed by the sound of the can opener, and the cat soon learns to run into the room at the sight of the red light.

91. This is called

   (A) second order conditioning
   (B) temporal conditioning
   (C) trace conditioning
   (D) vicarious conditioning
   (E) successive conditioning

92. Which of the following is the most reasonable prediction about this scenario?

   (A) the cat's response to the food will soon be extinguished
   (B) the cat's response to the can opener will be strengthened
   (C) conditioning to the red light will require more trials and will be easier to extinguish than the original conditioning to the can opener
   (D) conditioning to the red light will require fewer trials and will be more difficult to extinguish than the original conditioning to the can opener
   (E) exposure to both types of training will facilitate generalization

93. Activation synthesis theory proposes that

   (A) humans seek physical activity and arousal
   (B) dreams are the product of the individual's cognitive attempts to make sense out of essentially random neural activity
   (C) physical activity during sleep is frequent and often uncontrolled
   (D) people tend to try to organize their perceptions into meaningful units
   (E) group members with similar interests tend to engage more actively in the group

94. According to the learning principle of overjustification

    (A) subjects learn best through extrinsic motivation
    (B) motor skills are easily overlearned
    (C) cognitive skills are easily overlearned
    (D) intrinsic motivation for performing a certain behavior can be reduced by the offer of extrinsic motivation
    (E) punishment and reinforcement are equally successful tools in operant conditioning

95. The human ability to understand without specific training that there are different possible meanings of the sentence "Victor shot the man with a gun" supports

    (A) Chomsky's theory of the L.A.D.
    (B) linguistic relativity theory
    (C) the theory of prelinguistic utterances
    (D) the concept of self regulation
    (E) feature analysis theory

96. According to Erik Erikson, in the second stage of psychosocial development a child focuses attention on toilet training and other issues of control over his or her environment, thus wrestling with the conflict between

    (A) trust and mistrust
    (B) integrity and despair
    (C) assimilation and accommodation
    (D) generativity and stagnation
    (E) autonomy and doubt

97. Which of the following is a negative symptom of schizophrenia?

    (A) hallucinations
    (B) delusions
    (C) disorganized thinking
    (D) disorganized speech
    (E) flattened affect

98. The most plentiful excitatory neurotransmitter in the human brain is

    (A) glutamate
    (B) G.A.B.A.
    (C) serotonin
    (D) enkephalin
    (E) epinephrine

99. Volunteers in an experiment are given an injection of epinephrine, although they are not told this. The injection results in an increase in heart, pulse and respiration rates. One half of the volunteers, when placed in a room with a confederate of the researchers who pretends to be angry and agitated, interpret the physiological changes caused by the injection to be representative of anger. The other volunteers, given the same injection, are placed in a room with a confederate who pretends to be happy and excited; these volunteers report their physiological changes as being representative of excitement. These results most support which of the following theories of human emotional response?

(A) James-Lange Theory
(B) Cannon-Bard Thalamic Theory
(C) Schachter-Singer Two Factor Theory
(D) opponent process theory
(E) universality theory

100. Which of the following quotes would most likely be associated with Gustav Fechner, a 19th century researcher into "psychophysics"?

(A) "... each cell in the visual cortex seems to have its own specific duties."
(B) " ... there are wholes, the behavior of which is not determined by that of their individual elements."
(C) " ... the method of just noticeable differences consists in determining how much two weights have to differ so that they can be discriminated."
(D) "What a man can be, he must be."
(E) "The subtests of the W.A.I.S. are different measures of intelligence, not measures of different kinds of intelligence."

Sample Examination III

Section II

Directions: You have 50 minutes to answer BOTH of the following questions. It is not enough to answer a question by merely listing facts. You should present a cogent argument based on your critical analysis of the questions posed, using appropriate psychological terminology.

1. You own a factory in which you employ fifty workers constructing school classroom equipment. Suggest ways you might compensate and motivate your employees with specific reference to each of the following concepts:

    • incentive theory
    • the Premack principle
    • schedules of reinforcement (you need cite only one)
    • self efficacy
    • learned helplessness
    • unconditional positive regard
    • observational learning

2. Design an experiment to evaluate the effectiveness of a new weight loss product intended for use by the clinically obese. Make certain to include specific reference to each of the following in your design:

    • sampling
    • operational definitions
    • independent variable
    • dependent variable
    • placebo
    • double blind
    • control for one possible confounding variable
    • two controls for possible ethical issues

280

AP Psychology

Index

A

Absolute threshold 30

Abstract thinking 93

Acetylcholine 15, 17, 69

Accommodation as a depth/distance cue 36

Accommodation in development 92

Achievement motivation 109

Achievement tests 142

Acquisition 56

Action Potential 15

Activation synthesis theory of dreams 47

Active sleep (in reference to R.E.M.) 45

Adaptation 30, 32

Adaptive non-responding theory of sleep 46

Adler, Alfred 93, 98, 126, 128, 178

Adrenal gland 22, 54

Adrenaline/noradrenaline 22

Affective/mood disorders 153-154

Afferent/sensory neurons 17

Aggression 109

Agonists 17

Agoraphobia 155

Ainsworth, Mary 93-94, 98

Algorithms 80

All-or-none law 16

Allport, Gordon 122, 128

Altruism 107, 190

Altruistic suicide 107

Alzheimer's Disease 17

Amnesia 72

anterograde amnesia 72

retrograde amnesia 72

Amphetamines 48

Amygdala 21, 70, 156

Anal stage of psychosexual development 125

Androgyny 95

Anima 126

Animus 126

Anorexia nervosa 163

Anosmia 33

Antabuse 173

Antagonistic systems (sympathetic and parasympathetic systems) 18

Antagonists 17

Anterogade amnesia 72

Anti-anxiety medications 48, 177

Anti-depressant medications 155, 156, 177

Anti-psychotic medications 177

Anti-social personality disorder 161-162

Anxiety disorders 154-156

Anxiety hierarchy 173

Ape language 83

Apnea 47

Approach-approach conflicts 110-111

Approach-avoidance conflicts 111

Aptitude tests 142

Archetypes 126

Arousal theory 108

Asch, Solomon 189, 193

Assimilation 92

Association cortex 19

Atkinson, Richard 73

Atkinson-Shiffrin model of memory 67

Attachment styles 93-94

avoidant 93

disorganized 94

resistant/ambivalent 93

secure 93

Attention deficit hyperactivity disorder (A.D.H.D.) 160-161

Attitudes 191-192

Attraction 193

Attribution Theory 127, 190-191

Auditory cortex 19, 32

Authoritarian parenting 94

Authoritative parenting 94

Autism 160-161

Autonomic nervous system 18

Autonomy vs. shame and doubt 96

Aversion 56-57, 59

Aversive therapy 173

Avoidance-avoidance conflicts 111

Axon 15

B

Babbling 83

Bandura, Albert 60, 61, 126, 128, 173

Barbiturates 48

Basic anxiety 126

Basilar membrane 32, 33

Baumrind, Diana 94, 98

Beck, Aaron 174-175, 178

281

F

Facial expressions 112

Facial feedback hypothesis 112

Factor Analysis 122

Family systems therapy 176

Feature analysis theory 35, 37

Feature detector cells 35, 37

Fechner, Gustav 29, 37

Festinger, Leon 113, 191

Fetal alcohol syndrome (F.A.S.) 90

Fetal Stage 90

Fight or flight response 17, 21

Figure-ground images 36

Firing threshold of a neuron 16

Fixed action patterns 107

Fixed interval schedules of reinforcement 60

Fixed ratio schedules of reinforcement 59

Flashbulb memory 70

Flattened affect 158

Flooding 174

Fluid intelligence 138, 145

Flynn Effect 141

fMRI 22

Foot-in-the-door approach 188-189

Forgetting curve 72, 73

Formal operational stage of cognitive development 93

Fovea 31

Frames of reference 35

Framing and memory 72

Framing and problem solving 81

Free association 172

Free running rhythms 46

Frequency theory 33

Freudian Slip 123

Freud, Sigmund 7, 47, 49, 123-126, 128, 172, 178

Frontal lobes 18, 70, 154, 159, 176

Functional fixedness 81

Functionalism 49

Functional MRI (fMRI) 22

Fundamental Attribution Error (F.A.E.) 127, 190-191

G

"G" 138

Gage, Phineas 23

Gambler's fallacy 6

Gamma-aminobutyric acid (G.A.B.A.) 17, 156, 177

Ganglion cells 31, 32

Garcia, John 61

Gardner, Howard 138, 145

Gate control theory 34

Gazzaniga, Michael 20

Gender constancy 95

Gender identity 95

Gender role 95

Gender typing 95

General Adaptation Syndrome (G.A.S.) 111

Generalizability 2

Generalization in conditioning 56

Generalized anxiety disorder 155

Generativity vs.stagnation 97

Genetic predisposition 22, 23, 121, 154, 156, 159

Genie 82, 84, 89

Genital stage of psychosexual development 125

Genotype 22

Genovese case study 4, 190

Gestalt 35, 47

Gestalt therapy 175

Gibson, Eleanor 91, 98

Gifted children 140

Gilligan, Carol 98

Glial cells 18

Glutamate 15

Good continuation 35

Grasping reflex 91

Grieving 97

Group matching 2

Group polarization 186

Group therapy 176

Group think 186

Guilford, J.P. 138, 145

Gustatory system 34

H

Habituation 30, 91

Hair cells 32

Hallucinations 158,

Hallucinogens 48

Harlow, Harry 90

Heider, Fritz 127, 128, 190, 193

Heinz Dilemma 97

Heritability 22, 137

Heuristics 80
  availability heuristic 80
  representativeness heuristic 80

Hidden observer 48

Hierarchy of needs 109

Higher/second order conditioning 58

Hilgard, Ernest 48, 49

Hind brain 19, 69

Hippocampus 21, 69, 71, 72, 154

Histograms 6

Histrionic personality disorder 161

Hobson, J. Allan 47, 49

Holophrastic speech 83

Homeostasis 108, 112

Homosexuality 152

Hormones 22, 23

Horner, Matina 110, 113

Horney, Karen 126, 128, 178

Hospice movement 97

Hostile aggression 110

Hubel, David 35, 37

Hull, Clark 113

Humanistic theory 109, 128